# GENDER AND CHRISTIAN ETHICS

In this book, Adrian Thatcher offers fresh theological arguments for expanding our understanding of gender. He begins by describing the various meanings of gender and depicts the relations between women and men as a pervasive human and global problem. Thatcher then critiques naive and harmful theological accounts of sexuality and gender as binary opposites or mistaken identities. Demonstrating that the gendered theologies of Hans Urs von Balthasar and Karl Barth, as well as the Vatican's 'war on gender', rest on questionable binary models, he replaces these models with a human continuum that allows for sexual difference without assuming 'opposite sexes' and normative sexualities. Grounded in core Christian doctrines, this continuum enables a full theological affirmation of LGBTIQ people. Thatcher also addresses the excesses of the male–female binary in secular culture and outlines a hermeneutic that delivers justice and acceptance instead of sexism and discrimination.

ADRIAN THATCHER is Honorary Professor in the Department of Religion, University of Exeter. He is the author of twelve books, most recently *Redeeming Gender* (2016), and editor of *The Oxford Handbook of Theology, Sexuality, and Gender* (2015).

T0382338

# NEW STUDIES IN CHRISTIAN ETHICS

General Editor
ROBIN GILL

Editorial Board
STEPHEN R. L. CLARK, STANLEY HAUERWAS,
ROBIN W. LOVIN

Christian ethics has increasingly assumed a central place within academic theology. At the same time the growing power and ambiguity of modern science and the rising dissatisfaction within the social sciences about claims to value neutrality have prompted renewed interest in ethics within the secular academic world. There is, therefore, a need for studies in Christian ethics which, as well as being concerned with the relevance of Christian ethics to the present-day secular debate, are well informed about parallel discussions in recent philosophy, science, or social science. New Studies in Christian Ethics aims to provide books that do this at the highest intellectual level and demonstrate that Christian ethics can make a distinctive contribution to this debate – either in moral substance or in terms of underlying moral justifications titles published in the series

*(continued after the index)*

# GENDER AND CHRISTIAN ETHICS

## ADRIAN THATCHER
*University of Exeter*

Shaftesbury Road, Cambridge CB2 8EA, United Kingdom

One Liberty Plaza, 20th Floor, New York, NY 10006, USA

477 Williamstown Road, Port Melbourne, VIC 3207, Australia

314–321, 3rd Floor, Plot 3, Splendor Forum, Jasola District Centre, New Delhi – 110025, India

103 Penang Road, #05–06/07, Visioncrest Commercial, Singapore 238467

Cambridge University Press is part of Cambridge University Press & Assessment, a department of the University of Cambridge.

We share the University's mission to contribute to society through the pursuit of education, learning and research at the highest international levels of excellence.

www.cambridge.org
Information on this title: www.cambridge.org/9781108813235

DOI: 10.1017/9781108884204

First published 2021
First paperback edition 2023

*A catalogue record for this publication is available from the British Library*

*Library of Congress Cataloging-in-Publication data*
NAMES: Thatcher, Adrian, author.
TITLE: Gender and Christian ethics / Adrian Thatcher.
DESCRIPTION: Cambridge, United Kingdom ; New York, NY, USA : Cambridge University Press, 2020. | Series: New studies in Christian ethics | Includes bibliographical references and index.
IDENTIFIERS: LCCN 2020012172 (print) | LCCN 2020012173 (ebook) | ISBN 9781108839488 (hardback) | ISBN 9781108813235 (paperback) | ISBN 9781108884204 (epub)
SUBJECTS: LCSH: Sex–Religious aspects–Christianity. | Christian ethics.
CLASSIFICATION: LCC BT708 .T4439 2021 (print) | LCC BT708 (ebook) | DDC 241.081–dc23
LC record available at https://lccn.loc.gov/2020012172
LC ebook record available at https://lccn.loc.gov/2020012173

ISBN   978-1-108-83948-8   Hardback
ISBN   978-1-108-81323-5   Paperback

# Contents

vii

# General Editor's Preface

In 1996, Lisa Sowle Cahill contributed her widely praised monograph *Sex, Gender and Christian Ethics* to this Cambridge University Press series. Six years later, Adrian Thatcher contributed his *Living Together and Christian Ethics* to the series and, since then, has built a formidable reputation as a liberal theological voice on issues of sexuality and gender. In the last decade, the issue of 'gender' has received considerable fresh attention, partly as a result of changing medical and scientific understandings and partly as a result of radical cultural and political changes in the West. So a new volume from Thatcher on *Gender and Christian Ethics*, that takes full account of these changes, is particularly welcome.

There is a strong thesis running throughout his latest contribution, namely that the binary understanding of gender that has dominated recent Catholic, Anglican and some Reformed ecclesial reports and writings on sexuality is deeply misleading in terms of science, sociology, ethics and theology. He sets out clearly some of the medical and genetic evidence that suggests that human gender is more complex than a binary model allows. He examines some of the sociological and feminist studies that suggest that patriarchal culture shapes perceptions of sharp gender differences. He argues strongly that, at an ethical level, a binary model of gender does not do justice to individuals and groups that do not conform to it. And he develops a trinitarian theological position that sees gender as a (God-given) continuum. Finally he suggests that the gender binary continues to cause damage in the secular world, and explores different ways that hermeneutics within both Christianity and Islam can address sacred texts that appear to be patriarchal and discriminatory.

Adrian Thatcher's writing is always wonderfully clear, well-informed, challenging and creative. His new book admirably fits the two central aims of the series:

1. To promote monographs in Christian ethics which engage centrally with the present secular moral debate at the highest possible intellectual level.
2. To encourage contributors to demonstrate that Christian ethics can make a distinctive contribution to this debate – either in moral substance, or in terms of underlying moral justifications.

**Robin Gill**

# Acknowledgements

Academic writing can be a long and lonely slog, but it is always dependent on the prior efforts of co-labourers, too numerous to acknowledge.

I would like to thank my colleagues and friends in Theology and Religion at the University of Exeter for my continuing appointment as Honorary Professor in the College of Humanities. I retired from Exeter in 2011, but have continued a happy association with them ever since. Without access to the university's library and its ever-growing number of academic databases, further research for this retired academic would have been impossible. I am most grateful to them for proposing, and to the Vice Chancellor for approving, my present honorary appointment, and enabling me to make further contributions to Theology and Christian Ethics.

I have benefitted from the advice of several academics during the writing of this book. I enjoyed correspondence with Sister Susan Rakoczy at St Joseph's Theological Institute at the University of KwaZulu-Natal. Susan Gilchrist from TranschristianUK read and commented helpfully on all my references to gender-variant people. Dr Ronit Irshai, Senior Lecturer in the Gender Studies Unit at Bar Ilan University, shared her work with me on the Euthyphro Dilemma as I was writing Chapter 3. Professor Asma Barlas, at Ithaca College, New York, carefully and helpfully commented on my foray into her own work and that of other Muslim women academics in Chapter 10. Professor Gerard Loughlin, at the University of Durham, not only checked that I had read him aright but commented helpfully on the entire script. But I have benefitted most from the extensive knowledge of Dr Susannah Cornwall, Senior Lecturer in Constructive Theologies at the University of Exeter, who read the whole manuscript carefully and made several helpful recommendations.

My indebtedness is not only to my academic contacts and friends. I have been encouraged by the curiosity, enthusiasm and receptivity of medical students at the Plymouth University Peninsula Medical School.

For more than a decade I have taught short courses on kinship arrangements, gender and cross-cultural ethical issues, all within a medical humanities framework. The students have unwittingly helped me broaden my academic horizons, clarify my thoughts and pursue further research. For more than thirty years I have been a member, pianist and lay preacher in the congregation of Christ Church, Estover, a local ecumenical parish in Plymouth and the Anglican diocese of Exeter. The quiet, steadfast commitment of the small congregation at Estover has been inspirational in helping me bridge the gap between academic theology and the pressing vicissitudes of parish life on a housing estate. My long-standing membership of Modern Church, a voluntary society promoting positive, constructive Christian theology, has helped me to sustain my commitment to progressive theology more generally, and to making it more widely available to the churches. And not least I thank my partner, Caroline Major, for her unflagging interest and support over many projects, which helped me greatly to bring this long current project to its completion.

PART I

*Gender and Violence*

## CHAPTER I

# Aims and Key Terms

*Gender and Christian Ethics* builds on three convictions. First, that the problem of gender, in the world and in the world's religions, ranks equal to the problems of climate change, the failure to eliminate poverty, to secure world peace, and to eliminate weapons of mass destruction. Indeed all these problems intersect and are 'gendered'. Any reader detecting a whiff of exaggeration here is asked to suspend judgment at least until the end of Chapter 2. Unfortunately the conduct of relations between the sexes at all levels – personal, social, national, international, and global – is too often affected by the presumption of male power and privilege, to the detriment of women. Throughout the world shocking violence against women is increasing, and the complicity of the world's religions in endorsing and legitimising it is becoming better known. The book is a contribution to more peaceable, more equal relations between women and men, especially in countries and places where Christian faith is practiced.

Second, that a theology of sex/gender has recently become embedded in official Roman Catholic and some Protestant Reformed thought, which, I argue, may be seriously mistaken. Not only does it ignore (or tacitly encourage) the misuse of gender power, this new theology, signalled by the term 'complementarity', significantly alienates everyone whose bodies and desires do not fit its chafing complementarian assumptions. Some criticism of emerging gender orthodoxies must be made, not simply against the churches, but *for the sake of* the churches, since the new gender theology is offending countless people who do not and cannot locate themselves within it.

Third, that an alternative theology of gender, already rooted in Christian thought, is able to enrich the self-understanding of everyone within the orbit of Christian faith, whatever their sex, orientation, or gender identity. It is able to overcome violence with peace, and is therefore able to assist the churches in their wider ministries. Christian ethics has at its disposal already a rich theological tradition begging to be reread.

## Aims

The three main aims of the book correspond to each of these convictions, and the book is in three parts, each corresponding roughly to the aims. The aims are

1. To depict the relations between women and men as a pervasive human and global problem, in order to expand the range of theological thought required to address it (Part I);
2. To critique naïve and harmful theological accounts of the relations between women and men as binary opposites, to expose the harm they cause, and to replace them, and the exclusions they engender, with what will be called 'the human continuum' (Part II);
3. To demonstrate how the human continuum enables a more inclusive theological understanding not only of relations between women and men, but also among LGBTIQ people (Part III).

In the course of the book we will often encounter the uncomfortable and disturbing relation between religion and violence, raising the question (for Christians) how our sacred text has been allowed to justify it. So there remains a further, subsidiary, aim:

4. To contribute to a hermeneutic – an elementary method of interpretation of the Bible and tradition – which can never condone discrimination or oppression.

In my earlier years as a theologian I threw my energies into the intellectual commendation and defence of the Christian faith: in my later years I have come to see that the main barriers to belief for growing numbers of people are less likely to be intellectual, and more likely to be ethical. Sadly the continued association of the faith with violence against women and sexual minorities; the continued hostility towards LGBTIQ people; the continued practice of sexism in the churches; the toleration of the abuse of children on a global scale, and an inability to engage in self-examination and repentance for the crimes against them, can make it difficult for people of good will outside the churches to believe that there is Good News to be heard inside them. Despite the importance in the Bible of believing the testimony of witnesses, the testimony of lesbian- and gay-partnered Christians to their experience of the blessing of God on their unions is still called into question and their self-understanding has been rejected as erroneous. The moral crisis within Christianity cannot be ignored. Similar crises can be found in all the world's religions. As the argument develops in the book, the need for a different 'inhabiting' of the tradition bequeathed to us Christians, and a different way of interpreting the Bible, will become obvious.

## Key Terms

Already some key terms have been used – binary, continuum, gender, among them. The rest of this section explains how these terms will be used.

### Gender

'Gender' has become a complicated term. Definitions of gender proliferate (Bradley 2007: 14–25). It has long been a *grammatical* term that classifies nouns as masculine or feminine (or neuter). Its etymology retains traces of *genus* (Latin – 'type', 'class of things') and *genre* (French). Only since 1945 did the term begin to be used of the distinct social and cultural influences exerted upon individuals, already biologically classified by sex as either women or men (for a full history see Vigoya 2015). By the 1970s, 'sex' and 'gender' had become different realms, each contributing from different academic assumptions to the full understanding of the person. To add to the confusion, the acceptability of referring to sexual intercourse as 'having sex' probably led to the term 'gender' being adopted, in place of the term 'sex', to refer to the classification of a person as a man or a woman. Anyone applying for a passport or a driving licence now, knows this well. In the new century the distinction between sex and gender became blurred, largely because of the difficulties involved in assigning the origin of human behaviours and characteristics to either side of the sex or gender dichotomy. Consequently the compound term 'sex/gender' began to appear, less (one hopes) as an excuse for sloppy thinking, and more as an admission that sex and gender cannot finally be considered apart from each other.

In this volume, unless specified otherwise, gender will refer primarily to three broad areas. First, it clearly applies to 'the *relations* between women and men' (Bradley 2007: 1, emphasis added: see Porter 2015, xvii), whether at the personal, familial, social, cultural, religious, national, and international levels, together with the investigation of these. Many writings about gender rightly contain the caveat about the 'intersectionality' of gender, that, whenever it is discussed, it intersects with 'a range of social and material categories, including race, religion, ethnicity, class, age and sexual orientation' (Anderson 2012, xii). 'Gender is, above all, a matter of the social relations within which individuals and groups act' (Connell and Pearse 2015: 11). There are several advantages of emphasising relations or relationality in our treatment of gender. It provides a distinct focus. It accords well with the 'central position' which gender occupies in the human and social sciences, where 'it structures our investigations into the relations between women and men, and between human beings in general' (Heinamäa 2012: 216). And relations constitute the very being of God as Trinity – that glorious binary-busting doctrine – by reference to which striking theological contributions to the understanding of gender can be made. As Sarah Coakley observes, the 'ontological threeness' of the Trinity, 'always challenges and "ambushes" the stuckness of established "twoness", for '… in and through the Spirit we are drawn to place our binary "certainties" into the melting pot of the crucible of divine – not human – desire' (Coakley 2013: 330–1). It will not be forgotten that there are non-binary and intersex people for whom the male–female distinction causes pain.

Our second area understands gender to be 'a socially constructed system, one wherein our ideas about gender permeate and shape our ideas about many other aspects of society beyond male–female relations' (Duncanson 2016: 5). Christians are familiar with this idea. We have overarching beliefs which shape our lives and guide our actions, albeit in different ways. The Greek for 'creed' is *symbolon*. Our symbolic system has powerfully influenced the way we 'do' gender, and still does. In both areas, understanding how power is distributed will be crucial. The propensity for systems of belief to endorse violence will be examined. Our third area is 'gender *identity*'. Gender identity is an intensely individual matter, yet even this is experienced only in relation to other people of whatever sex, for 'our gender identity is formed by how we act in relation to two key things: our physical embodiment and social definitions of a man or woman's place in society, which we can conform to, reinforce, resist, subvert, and so on, in a variety of ways' (Duncanson 2016: 5). In all three areas comprising gender, there are very strong influences, often operating upon us unconsciously, often disguised as common sense or passed off as inevitable, natural, obvious, and so on. In all three areas, the power of these influences over us requires scrutiny.

### Binary

Like Coakley I too want to ambush the idea of a human or a sexual binary, challenging the 'stuckness' of much theological thought about sexuality and gender in binary opposites. 'Binary' is a key term in the book. A binary is a system or relation between two poles or opposites. From the Latin *bini* – 'two together' – a binary system of classification is 'one by which each group and sub-group is perpetually divided into two, the one with a positive and the other with a negative character, till individuals (or genera) are reached' (*Oxford English Dictionary*, online [*OED*]). Alert feminist readers will already have noted that 'positive' and 'negative' appear in this otherwise bland definition, already injurious to women if applied in a gendered context. A binary measure in music is one which has two beats to a bar. In such an arrangement the emphasis can be on only one of a pair. A binary system in astronomy requires two stars or suns, but does not require further information about their size, velocity, or orbit (*OED*). So there is nothing about a binary system that guarantees or even suggests equality or value of the items within the system, beyond the bare twoness of its operation.

Binaries appear to operate throughout academic discourse. Perhaps academics as a class capitulate to the temptation to assume that clean and sharp distinctions between concepts justify assuming equally clean and sharp distinctions between the complex and messy realities that concepts describe. 'Mind–body', for example, has often been understood as a binary of separate substances that then require to be reunited in some form of interactionism. We are now beginning to know how mental states and brain states are deeply and inextricably connected, while still being different. Even 'sex–gender' began to be treated as a binary, according to which biological and sociological facts could be neatly and conveniently separated out. Another popular binary, drawn from academic discourse, is the distinction between objective and subjective. I am sometimes told by medical students that humanities is 'subjective' (and justifiable for the cultivation of appropriate *feelings*), whereas *real* knowledge is *always* objective. Apparently there is a binary between objective and subjective knowledge dictating that only scientific knowledge is 'real' knowledge and has no human biases, whereas humanities, the arts, and ethics can be safely relegated to feelings and 'mere opinion'.

Binaries are overly simplistic: worse, they positively encourage oversimplification. That is why they are popular wherever people struggle with complexity, and prefer simplicity even at the cost of misrepresentation or at the expense of the truth. Even night and day are not binaries – without qualification they exclude dusk and dawn. 'In Genesis, God separates the dry land from the sea. But God also makes marshes, estuaries, and coral reefs' (Hartke 2018: 28). In all the instances just cited, what starts out as an important conceptual distinction drawing attention to difference, easily morphs into evaluation of one of the poles in relation to the other which can become unthinking and negative. Thus are binaries created, and once created they become difficult to unlearn.

A binary *sex* system is an overarching framework for organising and policing sexual relationships between human beings, which classifies them according to two, and only two, biological forms, male and female. The dark shadow of the biological binary is the orientation binary, by which the heterosexual–homosexual distinction pathologises and delivers moral judgement, depending on which side of the binary a person is located. 'Right' and 'wrong' are sometimes assumed to be binaries, but right and wrong are often better understood as points along a moral axis. That is one reason why moral choices are often controversial and difficult. They are rarely, as we say, matters of black and white.

A *theological* binary sex system determines in advance that there are just two and only two sexes; that one of these is more positive or 'prior' in relation to the other; that the two sexes are 'opposite'; that sexual desire (if we have any) in order to conform to the will of God and to our created nature as either male or female, must either be exclusively for members of the other sex, or be classified as sinful or deviant. Even 'married–unmarried' behaves as a binary in some theological thinking, since that neat distinction wilfully ignores the complex 'in-between-ness' of engaged people, and the options available to people who are post-married, and so on. I wrote about that distinction earlier in this series (*Living Together and Christian Ethics*)(2002). Gayle Rubin suggested removing twelve pairs of binaries in relation to her 'rethinking' of sex (Rubin 2011), but in this book I shall confine myself to three: female–male; homosexual–heterosexual; and feminine–masculine.

Jews and Christians have always believed, in accordance with Genesis 1.27, that God made humankind male and female. Reluctantly, I have come to the conclusion that a generation of theologians has sought to impose on this unsuspecting verse a modern, binary, theological sex system that has the consequences of misrepresenting our humanity to ourselves, and oversimplifying the known complexities of sexuality and desire (Part II). Perhaps with the best of intentions, the text 'male and female he created them' is made to endorse the 'biblical' equality of the sexes, in contradistinction to Genesis 2 and 3 where the woman is depicted in several ways inferior to the man and has been interpreted as such right down to the second half of the twentieth century. What looks like a welcome doctrinal innovation, that men and women were created by

God in some respects equal, carries with it other less welcome innovations: that there are two and only two sexes; that we are all one or the other; and that our sexual desires are or ought to be directed exclusively towards the 'opposite' sex. This new development is an excellent example of the meaning of gender as a 'symbolic system' or 'construction'. But it sidelines the Christian belief that the system valorising men above women has already been brought to an end by the Christ in whom there is no longer male and female (Gal. 3.28). The male–female binary is no more. A positive Christian ethic of gender should en*gender* more salvific ways of envisaging and living relations between women and men instead of generating and repeating binaries that treat them as opposites and generally evaluate them differently.

Binaries are dangerous in religion and theology. Binaries erect boundaries between what is thought to be holy and merely common; between what is pure and what is impure; between what is sacred and what is profane, and so on. Boundaries are policed with greater or lesser vigour, but it hardly seems possible that God may be honoured by exactitudes that divide. The only absolute binary that need be of concern to Christians is that between God and all that is not God – between uncreated and created being – and even this is no longer a binary, since in the arrival of Jesus Christ divine and human natures are united in one Person (Cheng 2011: 79). When the sexual binary is charged with assumptions about the 'other' sex being ontologically, morally, or physical inferior, then gender trouble begins. The distressing evidence is discussed in Chapter 2.

### Continuum

In the previous section we considered binaries, a binary system, a binary sex system, and a binary sex system endorsed by theology. We now come to what might replace the binary. The answer is a *continuum*. This too is a key term in what follows.

A *continuum* is 'a continuous sequence in which adjacent elements are not perceptibly different from each other, but the extremes are quite distinct' (*OED*). The Latin adjective *continuus* means 'uninterrupted' (from *continere* to hang together). A continuum allows for a wide difference between elements within it, while acknowledging their continuity within the sequence. That is why it is particularly valuable in undoing the understanding of women and men as opposites. The term has a similar meaning and use in at least the disciplines of mathematics, plant sciences, astrology, ecology, philosophy, physics, chemical engineering, and psychology (*OED*).

An alternative to 'continuum' is 'spectrum'. In 1993 Anne Fausto-Sterling referred, with tongue in cheek, to the male–female binary as a 'two-party sexual system', which is 'in defiance of nature' (Fausto-Sterling 1993: 20). Nature has provided 'many gradations running from female to male; and depending on how one calls the shots, one can argue that along that *spectrum* lie at least five sexes – and perhaps even more'. One particular meaning of 'spectrum' is 'a band of colours, as seen in a rainbow, produced by separation of the components of light by their different degrees of refraction according to wavelength', giving rise to the more general use where something is classified 'in terms of its position on a scale between two extreme points' (*OED*). It is now commonplace even for theologians to think of sexuality as a spectrum. 'Over the course of the twentieth century, the human sciences clearly established that human sexuality *exists on a spectrum*' (Davison 2016: 22, emphasis added). James and Evelyn Whitehead summarise the impasse reached by the religious repetition of the male–female binary:

> Often male and female have been presented as clear and distinct realities, understood in an either/or dichotomy that has been well-defended by cultural and religious decrees. Today we are aware that human nature is more variable, even more mysterious, than we had once assumed. Ongoing research – physiological and psychological – confirms that gender is experienced and expressed along a wide *spectrum*. (Whitehead and Whitehead 2014: 173, emphasis added)

The idea of a 'human continuum' is used in this book, both for the positive contributions it can make to the Christian doctrine of human being, and as an alternative to the modern theological binary sex-and-gender system. It provides a more fluid, less binary, understanding of humanity which resists firm categorisations, avoids inequality, preserves difference, acknowledges fluidity, encourages inclusion, develops tradition, and enables the churches to incorporate minorities gladly and without equivocation. As the idea unfolds, it will become apparent that it will assist in recasting each of the three binaries just discussed. Some of the difficulties associated with the concept are discussed in Chapter 7. The book is in part a positive theological response to the view that 'the division male/female has proved fuzzy on all levels of investigation ... that the sex characteristics of human individuals vary greatly, and on all levels, and that pure maleness and pure femaleness are two extremes on a *rich and multilayered continuum*' (Heinamäa 2012: 226, emphasis added). The human continuum is the way we are made and the way we find ourselves, even though it is distorted by divisions of wealth, race, class, nation, religion, ability, and so on. It is humanity before its jarring disjunctions erupt and explode in violence. It is broader than sexuality and gender, while it has a particular resonance for both topics. Even 'human' restricts it, for the disjunction between human and non-human animals remains a matter of much distress. As Part III will explain, the Christian faith professes another vision for humanity, incarnated in Jesus, and longed for as the *telos* of human striving, compressed in the all-embracing baptismal formula of Galatians 3.28, that 'There is no longer Jew or Greek, there is no longer slave or free, there is no longer male and female; for all of you are one in Christ Jesus.' In the area of sexuality and gender, the continuum replaces the binary of opposite sexes, but it does not replace sexual difference. It restores sexual difference to being what it always was – a matter, not of kind, but of degree.

Sexual desire or attraction also exists along a continuum. From the Kinsey Reports onwards scientists are increasingly confident that sexual attraction 'exists *along a continuum*, from attraction exclusively toward the opposite sex (OSA) to attraction exclusively toward the same sex, with attraction to both sexes equally in the middle' (Alexander 2017: 214, emphasis added). Within the particular domain of sexuality we might expect a large majority of people to be oriented towards reproducing the species (as the writer of Genesis 1 assumes), but it does not follow that we are all summoned to that task, or equipped with either the desire or the biological means to contribute to it. Our third pair of binaries, masculine–feminine, also awaits transformation. There are countless ways of being a man or a woman, and countless models of masculinity – from Pope Francis to President Trump – and femininity – from Lady Gaga to Mother Teresa. What is required here is the development of *human* characteristics and virtues that will enable us to love God and our neighbours more faithfully, not the separation of these into alleged masculine qualities such as dominance, action, rationality, and hardness, and allegedly feminine qualities of submission, passivity, emotionality, and nurturance. Even the idea of virtue, based on the qualities expected of the *vir*, or male human being, skews one of the most basic moral concepts available to us by its exclusionary and binary assumptions.

## Summary of the Argument

*Gender and Christian Ethics* offers a lot more than the liberal imperative that women and men are to be treated equally or that sexual discrimination is always to be exposed as wrong. It makes the claim that before God the troublesome male–female binary no longer matters because it has already been dismantled. To speak this way is to draw deeply on the meaning of the coming of Christ, and to risk incredulity and ridicule from post-Christian sceptics who rightly draw attention to the exemption of churches from laws removing sexual and employment discrimination against women, the stubborn veto against their ordination, and the opposition of most churches to same-sex love and marriage. Such critics and, sadly many Christians, are unaccustomed to hearing an account of 'male and female' that deserves to be identified as 'Christian', yet that actually concurs with Paul's vision that, while a myriad of human differences remains, the gender binary of male and female, like the racial binary of Jew and Gentile, and the class binary of slave and free, is abolished in the new humanity established by and existing 'in' Christ. When a binary is replaced by a continuum, 'male and female' can be differently described, evaluated, and lived, as Part III of the book will amply demonstrate.

In order to view the argument as a whole, shorter summaries of all the chapters are provided here. Chapters 2 and 3 expand each of the three broad areas constituting gender just discussed. Chapter 2 develops the first aim of the book, 'to depict the relations between women and men as a pervasive human and global problem'. It begins that task by focussing on the sheer scale of gender violence in the world. Using the trope of 'rape culture', it confronts examples of violence against women, and domestic and child abuse, including female genital mutilation. The chapter moves toward the second broad area of gender – the socially constructed systems of thought that endorse inequality and violence – and analyses how dominant interpretations of Christianity are complicit in violence against women and LGBTIQ people. Chapter 3 contributes to the discussion of personal identity– our third sense of 'gender' – and of sexual difference, modelling sexual difference on the basis of *divine* difference. It raises the question why believers sometimes act violently, believing it to be the will of God, and concludes that the ethical problems generated by adherence to the three binaries and the injury they cause, require a new theological anthropology and a new, non-violent way of inhabiting Christian traditions.

Part II, 'Double Vision: Catholics and Protestants on Sexual Difference', addresses the second aim of the book – to critique naïve and harmful theological accounts of the relations between women and men as binary opposites, and does so by examining two separate developments converging in the idea of 'complementarity', baptised into Christian theology as recently as 1981.

Chapter 4 revisits the theology of Hans Urs von Balthasar in order to draw attention to damaging features of his thought about gender that were to influence Popes John Paul II and Benedict XVI, and enter into official Vatican teaching. It traces how challenges to the basic gender binary became associated with other topics about which the Vatican became polemical in recent decades: same-sex relationships and marriage; alternative family forms; the diminution of sexual difference in science and social theory; and the achievement of the rights and recognition of transgender people. It describes how this escalating polemic became known within the Vatican itself as the 'war on gender'.

Chapter 5 revisits Karl Barth's contribution to the theological understanding of gender (in sections III.1 and III.4 of his *Church Dogmatics*). It identifies several features of his contribution that have proved harmful both to relations between women and men, and to the achievement of the self-worth and acceptance of LGBTIQ people. There is an evaluation of the legacy he leaves for Protestant thought. The emergence of the idea of complementarity in Anglican thought is traced, together with attempts to move beyond it.

Chapter 6 acknowledges the appeal of complementarity and that of the male–female binary it supports. It analyses in some depth the concepts of 'human difference' and 'human nature' in order to show that complementarity is not endorsed by binary accounts of either. It identifies further exegetical, ideological, theological, and logical difficulties with complementarity and concludes, reluctantly, that complementarity is little more than a 'conceit'; that its purpose may be to provide a different way of proscribing homosexual relations, in particular same-sex marriage; marginalising LGBTIQ people, maintaining the male priesthood, and so on.

Part III, 'The Human Continuum: A Place for Everyone', completes the second aim of the book (to replace the binaries described in Part II, and the exclusions they engender, with 'the human continuum') and addresses the third aim of the book – to demonstrate how the human continuum enables a more inclusive theological understanding not only of relations between women and men, but also among LGBTIQ people. It builds on the foundations laid in Part II. It derives the human continuum – a non-binary account of human being and human desire – from traditional doctrines, followed by the embracing of sex and gender minorities within it. The masculine–feminine binary is dissolved, but not before observing its exaggerated emphases in secular culture and suggesting theological alternatives.

Chapter 7 clarifies the idea of a continuum and uses it to describe both human biological sex and human sexual desire as continua. It then demonstrates that the human continuum idea is fully consistent with the doctrine of God and of the human being in God's image. The tension regarding women's full imaging of God, beginning with Paul, is noted. The new creation, in which there is 'no longer male and female', is shown to overcome the binary understanding of gender and the tension over inclusive participation in the divine image. The final section explores how the doctrine of the Trinity is itself non-binary, and grounds a non-binary understanding of human being.

Chapter 8 utilises the idea of the human continuum to sketch a theological affirmation of the being of intersex, trans, lesbian and gay, and bisexual people. The range of intersex and transgender conditions is described. An attempt is made to listen to the different experiences of intersex and trans people, and to what they want, and how theology (mis)treats them. The argument is made that the continuum of orientation removes the stigma attaching to the lives of lesbian, gay, and bisexual people and the devastating effects of traditional teaching are noted. Near the end of the chapter, bi theologians speak for themselves and the weakening of the binary in public spaces and institutions is discussed and assessed.

Chapter 9 addresses the third binary of our inquiry, that between masculine and feminine. It assesses two accounts of a distinctive masculine spirituality, and concludes that human spirituality is a genuine requirement of faith whereas gendered spiritualities perpetuate the very binary they purport to critique. Four excavations of masculinity and femininity, as they are found in secular culture, are undertaken, highlighting the damage they do, and showing they contribute nothing to the humanisation of anyone. The binary is dissolved in the theological resources of earlier chapters.

Chapter 10 addresses the final aim – to contribute to a hermeneutic that can never condone discrimination or oppression. It adopts a 'hermeneutic of analogy' – a means of comparing strategies for dealing with violent and patriarchal sacred texts. It describes, appreciatively, how some women interpreters of the Qur'an deal with texts that appear blatantly discriminatory, and then moves to describing common difficulties, similarities, criticisms, and even theological solutions between our two traditions. The final section suggests how the doctrine of God advocated earlier in the book enables a more peaceable and just reading of Scripture, and provides an antidote to the belief that God could ever legitimise unjust actions.

Readers familiar with my earlier *Redeeming Gender* (2016) will recognise the different approach to gender adopted in the present volume.

The earlier volume approached gender through the history of sexuality in classical, medieval, and modern times, and showed how ancient theories about human bodies developed into modern theories about two opposite sexes that were then borrowed by the churches. The present volume begins with distressing facts about gender violence in the present, and then moves to address epistemological questions about how such violence is encoded and embodied in symbolic systems of thought. The earlier volume examined the surprising influence of modern secular thinking about sexuality on official church teaching: the present volume devotes two detailed chapters to the influence of Hans Urs von Balthasar and Karl Barth on Roman Catholic and Protestant thought, respectively, and moves to a detailed critique of complementarity.

Not only are the approaches to gender different in each volume, so also are the theological proposals. In the earlier work I looked to the Gospels to discover how in the Reign of God the usual power relations, especially those of men over women, are reversed, and to find in Jesus Christ an alternative model of masculinity. Moving from the Gospel records I showed how considerations of theology and Christology helped to envision the redemption of human relationships, careful both to retain but also reduce in importance the idea of sexual difference. In the present volume I work throughout with the notion of a human continuum, using core elements of Christian doctrine – Trinity, Christology, humanity in God's image – to indicate that humanity understood as a continuum or spectrum not only overcomes harmful binaries but follows plausibly and directly from doctrinal foundations. In this later and longer volume, I go on to argue for the full belonging of LGBTIQ people within the human continuum on theological grounds, begin the task of critique of secular understandings of gender, and seek a hermeneutical reading of sacred texts across Christianity and Islam that addresses violent readings and substitutes peaceful ones.

I would like to think that each of the three parts has a distinct character: that Part I is descriptive and analytical; that Part II is critical; and that Part III is constructive. But these characteristics inevitably overlap to some extent. The critical elements sometimes predominate, and I worry lest the vigour of robust engagement with authors with whom I disagree sometimes obscures the charitable regard that we ought to have for each other. I make many claims in the book, but the claim to be right is never among them. All a theologian can do is to offer arguments to be heard in the churches in their efforts to seek the truth and think the compassionate mind of Christ. The Archbishop of Canterbury has called for 'good disagreement' among Anglicans, deeply divided over issues of sexuality and gender. My country is at present deeply divided over its political future, and my friends in the USA despair of the polarisation of politics there. Politics too suffers from the exaggeration of differences and the binaries that result from it. I would not wish, especially in a book that seeks to remove binaries from theology, merely to add to them by creating unnecessary conflict and polarisation.

CHAPTER 2

# The Global Gender Crisis

## A 'Rape Culture'?

*Rape Culture, Gender Violence, and Religion* is a powerful collection of essays (Blyth, Colgan and Edwards 2018) adopting the term 'rape culture' to describe the gender violence that 'has reached endemic levels in numerous countries and communities around the world, where sexual violence, family violence, homophobia, biphobia and transphobia have become a lived reality for many people' (Blyth et al. 2018: 1). Within this global context, the authors say,

> Christianity has, throughout its history and up to the present day, played a significant and often contentious role in shaping the social imaginary – or collective consciousness – surrounding gender violence. Within Christian interpretative traditions, certain biblical texts have often been used uncritically to support patriarchal gender hierarchies and cis-heteronormative discourses, which work to sustain and multiply forms of gendered violence. (Blyth et al. 2018: 1)

I am struck by how all twelve chapters require readers to face up to the unwelcome problem that some versions of Christianity and all fundamentalist versions of Christian doctrine (whether these are called 'imaginaries', 'collective consciousnesses', 'frameworks', *'epistemes'* [knowledges], etc.) suggest, condone and authorise violence against people who disturb their heteronormative and complementarian assumptions. The name given to the effect that overarching structures of knowledge have upon particular minorities of people who challenge them is (following Gayatri Spivak) 'epistemic violence'. The seemingly endless discussions about whether homosexuality, same-sex marriage and, more recently, the bodies of intersex and trans people can be incorporated, or licensed to appear, within these frameworks postpone the deeper issue: whether the whole imaginary is a framework of 'epistemic violence', one which requires everyone to be like its authors and proclaimers before they can be 'in Christ' and experience for themselves God's love and acceptance.

17

Testimony from around the world links patriarchy with violence. Here are just a couple of examples from many that could be provided. Sister Susan Rakoczy, writing from the University of KwaZulu-Natal, has described 'the insidious links between patriarchy, violence and Christianity and their effects on women as seen through the prevalence of domestic violence in South Africa' (Rakoczy 2004: 29). There is a very high level of violence there, and particularly domestic violence against women across all sectors of society. She is clear: 'Patriarchal structures in society and Christianity are not only violent in their effects on women's dignity as persons, but they undergird the epidemic of violence against women' (Rakoczy 2004: 34). In Oceania, where, according to the United Nations, rates of violence against women are among the highest in the world, the patriarchy of the churches is said to be a contributing factor, not least because the churches 'teach women that they must respect and obey men at all times' (Filemoni-Tofaeono and Johnson 2006: 106). Countries where Christians are most opposed to homosexuality are also the ones where inegalitarian gender relations and violence against women are most prominent. 'Despite the best efforts of affirmative or progressive churches, these discourses cannot be changed until the episteme is reconfigured to welcome and include a greater diversity of humanity' (Henderson-Merrygold 2018: 100).

Since I began writing this book, two remarkable global campaigns have spontaneously risen up and given courage and hope to millions of people (mostly women) who are now able to speak their experiences of abuse out of imposed silence and into the public domain. In October 2017, the *Me Too* campaign, which started as a hashtag on social media, developed virally as a movement against sexual harassment and assault, all around the world. In January 2018, Hollywood celebrities founded the *Time's Up* movement, protesting against sexual harassment in the film industry. The impact of the two campaigns has been huge, extending to many parts of the world. Whatever the criticisms of these campaigns, there is no doubt that they reveal the astonishing imbalance of power between men and women, a lack of respect for women and the sheer scale of the problem to be tackled. Perhaps the impact of these campaigns is beginning to be measurable? Research by the Fawcett Society in Britain shows that a majority of young men are 'more likely to challenge sexual harassment' since #MeToo, and that half of all people surveyed said that 'what is acceptable has changed' (Fawcett Society 2018).

It is impossible to think about violence against women in the West without including the ubiquity of pornography, its resulting eroticisation of inequality and its contribution to rape culture. Public discussion of pornography ranges from advocates who emphasise its entertainment value and regard it as somehow emblematic of a free society to those who emphasise a range of harms, including the likely neurological damage to its persistent viewers, and the social demeaning of women that much pornography assumes and to which it contributes. One suspects religious discussion is influenced by the suspicion of sexual pleasure, frustrated desire and the lack of body acceptance, while public discussion is hampered by the assumption that pornography appears in just one form. There are countless types of pornography, and the possibility cannot be discounted that the viewing of some of those may be beneficial to the viewers. However, I find most of the pornography I have viewed to be morally repugnant, and that is before sheer revulsion forbids clicking through to tabs such as 'forced sex', 'gang bang', 'anal fuck', 'gagging', 'pissing' and the like, all freely available. Repugnance based on empathy towards victims is not merely subjective and not diluted by appeals to the alleged consent of the 'actors'. Pamela Cooper-White contributes to theological discussion of pornography through her analysis of *eros*. '*Eros*', she writes, is 'that life force that reaches out toward the other for intimacy, mutual creativity, and exchange.' It is 'relational, empathic, whole, spirited, and imaginative'. Pornography on this under-standing is not erotic but anti-erotic. It is 'episodic, performance-oriented, fragmented, standardized, and addictive' (Cooper-White 2015: 493).

I remain confident that pornography contributes substantially to the rape culture, and that the violence associated with it is not merely physical or directly mimetic. Much of it is the visual form, not merely of physical violence against women, but of epistemic violence as well. Why? Review-ing the growing body of evidence, Jennifer Beste claims, 'online porn greatly influences teens and young adults' sexual expectations, patterns of arousal, sexual preferences, and sexual behavior' (Beste 2018: 235). It increases the likelihood of practising unwanted anal sex, and is associated with various harms, including treating sexual partners with little respect, and the belief that sexual satisfaction can be achieved without emotion or affection. It encourages the acceptance of 'rape myths', i.e., convenient but false beliefs that some men hold, such that women wear provocative clothing in order to invite aggressive responses, or that men, once aroused, are incapable of controlling their urges.

## Domestic and Child Abuse

The Crime Survey of England and Wales estimates that 1.2 million women experienced domestic abuse in the year ending March 2017, and an estimated 4.3 million women aged 16–59 have experienced domestic abuse since the age of 16 (Women's Aid 2018). In the UK, domestic violence accounts for 18 per cent of all recorded violent crime (Storkey 2015: 87). Men, of course, also experience domestic abuse, but the majority of partner violence is directed against women, who as victims also suffer disproportionately, being more likely to have endured continuous bouts of violence, and the fear of violence, whether or not it occurs. Women account for 83 per cent of high-frequency victims (i.e., of more than ten crimes). (In the year ending March 2017, the majority of defendants in domestic abuse-related prosecutions were men (92 per cent); Women's Aid 2018.)

The Jay Report into the sexual abuse of children in Rotherham – a medium-sized town in the north of England – reported that over sixteen years there were 1,400 female young victims of abuse (Jay 2014), and this has since been proved to have been an underestimate.

> Girls were raped by several men, trafficked to other towns and cities in the north of England, abducted, beaten, and intimidated. There were examples of children who had been doused in petrol and threatened with being set alight, threatened with guns, made to witness brutally violent rapes and threatened they would be next if they told anyone. Girls as young as 11 were raped by large numbers of perpetrators. (Jay 2014: 1)

It was not only the perpetrators who regarded their victims with contempt. So did the police, whose senior professionals refused to act on three earlier reports. Jay comments, 'By far the majority of perpetrators were described as "Asian" by victims, yet throughout the entire period, councillors did not engage directly with the Pakistani-heritage community to discuss how best they could jointly address the issue' (Jay 2014: 2). Fear of the charge of racism was a strong factor in their reluctance. In 2016–18, Britons were hearing almost daily of barely believable sexual exploitation of children by organised gangs of men in several cities and large towns in England. In 2017, a Royal Commission in Australia investigating the sexual abuse of children admitted that the nation had been gripped by an epidemic dating back decades, with tens of thousands of children sexually abused in schools, religious organisations and other institutions (Royal Commission 2017).

### 'Scars across Humanity'

Any sensitive person reading Elaine Storkey's *Scars across Humanity: Understanding and Overcoming Violence against Women* (Storkey 2015) is likely to be disconcerted by the range of emotions the book elicits: horror in the face of the appalling catalogue of violence against women throughout the world; despair that men are still capable of such cruelty and unthinking misogyny; empathy with the millions of female victims who bear the consequences of violence on their bodies and its scarring on their souls; admiration for the women who resist violence when they can, often at the cost of their lives; and perhaps gratitude that the full truth about gendered violence is beginning to be told.

In India, millions of unborn girls are killed by selective abortion and infanticide. As Storkey says, 'Violence begins before birth' (Storkey 2015: 18). 'Among the stock of women that could potentially be alive in India today, over 25 million are "missing".' The 'disposal' of newborn girls is commonplace. Despite the illegality of selective abortion, the law is barely enforced. The sex ratio is now far from balanced in parts of India. In Haryana there are 830 girls for every 1,000 boys, and the shortage of young women fuels the kidnapping and forced marriage of young women, while young men, angry at the shortage of young women, all too easily express their ire by violence against them (Storkey 2015: 26–7).

All over the world so-called crimes of honour represent another instrument of patriarchal control where the victims are almost always women. They encompass

> "honour killings", assault, confinement or imprisonment, and interference with choice in marriage, where the publicly articulated "justification" is attributed to a social order claimed to require the preservation of a concept of "honour" vested in male "family and/or conjugal" control over women and specially women's sexual conduct: actual, suspected or potential. (Welchman and Hossain 2005: 4)

Statistics about honour killings are very difficult to obtain. They may be the cause of death of up to 10,000 women in Pakistan each year (Storkey 2015: 61). In Britain 2,800 cases of honour-based violence were reported in 2010, a fraction of the actual number of cases. In Europe 96 per cent of the honour-killing perpetrators are Muslims, and the number of reported incidents all over the world is rapidly increasing. There is a 'conspiratorial muteness' (Julios 2015: 53) about honour killings. They are silently approved by families collaborating within communities and so have a collective corporate character. After investigating two decades of honour killings in Britain, Christina Julios concludes,

> Paternalistic mindsets together with distorted notions of family 'honour' and 'shame' will translate into extreme levels of domestic and sexual violence against women who defy such norms. In a testimony to the power of the collective over individual agency in 'honour' cultures; those who fail to acquiesce will pay with their lives. (Julios 2016: 67)

Storkey's chronicle of 'scars across humanity' continues with barely believable statistics and accounts of violence in the home, of trafficking and prostitution, of the crime of rape, and of sexual violence in zones of war. Former British Foreign Secretary William Hague has inveighed against the 'widely held view that violence against women and girls is inevitable in peacetime and in conflict', observing that at the present time 'we are clearly dealing with injustice on a scale that is simply intolerable, as well as damaging to the stability of those countries and the peace of the wider world' (Hague 2017a: 12; Hague 2017b). The recent introduction of the term 'state rape' to criminology is part of a welcome 'means of calling attention to State responsibility for widespread and systematic sexual violence as a particular class of atrocities' (Hagan and Morse 2014: 691). Since Hague spoke, most of the world has been shocked beyond words to have heard of the genocide of 27,000 Rohingya Muslims and the displacement of 700,000 more. UN investigators interviewed 875 witnesses who had fled their homeland of Burma and found that the military were 'killing indiscriminately, gang-raping women, assaulting children and burning entire villages' (Ellis-Petersen 2018).

It is impossible to describe the depth and extent of the gendered violence suffered by women in a few pages. Even aid agencies dedicated to the relief of suffering are not exempt. A report by the British House of Commons (Ratcliff 2018) complained that leading aid agencies had shown 'complacency verging on complicity' in responding to sexual abuse that was endemic across the aid sector. The authors of *Sex and World Peace* stake out a detailed claim that those countries with the most violence at the micro level (domestic) are also the countries with the most violence at the macro level of relations within and between states (Hudson *et al.* 2012). The recent rise of fundamentalism in the world religions is further evidence of this. 'The growth of fundamentalism', writes Vrinda Narain (with particular reference to Islamic fundamentalism in India), 'has resulted in the privileging of religious identity over all other identities' (Narain 2001: 76). Religious identity is then defined by the male fundamentalists, who speak with the loudest voices and achieve what Narain calls 'the masking of male agency' (Narain 2001: 77). The tendency to defer to loud fundamentalist voices is known in all the world religions.

## Female Genital Mutilation

At least 200 million women and girls alive today have undergone female genital mutilation (FGM) in the thirty countries with representative data on prevalence. In most of these countries, the majority of girls were cut before age 5 (UNICEF 2016). Could there be a more excruciating, barbarous practice ever devised by men in the name of honour and tradition? Efua Borkenoo, a Ghanaian activist, was the first to name the practice 'mutilation', not just 'cutting' or 'circumcision', and her book *Cutting the Rose: Female Genital Mutilation, the Practice and Its Prevention* (chosen by an international jury as one of Africa's 100 best books of the twentieth century) outlined in detail the horrific physical and psychological consequences of the practice (along with its history, cultural contexts, supposed justifications, and geographical distribution). As Hillary Burrage writes, FGM is 'not based on understandings open to rational-scientific debate, but often rather on deeply-held mores which brook no challenge and which are in effect invisible. FGM may not be mentioned, let alone questioned, in most practising communities' (Burrage 2015: 25). It is 'embedded almost inextricably in *a set of beliefs about sexual behaviours and gendered power hierarchies* which no amount of disclosure is likely to dislodge' (Burrage 2015: 25, emphasis added). A recent UK Government report estimates that around 103,000 women aged 15–49 and 24,000 women aged 50 and over who have migrated to England and Wales are living with the consequences of FGM, while around 10,000 migrant girls aged under 15 have probably undergone FGM (HM Government 2016: 8). Their pain must be unimaginable, while the medical and psychological consequences are severe, traumatic and permanent. Yet the practice is often presented as beneficial, often seen as a rite of passage into adulthood and generally carried out by women themselves.

But the scandal of FGM risks being complicated by the well-meaning and indignant remarks of liberal Western scholars like me, who may not stop to consider the deep contextual reasons for the persistence of the practice, or to align themselves with indigenous efforts to stop or replace it. The same caveat applies to all cross-cultural judgments. Spivak has famously warned (but in a different context) against 'white people saving brown women from brown men' (Spivak 1988). Practices such as FGM and veil-wearing, thought by many in the West to be disadvantageous and demeaning to women, can be maintained and even exaggerated, just because of the felt disapproval emanating from former colonising countries. The practices can then become part of 'resistance narratives constructed to ward off Westernization and the new form of colonization called globalization' (Kassam 2012: 410). Similar caution applies to child marriage, which represents another institution of patriarchal control over female sexuality and fertility. The United Nations reports that 'worldwide, almost 750 million women and girls alive today were married before their 18th birthday' (UNWomen 2017). In 2012 67 million women aged between 20 and 24 had been married as girls (United Nations Population Fund 2012: 6). Some of these girls were not even teenagers. Neither is the practice made more morally acceptable when it is said to be 'arranged' (as a UK Government Working Group once suggested (Home Office 2000)).

Daring to speak out about such matters is an exacting dilemma for liberal First World academics. On the one hand, I want to acknowledge the appropriateness of brusque postcolonial responses to moral censure. Critics of child marriage need to acknowledge that for most of Christian history it was possible to become betrothed at the age of 7, and married at the age of 12 (for girls) and 14 (for boys). Critics of the burqa as a cruel sexist device imposed on reluctant women by patriarchal men need to understand that the burqa also has feminist supporters who see it as an effective refusal of the male gaze and its corresponding expectation of full feminine visibility. On the other hand, criticism of cultural practices emanating from one society about the practices of another society need not imply the superiority of the criticisers. Critique immediately raises the problem of moral relativism, and here the philosopher Bernard Williams is my guide.

Williams influentially described moral relativism as 'possibly the most absurd view to have been advanced even in moral philosophy' (Williams 1973: 34). He illustrated the absurdity of moral relativism by means of three contradictory propositions: 'that "right" means ... "right for a given society"; that "right for a given society" is to be understood in a function-alist sense; and that (therefore) it is wrong for people in one society to condemn, interfere with, etc., the values of another society' (Williams 1973: 34). Moral relativism is false, argued Williams, since the contention that a particular society may decide a certain action is right does not entail the stronger contention that it is universally right not to interfere or criticise it. He also thought that relativism produces indifferentism, the view that no one is justified in protesting against any moral wrong at all.

I follow Williams here, not for the sake of a particular moral theory, but for the sake of human solidarity. All people feel pain, need food, shelter and so on. Rights theories presuppose this. There *are* universals in moral-ity, and the damage done to women by the practice of FGM can be called, in the name of a common human morality, an outrage. At least two volumes in this series warn against the demoralising effects of relativism. Lisa Cahill, in *Sex, Gender and Christian Ethics*, finds 'the academic game of theoretical relativism' to be 'frightening' in its power to diminish the impetus for practical moral action (Cahill 1996: 31), while Susan Parsons, in *Feminism and Christian Ethics*, argues for an 'appropriate universalism' (Parsons 1996: 198): 'universal' because creaturely life is sustained by God and is the universal context for compassion and compassionate relation- ships to develop; and 'appropriate' in acknowledging its own cultural foundations and owning up to the past practices and present possibilities of cultural arrogance. Both Cahill and Parsons appeal to human solidarity rather than directly to reason, but both approaches are needed. It does not follow that people affirming an appropriate universalism are free from moral hypocrisy in other respects, or that they are morally superior, or neglectful of horrendous moral mistakes their societies have made in the past. Even with FGM it may be the case that certain benefits (rites of passage, social approval, personal reward, etc.) sometimes follow from the practice. *Any* ideology assuming the inferiority of women is to be chal- lenged, intellectually and practically. Quiet advocacy, conscientisation, support for United Nations initiatives, the empowerment of individuals and support for the growing number of charities working to end the practice will be more successful than indignant moral expostulation.

## Gender as a Symbolic System

Storkey's analysis of the violent relations between men and women quickly elides into explanations of the violence by reference to gender as a symbolic or socially constructed system. This is the second sense of the term gender defined earlier. She is right to claim that 'violence on such a scale could not exist were it not structured in some way into the very fabric of societies and cultures themselves. It could not continue if it were not somehow sup- ported by deep assumptions about the value of women, or some justifica- tion of the use of power' (Storkey 2015: 2). Religion is deeply implicated in all three of these areas – the fabric of societies and cultures, deep assumptions about the value of women, and the justification of the use of power. The ability of religions to address their partial responsibility for misogyny is the key to the survival of their academic integrity in the present century and to the vindication of their claims to offer salvation, well-being, union with God and so on. A radical upheaval in the doctrine of human being is urgently needed, not just for the sake of the 'believ- ability' of Christian or other claims about God and God's love, but for the sake of future potential victims of male domination.

The previous section drew attention not only to the pandemic of gender violence; it also made suggestions about some of the causes of it. There are many competing theories about this (Storkey 2015: 152–69), and in our descriptions of it thus far, phrases such as 'deep assumptions about the value of women', 'a set of beliefs about sexual behaviours and gendered hierarchies', 'the masking of male agency', have appeared. Patriarchy, then, beyond the many proximate causes, may be seen to be the ultimate cause of violence against women, but patriarchy has itself been critiqued as an explanatory concept, including its generality, and its imposition (as we have just observed) of postcolonial assumptions upon the Two-Thirds World (van Klinken 2013: 14–16). Mindful both of its generality and its overuse in the culture wars, I nonetheless agree with Storkey, who calls it 'an overriding but complex term for the processes by which male power is grasped and imposed, and the ideologies and practices which reinforce women's vulnerability' (Storkey 2015: 185). 'What shapes patriarchy', she asks, 'if it is not the institutions, ideas and attitudes which are devised by human persons?' (Storkey 2015: 185–6). Everyone knows that bad beliefs shape bad behaviour, and it is not hard to see how, once half the human race is regarded as inferior by the other half in any belief system, misogyny becomes justifiable, practicable, and to some extent inevitable.

Thomas Laqueur (1990) has convincingly shown that Greeks and Romans, and indeed Christians until roughly the eighteenth century, thought about bodies and their capacities for reproduction, and about their corresponding status in familial and social life, very differently from people today. His thesis is well known, and both appreciated and criticised in equal measure. I have commended his thesis extensively (but not uncritically)(Thatcher 2016), and so I will do no more here than mention its outline very briefly. He argues there was, until relatively recently, thought to be a default male body, not two sexes. The female body was an inferior version of the same male prototype. This 'one sex' body, in different versions, was thought to be demonstrated biologically by *similar* genitalia in men and women, the male genitalia located outside the body, and the same genitalia located *inside* the female body. So there are two, or multiple, versions of the same one-sex body. That is what it means to say the ancients believed in a single sex, not two sexes. Luther held the then common view that women emitted seed, and that 'if this seed was not released on a regular basis, it would build up in the body and putrefy' (Crowther 2012: 671–2).

The reason why common human genitals were, in women, held inside the body, was due to a lack of heat. While this sounds extraordinary to the modern ear, an elemental theory of everything (however fantastical) makes sense of it. If everything is a combination of fire, water, earth, and air, these elements (or the lack of them) will be differently arranged in all beings. Heat and cold are differently present in the seasons, for instance (like wetness and dryness, hardness and softness), and these are the basic contrasts between a male and a female body. Bodies exist on a continuum of elements and humours. An essential premise underlying the whole scheme is that to have greater heat is to be more perfect, so women will always be imperfect vis-à-vis men. Bodily difference underwrote countless gender differences. So men 'were described with cultural superlatives that reflected their perfect "natural" state: physical and political strength, rationality, spirituality, superiority, activity, dryness and penetration'. Women, conversely, were thought to embody the negative qualities of 'physical and political weakness, irrationality, fleshliness, inferiority, passivity, wetness, and being penetrated' (Swancutt 2003: 198).

Arising from this analysis of classical physiology I select two general conclusions. First, the understanding of human beings and their bodies as comprising two separate sexes was shockingly new in the modern period (for the full story, see Schiebinger 1989, 1993). 'The dimorphic model is so commonplace to us now', writes Sara Heinämää, 'that it is hard for us to imagine any other way of conceiving sex and discussing it' (Heinämää 2012: 223). However, she continues (following Dreger 1998),

> a series of studies in the history of sex-concepts show that prior to twentieth-century maleness and femaleness were not conceptualized as mutually exclusive features. Individuals with mixed or ambiguous genitals and gonads were considered exceptional but not medically or physiologically abnormal. Similarly, women with male bodily features, such as a beard, and men with female bodily features, such as breasts, were considered as normal variations of human embodiment. (Heinämää 2012: 223)

Former ways of conceptualising the human body throw into relief the social and medical novelty of opposite sexes. From the seventeenth to the twentieth century the opposite-sex binary became what the French anthropologist Pierre Bourdieu called a *doxa*, a feature of the established order of things that no one thinks of questioning. Bourdieu too takes for granted that men and women were 'perceived as two variants, superior and inferior, of the same physiology' (Bourdieu 2001: 14–15). Second, the story powerfully shows what philosophers warn us against, that values cannot be derived, at least directly, from facts. The body, whether male or female, cannot be the basis for making discriminatory judgements of any kind, whether about its status, worth, or role. Rather it is prior beliefs about superiority and inferiority with regard to gender that shape how bodies are read and what unjustified burdens are imposed upon them.

That is why Christian ethics is able to make a contribution to the clearing away of unfounded assumptions about gender instead of replicating them in the new guise of a new theory of opposite sexes.

## The Medieval Continuum

Several medievalists have drawn attention to the persistence of the ancient gender continuum in medieval Christian thought and its amalgamation with Christian theology. Jacqueline Murray speaks of the medievalists' 'attempt to break out of the tyranny of binaries, the dyads of men/women, male/female, and masculine/feminine, given the tyrannical binaries that dominate the study of the Middle Ages: lord/serf, orthodox/heretic, and secular/ecclesiastical' (Murray 2008: 36). Medieval theology considered relations between male and female 'to be binary and hierarchical: the weak and passive female compared to the strong and active male'. These relations however,

> were not static; they were placed on a continuum and human beings could be found at different points along it. Generally women were found on one end, men on the other, and 'unmen,' such as slaves, would be located somewhere in the middle. It was the characteristics at either end of the continuum that established and reinforced the ethical and moral qualities that contrasted men and women as a series of binaries: intellect/body, form/ matter, active/passive, rational/irrational, reason/emotion, selfcontrol/lust, judgment/mercy, order/disorder, and, most important, perfection/ imperfection. (Murray 2008: 39)

Murray emphasises that this ancient continuum was 'value laden':

> men were considered to be fully human and perfect and without mystery, whereas women were the marked category that needed investigation and explanation. Women were by nature colder than men and their internal genitals were smaller, underdeveloped, and inferior to those of men. Women were also wet and porous, whereas men were hot and contained. Women were able to balance their humors naturally and regularly through menstruation, which helped to dry out their excessive wetness. Men expelled their excess heat through sweating, which accounted for the fact men had more pronounced veins than did women. (Murray 2008: 39)

The lengthy description of the medieval continuum concurs entirely with Laqueur's description of the classical one. When the classical continuum was combined with reflection on Genesis 2, 'the general conclusion was that men and women were both fully in the spiritual likeness of God, but this was not reflected in their biological differences, which ultimately kept women removed from "fully human status"' (Murray 2008: 41). Many examples are cited of women who act in masculine ways (more perfectly) and men who act in feminine ways (shamefully). 'The notion that men and women were not so much equal as capable of becoming more similar as they moved along the continuum was most frequently used to suggest that women should, and would as they became more spiritual, move toward the masculine end' (Murray 2008: 42). The continuum must therefore be construed as damaging to female human being, capable of sometimes accelerating into outright misogyny, but always reminding women of their permanent inferiorities.

The medieval continuum cannot therefore be helpful as a source for inspiration for a realisation of more just relations between women and men. That is because it does not operate in an equilibrium: it is a slide from strength to weakness, perfection to imperfection, and so on. However, once the gradient is removed and humanity conceived as a single kind, the possibility exists for a different basis altogether in the establishment of just gender relations (Part III). That possibility is considered in more detail in Chapter 7.

## 'Eternalizing the Arbitrary'

I want to pursue a little further the question how harmful gendered beliefs embed themselves in cultural and religious practices where they successfully pass themselves off as normative, thereby escaping analysis. Here, the French sociologist and anthropologist Pierre Bourdieu is a helpful guide. Perhaps no one has done more to unmask the near ubiquitous presence of symbolic systems that devalue women than Bourdieu. He finds himself (like me) in a 'relationship of sympathetic externality' to the 'immense body of work encouraged by the feminist movement' (Bourdieu 2001: 116). His *Masculine Domination* begins with observations from his residence for several years among the Berbers of Kabylia, and moves outwards to the replication of these gendered norms in more modern societies, indeed 'at the two extremes of the space of anthropological possibles, among the highland peasants of Kabylia and among the upper-class citizens of Bloomsbury' (Bourdieu 2001: 81). We will stay with Bourdieu for a few pages in order to take in the scope, this time, of the task of understanding what he calls the 'androcentric unconscious' that lies undetected in most (all?) societies, prior to attempts to dissipate it. 'Eternalizing the arbitrary' (Bourdieu 2001: vii) is what patriarchy allegedly does, that is, it makes arbitrary social arrangements that favour men and devalue women adopt a permanent character. These arrangements constitute a *doxa*. There is, Bourdieu claims, an unquestioning or 'paradoxical' submission to the way the social world is organised, and 'masculine domination, and the way it is imposed and suffered' is the 'prime example' of it.

The naked violence we have just examined is supported by another type of violence – a violence so *gentle* that it does not register as violence at all. This is the 'symbolic violence, a gentle violence, imperceptible and invisible even to its victims, exerted for the most part through the purely symbolic channels of communication and cognition (more precisely, misrecognition), recognition, or even feeling' (Bourdieu 2001: 1–2). This is the violence that transforms history into nature, and 'cultural arbitrariness into the *natural*' (Bourdieu 2001: 2, author's emphasis). It resides in the 'unconscious schemes of perception and appreciation' that constitute the 'androcentric unconscious' (Bourdieu 2001: 5), and are shared by both women and men. Just because they are unconscious they evade recognition and justification. In Kabylia (if not in London or Washington),

> The social order functions as an immense symbolic machine tending to ratify the masculine domination on which it is founded: it is the sexual division of labour, a very strict distribution of the activities assigned to each sex, of their place, time and instruments; it is the structure of space, with the opposition between the place of assembly or the market, reserved for men, and the house, reserved for women, or, within the house, between the male part, the hearth, and the female part – the stable, the water and vegetable stores; it is the structure of time, the day and the farming year, or the cycle of life, with its male moments of rupture and the long female periods of gestation. (Bourdieu 2001: 10–11)

All this sounds far removed from Western societies where, thanks to feminist protest, much progress has been made in desexualising labour and space. In the UK, in 2017, 58 per cent of doctors in training were female (General Medical Council 2017: 28). Over half of new ordinands in the Church of England in 2016 were women (Anglican Communion News Service 2017). The percentage of female Members of Parliament in the UK rose from 18.2 per cent in 1997 to 32 per cent in 2016 (Parliament UK 2018). In 2018 in the UK, the gender pay gap for full-time employees fell close to zero for people aged between 18 and 39 years (ONS 2018). If these statistics were pointed out to Bourdieu (he died in 2002), he would probably, without disputing them, remark that the cognitive structures of sexual difference still remain buried within the appearance (*doxa* in Greek) of things. He might draw attention to his claim that 'the sexual act' is still regarded 'as a relation of domination. To possess sexually, as in the French *baiser* or the English "to fuck", is to dominate in the sense of subjecting to one's power, but also to deceive, mislead, or, as we say, "to have"' (Bourdieu 2001: 19). Young men are said generally to think of sexual experience with women in terms of 'conquest', of 'possession', whereas women think of it very differently. Even the giving of pleasure in this shifting atmosphere of domination is suspect, for within it

> the faking of [female] orgasm is 'a perfect example of the male power to make the interaction between the sexes conform to the view of it held by men, who expect the female orgasm to provide a proof of their virility and the pleasure derived from this extreme form of submission'. (Bourdieu 2001: 20–1, citing Mackinnon 1987: 58)

Gentle violence, then, is never gentle for long. Bourdieu claims the 'sexual relation' *is* 'a social relation of domination'. Why?

> ... because it is constructed through the fundamental principle of division between the active male and the passive female and because this principle creates, organizes, expresses and directs desire – male desire as the desire for possession, eroticized domination, and female desire as the desire for masculine domination, as eroticized subordination or even, in the limiting case, as the eroticized recognition of domination. (Bourdieu 2001: 21)

Boys, he continues, must pass through a process of 'virilization' or 'defeminization' (Bourdieu 2001: 25–6), which may involve endless sexual 'conquests' and 'frantic investment in all the masculine games of violence' (Bourdieu 2001: 51). Women, destined for the passive role, appear as men would like them to appear, from being fully veiled to being hardly covered at all. The 'controlled exhibition of the body as an index of "liberation"' turns out to be 'very obviously subordinated to the male point of view' (Bourdieu 2001: 29).

When I read theology at Oxford in the early 1960s, George Berkeley's 1713 work, *Three Dialogues between Hylas and Philonous*, was a set text for one of the philosophy of religion examinations. In this work Berkeley propounded the peculiar philosophical doctrine that to be is to be perceived: *esse est percipi*. We know objects continue to exist when no one is perceiving them, he averred, because God perceives them. Bourdieu takes the slogan *esse est percipi* out of the eighteenth-century squabble between empiricists and idealists and uses it to elicit sympathy for women under masculine domination, which, he says, 'constitutes women as symbolic objects whose being (*esse*) is a being-perceived (*percipi*), [and] has the effect of keeping them in a permanent state of bodily insecurity, or more precisely of symbolic dependence' (Bourdieu 2001: 66 emphasis added).

More than twenty years on (the original French edition of *Masculine Domination* was published in 1998), there are obvious difficulties with Bourdieu's analysis. The large generalisations do not account for the complexities and particularities of gendered relations. They can be readily, and fashionably, rejected as 'essentialist'. They have limited and different application in different societies. Bourdieu may underestimate the achievements of women in overcoming some of the difficulties of which he complains, or the degree to which resistance to male power is possible. But when lamenting violence against women we needed to have recourse to broader explanations of it which took account of its pervasive breadth and depth, and Bourdieu's work is a strong contribution to that. In a side-swipe at Judith Butler (who is unnamed) he contrasts the 'strength of the structure' of unequal social relations with the lame 'act[s] of performative magic' and the spurious 'subversive voluntarism' that seeks reform of the structure by transgression. No, the problem lies elsewhere, in the 'schemes of perception and appreciation not readily accessible to consciousness' (Bourdieu 2001: 95). It is the system, not the self, that requires radical amendment, but these are intertwined. Individuals are not powerless. 'Structures shape people's practices, but it is also people's practices that constitute (and reproduce) structures. In this view of things, human agency and structure, far from being opposed, in fact presuppose each other' (Sewell 1992: 4).

## The Abuse Crises

The abuse crises in the Catholic and Anglican churches have appalled nearly a generation of believers and unbelievers alike. Nancy Dallavalle laments the 'general failure to grapple with gender and sex and sexuality in the Catholic intellectual tradition as a whole' (Dallavalle 2016: 126). She argues the positive emphasis on heterosexual sexual intercourse as 'the basis for new life has led to *a problematic rigidity in the understanding of biological difference* as this pertains to gender roles and sexual orientation' (Dallavalle 2016: 126, emphasis added). This rigidity is the elevation of the male–female binary. On the other hand, she continues, 'the evidence of genuine sexual variety, both in terms of gender identity and in terms of sexual orientation, has led to a sense that embodiment can be theorized apart from bodies' (Dallavalle 2016: 127). The clerical abuse crises, principally but not exclusively in the Roman Catholic Church in the previous fifty years, provide overwhelming evidence for this (see Hogan 2011 for references).

The abusers were men in powerful positions, and they misused their power over vulnerable others. The 'malignant nexus of sexuality and power' undermined the Catholic tradition 'completely' (Hogan 2015: 336). But there is an aetiology to the abuse crisis, a major strand of which 'is the poisonous legacy of a long tradition of contempt for human sexuality in an institution which has privileged secrecy and unaccountable power over transparency and participation' (Beattie 2010). Her tradition, she explains, is one

> in which sexual desire has been portrayed as the enemy of those who seek spiritual union with God. In a religion in which the main focus has been the development of men's spirituality through the suppression of their sexuality, this has meant that male priests and monks have regarded the sexual female body as the greatest threat to their spiritual well-being, and the control of female sexuality has been and continues to be a major preoccupation. (Beattie 2010)

How would the misogyny of the tradition help to explain the abuse of boys and young men within it? The answer comes in three highly plausible stages. First, 'the accumulation of power over other people's bodies ... allows men to believe that their primary spiritual responsibility lies in the area of sexual discipline, and the use of power becomes a means to inhibit and punish sexual desire'. Next comes 'a dark spiral of temptation, guilt and punishment focused on the "sin" of sexual arousal and the bodies which cause it – whether those are the bodies of women, children or men, or indeed one's own (which becomes subject to extravagant masochistic practices of chastisement)'. But now that many gay men are out of the closet, 'homosexual bodies have also become highly visible sources of temptation for a religious hierarchy which includes many homosexuals among its ranks', with the result that 'the "problem" of homosexuality has now been added to the age-old "problem" of female sexuality with which the men of the church must do battle' (Beattie 2010).

An exclusive male priesthood combined with compulsory celibacy is deeply implicated in the abuse crisis. It is also hopelessly incompatible with the Catholic Church's recent teaching about complementarity. Not that the priesthood attracts paedophiles: rather, as Marie Keenan has shown in her detailed and sensitive study, based mainly in Ireland, priests who abuse are not especially bad men, but good men 'whose clerical masculine identity and way of "doing" priesthood or religious brotherhood is built on a life that is impossible to live' (Keenan 2012: xv). Many never achieved the sexual maturity required of them because of their physical and spiritual distance from women and their theological beliefs both about women and about themselves. Beattie has complained that the teaching of the Roman Catholic Church about sexuality is 'rooted in an ahistorical, absolutist approach, seeking to uphold timeless and universal truths about the meaning and purpose of sexuality, as a way of resisting changing social values' (Beattie 2010, cited in Nixon and Cornwall 2017: 385). The institution of the church failed them in their training, failed to support them in facing almost inevitable emotional and sexual difficulties, and failed to support their victims. That failure was systemic (Hidalgo 2007). Keenan charges that

> The Church still promotes an institutional practice that is bound to fail. Cruelty and abuse are bound to arise from such impossible tasks. The power and control game (control men's bodies and you control their minds) has turned into a cynical exercise against better knowledge. Just for the purpose of order and maintaining the institution, human lives are now sacrificed and destroyed, lives that include the identifiable victims of Catholic clergy, whose stories of pain resound around the world, but lives that also include the clergy themselves. (Keenan 2012: 263)

I have no wish to dwell on the tragedy that is the clerical abuse crises and the failure of the church to deal with it at every level. In any case explanations are complex. I *do* wish to draw attention to the ways it exemplifies the fault-lines surrounding sexuality and gender discussed in Chapter 1, namely the misuse of gendered power; the symbolic system which engenders injustice and violence, and the lack of recognition of personal identity. All three are instantly recognisable both in the church as an institution, and among the abusing priests themselves. Indeed the identity of priests becomes a crucial problem, since it is always worked out in social space and is never a matter of pure interiority. Yet the social space of priests is inhabited and inhibited by the masculinist culture within the church at all levels. Neither is the Anglican Communion exempt from similar failings. The 'culture of abuse and cover-up', which pre-existed the most recent exposure of clerical abuse in the Church of England (which the Gibb Report [2017] uncovered), was 'often hidden behind a veil of religious excuse' that served to confirm 'the frequently distorted psychology of religious institutions' (Selby 2017). Insofar as churches can be regarded as, or analogous to, corporate individuals, the manifestation of silence, denial, and cover-up, manifests a deep malaise of soul. The Decade of Evangelism (1990–9), declared by the Lambeth Conference in 1988, 'seems now, tragically, the Decade of Disgrace' (Gill 2019: 21).

In 2018, the Independent Inquiry into Child Sexual Abuse (IICSA) began its preliminary inquiry into the systemic failure of the Church of England and the Church of Wales, regarding the safeguarding of children.

Part of the brief of IICSA was to investigate 'the extent to which the culture within the Church inhibits or inhibited the proper investigation, exposure and prevention of child sexual abuse' (IICSA 2018: 2:3). Martyn Percy, a senior Anglican, spoke for many of us when he confessed to a sense of shame at the exposed incompetence and lack of concern for the victims of abuse, streamed live to the nation over three long weeks:

> To know that you belong to a body where you can no longer believe or trust the account of the polity and practice that is being offered in defence of its behaviours by its own leaders. To know that the real victims in this tragic farce who are still waiting for basic, fundamental rights that should be givens for the church – recognition, remorse, repentance – are abused twice over. In the first instance, it is by their actual abuser. The second time, and far worse, is the subsequent abuse perpetrated by the church. (Percy 2018: 4)

The safeguarding problems, he wrote,

> are rooted in warped attitudes to gender and sexuality; cultures of obeisance that do not challenge or question the competence of clergy and bishops, instead putting them on a pedestal; failures to invest in training for seminarians and clergy in the basics of law, good practices, and relevant social and psychological theory; patronising attitudes towards laity; and lazy, naïve assumptions about human nature. These things will not be fixed by hiring a few more safeguarding officers. The problem runs far deeper, and extends far wider. The Church of England has not even begun to reckon with the ecclesial ethos and traditions that offered the best petri-dishes for developing and growing cultures of abuse. (Percy 2018: 3)

Churches, everyone knows, have been slow to react to the abuse crises. There is a growing number of highly critical analyses of the continuing cover-up in the Church of England (see e.g., Harper and Wilson 2019; Fife and Gilo 2019; Oakley and Humphreys 2019). But academics too have been slow to react. Sîan Hawthorne shows how religious studies as a discipline is slow to react to the marginalisation of misogyny towards women in religious traditions, being nudged only slowly and reluctantly by the social sciences to own up to 'the distorted accounts of religious phenomena that result from the failure of religious studies scholars to attend both to gender differences and to the broader ideological dimensions of its own history' (Hawthorne 2011: 134).

This depressing judgment is *a fortiori* more likely to be true in theology, especially when the veil of sacredness is laid over troublesome texts inhibiting revisionary interpretations, and where emerging scholars are (with notable exceptions) likely to steer away from controversial topics.

In the Roman Catholic Church 'There is little to no recent discussion of
sex and sexual morality within Catholic parishes and congregations, reflecting a significant and damaging crisis of authority' (Tentler 2016: 100).
While churches exist to proclaim and embody the Good News of the
gospel, the *bad* news is that the demands of the gospel require a fresh
understanding of it in every generation, which will only be achieved
through painful disagreement, not by circumventing it. As Charles Taylor
succinctly puts it, 'The attachment to a rigid code, as well as the sense of
being an embattled band of the faithful, developed through the defensive
postures of the last two centuries, makes it almost impossible to find the
language' (Taylor 2007: 494).

In this chapter I have elaborated the first two senses of gender outlined
in Chapter 1, postponing the third sense (that of identity) to Chapter 3.
I have not merely provided copious examples of gendered violence, which
in themselves are morally reprehensible, but attempted to explain how
systems of thought can condone and perpetuate it, and (for a time, hide or
deny that they are doing so). The groundwork of exposing the gender
binary and the damage it causes is well under way. When this groundwork
is completed, the possibility of an alternative theological vision for
Christian ethics, both non-binary and non-violent, will come into view.

## CHAPTER 3

# Gender Binaries as Theological Problems

## Personal Identity

In 2014 the social media platform Facebook introduced a growing list of gender categories, up to 71 at one point, which users could select and make public, including 'asexual', 'polygender', and 'two-spirit person'. As I write (October 2017), the choice in the gender box is 'male', 'female', or 'custom'. Selecting 'custom' enables any Facebook user to apply to themselves their preferred gender adjective, together with their preferred pronoun for use by other people when referring to them (he/his, she/her, or they/their).

There are many ways of analysing the explosion of gender awareness exemplified by the Facebook registration process, some of them contemptuous and dismissive. Is the gender menu an extreme example of 'expressive individualism' (Taylor 2007: 473), assisted by popular, half-understood science, celebrity gossip, and social media sites and posts? Is it the extension of consumer choice into the very heart of the self? Is it a full-blown example of 'reflexive essentialism', an unguarded public display of interiority combined with the belief that something called 'sexuality' is 'the definitive aspect of our social identities' (Rahman and Jackson 2010: 149)? Is it to be dismissed as cultural superficiality? Or psychological indulgence? Or an ideological assault on traditional beliefs? Or an example of incoherent language use, in that referring expressions are allowed to refer uncomplicatedly to supposed inner states? I approach the gender menu as evidence for the welcome breakdown, variously, of the three sets of binaries, male–female, heterosexual–homosexual, and masculine–feminine, and the attempt to move beyond them. As such, a promising theological and pastoral approach to gender diversity will require recognition, first, that the old binaries are unserviceable for growing minorities of people; second, that gender orthodoxy is not a precondition for people of faith; and third, that condemnation of alternative identities is a flight from pastoral responsibility.

Questions about identity are always more than they seem. Philosophers have discussed personal identity for centuries. Outside of philosophy, writes one philosopher, "'personal identity' usually refers to certain properties to which a person feels a special sense of attachment or ownership. Someone's personal identity in this sense consists of those features she takes to "define her as a person" or "make her the person she is"'" (Stanford 2015). In this section I shall examine three questions arising from personal identity statements – epistemological, linguistic, and theological. Is the self-knowledge expressed in identity statements always incontrovertible? Second, identity statements can only be made with the tools of language, but perhaps the tools are inadequate for the task? Perhaps, to change the metaphor, the linguistic prompts available to us may actually mislead us? Third, can the claim made by Christians, that being Christian defines their identity more than any other feature of their lives, and especially more than their gender or sexuality, be justified?

When the philosopher Ludwig Wittgenstein was wrestling with the problem how our language was able to refer intelligibly to our supposed inner states, he took as an example the experience of pain, and asked rhetorically, "'What would it be like if human beings shewed no outward signs of pain (did not groan, grimace, etc.)?' Then it would be impossible to teach a child the use of the word "toothache"'" (Wittgenstein 1953: 92, para. 257). The point of the question was to indicate that naming toothache is not, or not just, applying a label to a sensation, because the word 'toothache' already exists in the language where its use is also accompanied by groans, grimaces, painkillers, and visits to the dentist. What appears to be the child's self-referring expression ("I've got toothache") requires not just sympathetic carers who believe her but a whole community using a particular language (or playing a particular 'language game') and having the experience of toothache. Identifying oneself as, say, gay, is also an act of naming. Wittgenstein's discussion of the impossibility of a private language may seem distant from the reflexive knowledge required when we make statements of identity. But I think it shows that the self-knowledge expressed by identity statements cannot be simply dismissed as inner feelings or states untested in the crucible of experience. 'Coming out' is always more than an externalising of secret, inner states and declaring the content of these states to a potentially hostile public. The self-knowledge imparted is already the product of relations with other people, of shared solidarity, of proven desires and longings, and cannot be dismissed in the way a private language can.

Perhaps it is too easy for straight people to identify as straight? Being straight can lead to a complacency, to a failure to examine the assumed normativity the term suggests or even imposes. As Eric Reitan remarks, 'most Christians aren't sexually attracted to members of the same sex. And this means that, for most Christians, it is incredibly easy to avoid the supposed sin of same-sex sex' (Reitan 2017: 25). Heterosexuality, we might say, is part of the *doxa*. However, even this is not made on the basis of some inner private illumination which comes to me when 'I' interrogate myself, and then express by selecting the appropriate available medical label. What confirms me as a straight person is how I live as one among many men and women, and as I interact with them and they with me at different stages of life, beginning probably in the nursery or preschool, or even before. I soon come to understand myself as more attracted to some people than others, perhaps more at ease in their company, more eager to experiment with attachments or romantic engagements with them, and so on. I find out who arouses me, even involuntarily. This is the *phenomenological* recognition of 'my' sexuality, because it is already my experience, and I am intuitively and directly aware of it. But this knowledge is brought to me as much by others as it is found 'within' me or brought to me by 'privileged access', or subsequently confirmed by the hard sciences. It is never a question purely of identity. Only in countless exchanges, communications, and interactions, at many times and in many places, do I arrive at some provisional knowledge about myself. This knowledge is to be trusted, even though, along with ourselves, it will develop. *Sociality* is a precondition of my identity as a person. Only in relation am I who I am. Self-knowledge is always also relational knowledge.

I think Wittgenstein's imaginary world where the expression of pain is impossible may help to better frame the experience of trans people (though of course I cannot speak as one, and I do not assume trans people all have the same experiences). While locating the embeddedness of "I've got toothache" in the child's surrounding social world is supposed to settle how the child learned to express dental pain, it does not settle whether the child is lying (lying, of course, is another language game, along with its detection). Here the distinction between sceptical or extreme doubt (which some philosophers like to discuss under the rubric of the 'other minds problem') and reasonable doubt becomes useful. Behind widespread assumptions about trans people is a similar kind of extreme doubt – the doubt whether there really are people who have a gender identity or gender expression that differs from their sex assigned at birth. This is a doubt that can be exposed as extreme. And that works by listening to the experience of trans people. It becomes an issue not of proof but rather of trust (a distinction that religious people should know rather well).

And trust can be corroded. There may be occasional biologically male individuals who disguise themselves as women, or pretend to be trans women, in order to gain access to accommodation reserved for women only, and to attempt to act nefariously. There are also rare cases of people who have undergone gender reassignment surgery and subsequently regret it. It is obvious that such cases will be used by conservative media to discredit trans people generally and to reinforce the gender binary in which they remain heavily invested. The very existence of other people who may find sexual binaries intolerable is disturbing, even threatening, to hetero-normative majorities. It is easier for us to say it is they, rather than we, who are mistaken. It is unreasonable to suppose they are lying. But might they not be mistaken, even deluded? That question raises another: the suitabil-ity of language to express it.

## Identity and Language

The suitability of language seems to be a pointless question. What else do we have? But the idea of language games will not let us abstract language from the various contexts, uses, practices, and so on, where language is used. The language of gender identity begins in pathology. 'Homosexuality' begins to be used, in German, in 1869 (Loughlin 2015: 613), and 'bi-sexuality' and 'heterosexuality' probably as late as 1892 (both in R. von Krafft-Ebing's *Psychopathia Sexualis*). Not only are these terms more recent than is commonly supposed, they pathologise, and so are inherently unsuited to the delicate personal project of identifying who one is. Beginning in 1922, and gradually through the twentieth century, homo-sexual men appropriated the term 'gay' in order to neutralise the stigmatising accusation carried by 'homosexual' (*OED*, and see Vasey 1995: 135). The term 'hermaphrodite', borrowed from the Greek myth of Hermaphroditus (who acquired male and female characteristics by bathing in the fountain of the nymph Salmacis) is clearly a medical one: its earliest known use in English (in 1348) condemns hermaphroditism as an imperfect form of human being. 'In harmofroditus is founde bothe sexus male and female: but alway vnperfyte' (de Glanville, 1495, cited in *OED*). Now the term 'intersex' is generally preferred. One exasperated intersex writer called the process of definition 'a channel through which intersex people can be assessed, judged, manipulated, and coerced' and found to fit, or not, within medically approved categories (O'Brien 2016: 53).

Darlene Weaver, in *Self-Love and Christian Ethics*, rightly argued, as I am doing, that self-knowledge is arrived at through relations with others, and for Christians, with God (Weaver 2002: 141). While the idea of language games still teaches us to understand language within the totality of its embeddedness in linguistic communities, it still reflects the ordinary-language philosophy of the 1950s, half a century before the arrival of Facebook, Instagram, Tinder, Tumblr, Pinterest, and many more social media sites. This part of the online world contains 'communities' where prejudices are fuelled and fanned, exploitation is a constant threat, and misinformation is rife. It is an uncertain and dangerous place for self-knowledge to be acquired. Here it is possible for minorities to network with each other supportively, but also to lay themselves open to its many dangers. Adolescent and even prepubescent children are increasingly prone to anxieties about body image, sexuality, and of course gender identity. When they express these anxieties it will be by means of the language games they may have only half learned and scarcely been able to understand. Families need to be supportively informed and proactive regarding their children's learning. Are there church communities in which growing self-knowledge can come about in an atmosphere of acceptance, shaped by the Good News that God accepts us not merely as we are but as we come to be?

We shall see that 'transgender' is an umbrella term, one (to continue the metaphor) that fails to protect trans people from the deluge of objectification. 'Queer' too has become another umbrella term, in fact, a double umbrella term, covering 'folk who are outside of the mainstream: both the cisgender/heterosexual mainstream and the conventional LG(BT) mainstream' (Barker and Scheele 2016: 36). Bourdieu's account of the effect of objectifying language on people's lives throws light on the justifiable complaints of sexual minorities, at least about their medicalisation. His analysis of masculine domination led him to describe in detail what he called a 'social programme of perception' beyond the facts of gendered life, 'a mythic vision of the world' that encompasses even our thought processes. 'Acts of *cognition* are, inevitably, acts of *recognition*, submission' (Bourdieu 2001: 13 author's emphasis).

Bourdieu (remember he writes in 1998) has in his sights the male–female binary, but in the heterosexual–homosexual binary he sees a similar 'scheme' that metes out 'symbolic violence', one of whose forms is 'a denial of public, visible existence' (Bourdieu 2001: 119), of just the kind that trans people and lesbian and gay people have, or have had, to endure. Alongside practical action to diminish injustice, 'there is always room for a *cognitive struggle* over the meaning of the things of the world and in particular of sexual realities' (Bourdieu 2001: 13–14, author's emphasis). The cognitive struggle is nowhere more obvious than in endless church reports and official documents where there is generally no softening of the dominating, 'otherising', stigmatising edge to the language of sexuality. The symbolic violence of its deployment remains an awkward factor among language users who have no malign intent. But the reifying and marginalising effects of language are not confined to church documents. There is a danger that when we Christians talk about sex we refrain from using the language of love and of relationships, of justice and of sacrament, preferring instead medical terminology and sexual 'acts' (Davison 2016: 15). Even the familiar chain of letters LBGTIQ is also capable of being read as a lumping together of an assortment of awkward cases that mainstream theology must decide whether to accommodate or not, mere 'inconsequential statistical outliers insufficient to challenge the basic view of humans as naturally dimorphic' (DeFranza 2018: 66; Barker and Scheele 2016).

## Christian Identity

The prevalent view about sexual identity in official church documents, Catholic and Protestant, is a binary one. We are either male or female (with no deviations, no ambiguities or fluidities, no concessions to our orientation, no reliance on what we hold ourselves to be at the deepest level of our intellectual and emotional selves). Homosexuality remains an aberration from divinely intended complementarity, perhaps inviting toleration or compassion, whereas intersex and trans people are rendered inexplicable and incomprehensible. In 1997 an influential statement by a group of concerned theologians – the St Andrew's Day Statement – affirms, 'There can be no description of human reality, in general or in particular, outside the reality in Christ. We must be on guard, therefore, against constructing any other ground for our identities than the redeemed humanity given us in him' (Bradshaw 1997: 7). This is how their argument runs:

1.  there are competing accounts of identity (for example, straight, gay);
2.  within the Church a new identity is conferred on believers by their faith and baptism;
3.  this new identity becomes the ontological basis for any other contingent identities, particularly sexual identities, that Christians may affirm.

However, the signatories to the Statement have no doubt that Christian identity is certain; that male and female identity is exclusive, binary, and ultimate; and that minority identities are open to false consciousness or delusion:

> Those who understand themselves as homosexuals, no more and no less than those who do not, are liable to false understandings based on personal or family histories, emotional dispositions, social settings, and solidarities formed by common experiences or ambitions. Our sexual affections can no more define who we are than can our class, race or nationality. At the deepest ontological level, therefore, there is no such thing as 'a' homosexual or 'a' heterosexual; there are human beings, male and female, called to redeemed humanity in Christ. (Bradshaw 1997: 7)

This position however, is less clear than its authors might like. Christians, they say, have an ultimate identity that renders all other identities proximate. But just what is included 'at the deepest ontological level'? Does 'male and female' operate at the proximate or at the 'deepest ontological' level? Is it 'creational', as some say, 'difference all the way down', or is it more a cultural exaggeration based on a few dissimilarities? The authors have smuggled the 'male and female' binary into the category of ultimacy, leading a keen-eyed respondent to the Statement's authors to confess herself 'fascinated by the fact that you do appear to attribute the deep ontological meaning you deny to heterosexuality and homosexuality to maleness and femaleness' (Stuart 1997: 77). Elizabeth Stuart recognises that the categories of male and female, while not to be understood as ultimate, rivalling identity 'in Christ', *are* regarded by the statement's authors as ultimate and exclusive, nonetheless, in relation to sexual identity. We will be returning to the 'deepest ontological level' in Part III, and discovering that, at that level, 'male and female' is the very state of affairs which no longer counts for anything. A more immediate problem raised by the Statement is the challenge to self-knowledge that it explicitly raises.

## The Metaphysics of Sexual Difference

Linda Alcoff, at the start of her *Visible Identities: Race, Gender, and the Self*, sagely observed, 'When I refuse to listen to how you are different from me, I am refusing to know who you are. But without understanding fully who you are, I will never be able to appreciate precisely how we are more alike than I might have originally supposed' (Alcoff 2006: 6). There is much wisdom in this simple observation. Trying to understand the diverse shades of human difference is a moral imperative, since without it, the failure to love the neighbour, the ethical imperative of faith, is all but inevitable. Understanding difference is the key to solidarity among human beings. Jesus affirmed his solidarity with people lacking food, clothing, shelter, medical care, or a friendly visitor in prison (Mt. 25.31–46). His solidarity with them even reached to the point of *identity*. Calling such people members of his family, he taught that the judgment of nations rests on their ministry to such people – 'Truly I tell you, just as you did it to one of the least of these who are members of my family, you did it to me' (Mt. 25.40). Differences between Jew and Gentile are overcome in the new human solidarity intended by Jesus. But sexual difference?

Judith Butler has famously attempted to dissolve the idea of two different sexes. Leaving aside her popular idea of gender as something performed, or her apparent dissolution of the human subject, her contention that sexual difference is written onto bodies rather than generated by them, must be taken more seriously. In *Gender Trouble*, she 'demanded a reconsideration of the figure of the body as mute, prior to culture, awaiting signification' (Butler 1999: 99). 'Sex', 'gender', even 'sex/gender' are all deconstructed:

> From a political analysis of compulsory heterosexuality, it has been neces-sary to question the construction of sex as binary, as a hierarchical binary. From the point of view of gender as enacted, questions have emerged over the fixity of gender identity as an interior depth that is said to be external-ized in various forms of 'expression'. (Butler 1999: 99)

But sexual difference cannot collapse so easily. Neither should it. One of Butler's great intellectual achievements is to show the extent to which language and culture overlay the sexed body. That is the meaning of the idea of the body as 'mute, prior to culture, awaiting signification', predis-cursive. However, there remains a visible facticity about most human bodies as soon as they come into the world (and even before). When the sexed terms 'boy' and 'girl' are applied to most but not all babies, are these to be understood as misleading cultural signifiers, saying too much, or truth-telling designations making an important distinction about what type of body the newly born has and is? I take the latter alternative, yet as soon as the boy–girl distinction is amplified by congratulatory greeting cards, colour-coded clothes, and gender-specific nursery toys, the force of Butler's strictures is quickly apparent. Yes, there is sexual difference. Affirming this is to affirm at least a version of 'gender realism' (Barnes and Norton 2015: 140). There are sexed bodies, but our access to them is still mediated via language and culture.

In what then, does sexual difference consist? Can it be simply what an infant has between his or her legs? Or ears? Hardly. Alcoff argues, subtly, that 'The objective basis of sex categories is in the differential relationship to reproductive capacity between men and women' (Alcoff 2006: 151). Yes, there is an objective basis for sex difference, but the difference lies in the *possibility only*, of the relationship of women to reproduction, in that conception and lactation for most (i.e., fertile) women (and for no men) are possible. Whether or not fertile women wish to make use of their biological capacities remains a separate question, and whether they *ought* to do so is another. Yes, there are *behavioural* differences between females and males (Hines 2004: 3–19), but these have been hugely exaggerated, not least by 'over-reporting of significant differences' and the 'influences of stereotypes about sex differences on the perceptions of researchers and research participants' (2004: 5). 'Variation within each sex is great, with both males and females near the top and bottom of the distributions for every characteristic' (2004: 18). Sex difference is best understood along a continuum: 'In fact, although most of us appear to be either clearly male or clearly female, we are each complex mosaics of male and female character-istics' (2004: 19).

Sexual difference continues to be a marked feature of cultures, not least because it is a principal reason for becoming a victim of sexual violence. That is why abstract questions about difference are so important. Skewed metaphysics validates malpractice. Any disequilibrium between the sexes can be a cause of discrimination, and may already be the product of it. But there is a more important question based on the facts of sexual difference, namely 'whether this biological or material infrastructure for sexual differ-ence yields a metaphysics of sexed identity' (Alcoff 2006: 166)? Put another way, the issue is whether sexed identity is a 'natural kind', that is, to be a man or a woman is to belong to 'a group that shares a common essence'? Or whether it belongs to 'an objective type', that is, 'a unity without an underlying essence' (2006: 168)? Admittedly the question takes us to the limits of abstraction, and to the need to say where essence ends and unity begins. I follow Alcoff's resolution of the problem (as she engages with Haslanger (2000)). We are *not* so trapped within our lan-guage and so unable to characterise sexual difference (and everything else) except by all-enveloping discourses (which turn out to be the fictions of patriarchy). Gender realism is true! 'Yes, we use concepts to know the world; no, that does not mean that we cannot say anything about the world but only about other concepts' (Alcoff 2006: 170).

But here it is *theological* metaphysics which convinces me, as Part III will show. The reasons why I want to deny that 'man', 'woman', 'intersex', and so on are groups each with a separate essence, are theological. Once they are divided, they can be set against each other. God has a single essence. God is One. The essence of God is single and indivisible. There are distinctions within God's essence or being – they are called Persons – and they do not divide the divine essence. Human being collectively and individually is, as all Christians testify, made in the image of God. Human beings together have a single common essence: their myriad differences, including sexual difference, all presuppose what they have in common, their having been made by God in order to enjoy sharing in God's life forever. Human beings are an inclusive continuum prior to sexual division.

Humans are one kind – humankind – not two or more kinds, male and female. Once the unity of humankind is safeguarded, it becomes possible to acknowledge the many objective types the Creator has let be. An 'appropriate universalism' finds a broad solidarity among and between human beings, broader even than the binary of sexual difference. The human nature of Christ is also crucially important in relation to sexual difference. The Christ has two natures – one divine, one human. It would be misleading, not to say devious, to claim that Christ had a male nature, even though he was a man. If Christ's human nature is, at root, a male nature, women play no part in the redemption he secures. Following Gregory of Nyssa's oft-quoted dictum from his *Epistle 101*, 'The unassumed is the unhealed', I have suggested elsewhere (Thatcher 2016: 98) that if Christ's maleness is primary, his lack of a female nature renders the inclusion of women in redemption 'debatable' (which of course is why it was endlessly debated). Ambiguity on such a point is enough for gendered relationships to be poisoned by misogyny.

Sexual difference, I am suggesting here, is *literally* 'inessential'. There is no male essence or female essence; and no male nature or female nature. But that is not to say sexual difference is unimportant or non-existent. It is inessential both because 'man' and 'woman' lack a metaphysical essence, and because it lacks ultimate significance in this world and in the next. It is the binarists in theology who accord ultimacy to it. It does not manifest itself as a binary, and sexes, where they are unambiguous, are not 'opposites'. And that position is currently *not* widely held in Christian theology or in the churches. Part III of the book addresses that problem.

## Epistemology and Ethics – Christian and Jewish

The authors of the St Andrew's Day Statement are clear that there is a range of false understandings to which everyone, but especially gays, are prone. Reflexive knowledge is not to be trusted. Since the heterosexual–homosexual binary is primary in their theological ontology and the preservation of it the *raison d'être* of the statement, gay self-understanding appears doomed. The epistemological problem is now a *moral* one, that of not believing what people think and say about themselves. This is precisely the flawed reaction to difference with which the chapter began – 'When I refuse to listen to how you are different from me, I am refusing to know who you are.' That is why another respondent, Rowan Williams, observes the statement 'makes it plain that homosexual desire is of its nature a pointer to something in need of healing and correction' (Williams 1997: 15). Homosexual persons 'are told that they are tolerated, even respected; but their own account of themselves before God is not to be recognised' (Williams 1997: 17). Their self-knowledge is mistaken. Their testimony that God blesses same-sex love can be safely disregarded. On the same premises, intersex and trans people are *a fortiori* in an even worse, collapsed, state of self-knowledge.

This grave matter – refusing to believe the testimony of others – is compounded by two others. I will call one the 'noetic damage theory', whereas the other, which we will get to in the next section, is about how Christians think the will of God can be known. Twenty years after the St Andrew's Day Statement, A. T. B. McGowan turns the binary-imposing screw more tightly, and states that all of us, but especially homosexual, trans, polyamorous, and paedophile people (yes, all lumped together), should understand their unfortunate condition as a consequence of the biblical Fall:

> ... the sexuality of each one of us has been damaged by our inherited fallenness, in different ways and in different measures. For some of us that will mean that they experience same-sex attraction, some will experience gender confusion, others will be sexually attracted to children, yet others will only be sexually satisfied with multiple partners, and so on. (McGowan 2017: 182)

The Fall, he explains, has a universal 'noetic effect' (2017: 183). While it wreaks havoc on particular bodies, it contaminates their minds, together with the minds of those non-Christians who write about such bodies, and more liberal Christians who think differently about sexuality and gender. 'The unbeliever, then, has a "mindset" which is opposed to God and unbelievers are enemies of God in their *minds*' (2017: 183, author's emphasis). Warming to his theme, he alleges unbelievers 'cannot accept the biblical arguments about human sexuality because their minds are blinded, such that they cannot see and understand biblical truths' (2017: 185). That is why 'those who oppose a biblical view of homosexual acts' should not be given 'too much credence' (2017: 185). '[T]he dialogue between the believer and the unbeliever does not consist in a disagreement over the facts but rather in a radical difference in *epistemology*' (2017: 186, emphasis added).

If McGowan's view were to be taken seriously by LGBTIQ people, it would doubtless intensify the opportunity for further guilt and self-loathing. It would strikingly affirm their cosmic undoing and give divine authority to the theological supporters of compulsory heterosexuality. Laying aside problems associated with the Fall when it is understood as a historical event within the Garden of Eden, all Christians acknowledge that the world and everything in it is not altogether as its Creator intended. That is why its redemption is needed and given. McGowan seems rather oblivious to a series of morally problematic questions. Why think that sexual minorities are to be characterised as the principal and unwitting victims of this cosmic disorder? Might it not also be considered sinful, wilfully to disregard the testimony of non-heterosexual Christians to the presence of God in their unions? Is it not an instance of hubris to assume only one particular theological understanding of sexuality (his) is free from noetic damage? Is the same disrespect for contrary testimony to be extended to the sciences when they too appear to be at odds with conservative theological norms?

McGowan is right to say there is a 'radical difference in epistemology' between his view and those who differ from him. He believes he has privileged access to undamaged noetic understanding that, if accepted, may profoundly damage others. Gently and respectfully, Eric Reitan exposes much of the opposition to homosexuality and same-sex marriage as a failure to love one's neighbour (Reitan 2017). McGowan is right that we can all be mistaken, and that Christians can rightly access wisdom from a source unrecognised by the secular world. I suggested earlier that the language through which we express our self-understanding is limited in several ways. However, it is a sound principle that the testimony of people is to be believed, and not a priori disregarded, unless there are strong reasons for doing so. Perhaps the preference for strenuous moral judgement against sexual minorities on the basis of biblical certainty is a betrayal of the Great Commandments and the Golden Rule, and his 'noetic effect' an example of epistemic violence, pegged to the divine authority of the Bible?

## Knowing the Will of God

The second epistemological problem is broader. I have suggested that the charges of deluded self-knowledge and distorted comprehension of sexuality are morally questionable and damaging to those to whom they are directed. That leads to the question why, in the history of Christian thought, belief in divine love was often severely compromised, and deemed consistent with many demeaning attitudes that, for example, not only regarded women as lesser persons than men, but justified the horrors of the trade in slaves. '[T]here are exceptionally problematic, not to say disastrous, pastoral and missiological consequences of conservative positions' (Song 2014: 79). At a time when many people outside the churches believe the churches' teaching about sex and gender is blatantly discriminatory some account needs to be provided of the apparent dichotomy between the belief in infinite divine compassion and harsh human regulation.

One strand in an explanation of this antinomy involves a particular kind of theological thinking exposed by the Euthyphro Dilemma. This dilemma, which originates in a question put by Socrates in Plato's dialogue *Euthyphro*, is often presented in its modern form by the question, 'Are morally good acts willed by God because they are morally good, or are they morally good because they are willed by God?' (Philosophy of Religion, n.d.). I draw attention to the dilemma, not because I want to resolve it (as Simin (2009) and Zangwill (2012) try to do), but to point to different ways of thinking about the will of God that are represented in the dilemma itself. The first alternative, that morally good acts are willed by God because they are morally good, suggests the goodness of such acts is intrinsic to the acts themselves, and can generally be recognised and performed by agents whether or not they believe in God. The second alternative, that morally good acts are morally good because they are willed by God, suggests that God alone is the arbiter of what counts as a morally good act. This alternative has a consequence that if God alone can judge what is a morally good act, human judgment is irrelevant. This way of thinking about God leads to what is sometimes called the 'problem of abhorrent commands'. Believers give themselves the license to hold that God might require, for God's inscrutable reasons, morally abhorrent acts such as rape, torture, and genocide, leading them to suppose that they must obediently carry them out.

I suggest that something like this alternative view has in fact been held, and continues to be held, within the religions. According to the 'divine command theory' of ethics (or at least some versions of it), what is morally good is what God commands. The knowledge of what God commands is known through the totality of God's self-revelation in Christ, and derivatively in Scripture, tradition, and reason. However, once some of the commandments or texts of Scripture are combined with particular ways of reading them and identified with what God wills, abhorrent acts receive their justification. If an individual, a church, or religious group, a nation, an empire, a ruling class, or a male élite can persuade itself that God commands them to do *x*, then any human reservation based on solidarity with the victims of *x* is stifled. If God wills hierarchical social structures, God surely authorises punitive measures to maintain what God has willed. Given the ease with which humans act wrongly in order to preserve their self-interest and their power over others, the conviction that God commands them to act unjustly provides the ultimate self-justification for acting viciously in the guise of virtue. It doesn't matter that the commands of God are cruel or malicious: what matters is God's will, not ours. Since the commands of God are inscrutable, who are we to scrutinise them? Abhorrent commands may even be abhorrent by *our* standards, but who are we to judge the mind of God? God alone is the righteous Judge. God has the benefit of omnipotence and omniscience, so if the longer-term beneficent purposes of God extend beyond the myopic horizon of human calculation, then from horrendous evils good may surely come.

Supporters of divine command theories (at least in this version – which I think is far from a caricature) may accuse me of outrageously misrepresenting them. The two Great Commandments and the Golden Rule of Christian ethics require obedience, they may say. There is surely room for obedience among other descriptions of Christians' relationship to God. I'm much more worried about the psychological and anthropological 'mechanisms' that allow authorities to believe (too easily) that God wills them to act unjustly or cruelly. Indeed many unjust actions do not appear horrendous or cruel at all – they may simply belong in Bourdieu's category of 'a gentle violence, imperceptible and invisible even to its victims'. The long history of colonialism, racism, anti-Semitism, and slavery within Christian empires makes better sense when belief in divine command is identified as a strand in its tawdry self-justification.

## Help from Halakah

I have learned much from a Jewish feminist scholar about the Euthyphro Dilemma. The contortions it produces in Jewish thought is similar to the impact we have been discussing. Ronit Irshai, in separate essays, sets out the religious dilemmas that believing male homosexual Jews and believing Jewish feminist theologians painfully encounter in regard to the observance of Jewish law or *halakhah*. In the former case, as Irshai explains, 'For Modern Orthodoxy, even if God commands certain things that on the surface clash with contemporary moral concepts, individuals are expected to sacrifice or "bind" their inclinations, including their moral values, to comply with the divine injunction' (Irshai 2018: 19). The binding (Hebrew, *aqedah*) of inclinations is a metaphor with a special force, since Abraham bound Isaac as an intended sacrifice to God before the ram was provided as a substitute (Gen. 22.1–19). Here is a most abhorrent divine command: to murder one's own child. And here is the lesson: only as God's command is obeyed without question, and against one's most basic moral convictions, does relief occur.

Except that for homosexual Jewish men, relief does *not* occur. The Torah prescribes that a man lying with another man as with a woman should be put to death (Lev. 18.22; 20.13) and no amount of trusting in God is going to provide relief from the desires and longings of gay men. The acute dilemma (varying the 'binding' metaphor) is between 'bowing to a yoke or subordinating oneself to a higher normative order which may require giving up desires or needs' (Irshai 2018: 20). While bowing to the yoke of halakhah is not necessarily problematic, since every religious person is willing to give up desires or needs, homosexuals are not required just to give up 'desires', like a religious Jewish person who wants to eat cheeseburgers but can't because of dietary laws (Irshai 2018: 20). The Jewish religion celebrates sexuality and intimacy and here halakhah condemns homosexuals to total sexual abstinence and solitude to the rest of their lives. This, in contrast to the cheeseburger example, *is* a moral problem (Irshai, private correspondence).

Irshai points out that the sacrifice required of observant gay Jews includes 'all individual proclivities, desires, and needs, *including one's ethical values*' (Irshai 2018: 21, author's emphasis). Orthodoxy requires that the genuine moral insights of believers must be sacrificed 'to what is interpreted as the divine injunction' (Irshai 2018: 29). But the continuing faith of many gay men, and the realisation that homosexuality is a natural condition, has led to the charge of immorality being withdrawn and redirected instead against those who would proscribe homosexuality: 'Not only is male homosexuality no longer viewed as a moral abomination, but precisely the contrary: those who would deny homosexuals the chance to realize their orientation are now on the defensive' (Irshai 2018: 22). Elsewhere, with Jewish religious feminism to defend, Irshai raises the question 'whether the ethical and moral are totally congruent with Divine injunctions and in fact determined by the latter; or whether God does not define good and evil but only wishes to make human beings aware that they exist and commands them to choose the good' (Irshai 2016: 1). The question is a further concise version of the Euthyphro Dilemma, impinging this time on believing Jewish feminist scholars who want to remain faithful to God's commands and critique patriarchy at the same time. The Aqedah theology requires women to sacrifice their subjecthood, where necessary, in the service of husbands and, she testifies, is deeply unjust.

It should be emphasised that the position Irshai takes implies no diminution in obedience to God. It differs from conservatism not by the suspension of inconvenient commands, but in the method of discernment of God's will. It does not shy away from the need for personal sacrifice within religious commitment: it challenges the injustice and immorality of halakhah toward women that mistaken patriarchal interpretations of Scripture enjoin. Her resolution of the dilemma requires recognition of the historical context to which Divine Law is directed, and the possibility of progressive revelation, especially through the voices of the marginalised. Obedience to God does not require ignoring or misrepresenting the facts of nature. Neither does it require ignoring morality, since (for Irshai) morality is an autonomous realm and God's commands follow morality. That's why we should interpret them so they won't clash with moral notions or compromise or sacrifice core beliefs in God's goodness and justice. (We will listen later to women's voices within Islam grappling with similar questions and moving towards similar solutions.)

## Beginning with Love

Before we leave the Euthyphro Dilemma, we will draw on its other prong (but not impale ourselves upon it). As I described it, morally good acts are willed by God because they are morally good. Believers in God can recognise what is morally good and believe good actions coincide with what a morally good God wants. Of course they can be wrong. They require the gift of discernment. People of faith regularly cooperate with people of no faith in performing morally good acts because they are morally good. But Christian people have an additional and compelling reason for performing just and good actions, for they understand God to be Love, to have been made known as Love through Jesus Christ, and to inspire the practice of Love through the Holy Spirit, whether through the Christian faith, or through people of different faiths, or through people of no faith at all. This is a better way of being Christian than the way of obedience to 'divine' commands that sometimes turn out to be unjust and cruel. Beginning with Love is where Pope Benedict XVI began in his first encyclical as Pope (Pope Benedict XVI 2005). Discipleship may be better understood as being 'in Christ', a participation in the divine love which manifested itself in the life of Jesus and manifests itself still, in his extended body. *Ubi caritas, ibi deus est.* Beginning here enables the practice of faith to be an exercise in love. It leaves the Euthyphro Dilemma behind because it identifies God's will with God's love revealed in Christ and participates in it. We are searching for a theological worldview, a metaphysics that doesn't tip over into treating anyone at all as other, or worthy of less respect; that attends to and prevents the disastrous pastoral consequences of brittle and uncharitable Christian teaching; and that refuses to compromise the radical nature of God's love by endless qualifications and exemptions.

My grounds for resolving the Euthyphro Dilemma are based on divine love. Asked by lesbian and gay students why an inclusive theology is more likely to be embraceable than one that requires from them a life of sexual abstinence and struggle, I answer a theology that embraces them and wills their flourishing is the one to choose: one in which God's love may be found in the intimacies of their relationships; one which does not require unnecessary pain and struggle, even though both may come their way. The biblical position that God is love is the ultimate motivation for just actions in sexual ethics (though another book may be needed to defend this claim). There is no 'special theology of same-sex love':

> Same-sex relationships can be good . . . for the same reasons that opposite-sex relationships can be good . . . The reasons for supporting them are therefore the same . . . When two men, or two women, want to commit themselves to a life lived together, through thick and thin, the reasons for blessing them . . . are the reasons why we'd bless anyone: because we are thankful for them, and their commitment . . . because we know our frailty and we want God's protection for it, and because there is a commitment in front of us that points to what God's coming kingdom is all about. (Davison 2016: 76–7)

There are of course those who heroically and sincerely attempt a different way. Shunning 'homosexual', they speak of 'same-sex attracted Christians' (Allberry 2015: 10; Deyoung 2015: 147; Berry 2016; Fisher 2017) and shun same-sex intimacy (but not friendship). Same-sex desire is something 'unwanted', a designation akin to that of a burglar as an unwanted visitor, or a puncture as an unwanted event on a bicycle ride. In agreement with Cardinal Ratzinger's words, they may believe themselves 'called to enact the will of God in their life by joining whatever sufferings and difficulties they experience in virtue of their condition to the sacrifice of the Lord's Cross' (Ratzinger 1986: para. 12). Internalisation runs deep. But the question arises why gay people should suffer *at all* as a consequence of the way God made them? The narrative of self-denial is central to the Christian tradition but context is always central to its being virtuous (see Stuart 1997: 79). More central still is the command to love one's neighbour *as one loves oneself.* Weaver reminds us that 'self-love is a positive moral obligation in its own right' (Weaver 2002: 140–1). Much of the suffering of lesbian and gay Christians is directly attributable to the mistaken teaching and condemnatory ethos of the very churches to which they are drawn. Why accept the pathological judgement about their very being any longer, especially if it makes the obligation of self-love difficult or impossible? A similar question was raised by Margaret Farley in relation to intersex people – 'The question for all of us is not only what treatment should be given for a condition considered to be pathological, but whether the condition is pathological or not' (Farley 2006: 151).

I think that in the three areas constituting gender discussed in this and the previous chapter, believers of all faiths have wrongly concluded that God legitimises unjust actions. Any belief, whether unreflectively held or dogmatically proclaimed, that women are inferior to men (whether physically, psychologically, socially, morally, ontologically, and so on) is enough to justify differential treatment that may result or escalate into violence, exclusion, or exploitation. The passage from macrocosmic theories about God and the world (theology) to microcosmic practices in the power relations between men and women (gender) and the unjust treatment of minorities may be difficult to plot, but it is more difficult to deny.

### Banishing the Binaries

The binaries discussed in previous chapters illuminate these dark shadows of our social and theological history. On a one-sex theory, women are defective men. On a two-sex theory, women are so different from men they are the 'weaker' sex. When legislation began to be passed to require more equal treatment for women, the new male–female binary became the basis for a new counterblast against the advances of lesbian and gay people – first the decriminalisation of sexual relations between men, next the achievement of equal rights, and eventually the right to marry. The male–female binary that enshrined the dominance of men over women was given a new use. It applied only to a particular sort of male – the heterosexual (real or imagined) – whose fulfilment could be guaranteed only by the provision of a female. As appeals to various texts of Scripture that were supposed to proscribe love between men became increasingly

implausible, the very being of a homosexual person became newly pro-
blematised. It was not enough even to be celibate. To be non-heterosexual
was already to have the suspicion of moral deviance stamped on one's
being, mitigated only by the stoic refusal to engage in 'same-sex practices'.
Once the reservation of the priesthood to men began to be scrutinised, the
maintenance of the binary had another new and urgent purpose. These
binaries created further problems for intersex and trans people as they too
emerged from the closet.

Millions of Christian people are hurting as a consequence of these
binaries. Women who are called by God to the priesthood must generally
serve in some other capacity instead. While most churches (as far as
I know) will test a vocation to ministry, in most cases of applications from
women no test will be offered. Either the Holy Spirit is a priori mistaken,
or the applicant confused or deluded. Women and men who would like
the option of confession to and absolution from a woman priest can
whistle in the wind. Indeed the absence of women priests and ministers
severely compromises the overall effect of Christian ministry as a whole,
causing eucharistic famine in large areas of the world. Christian women all
over the world have to endure, or insulate themselves from, the demeaning
effects of sexist language and liturgy.

The well-being of each of the groups in the LGBTIQ designation would
be much improved if the symbolic system requiring binary oppositions
were to be permanently modified, and that is what I attempt in Part III of
the book. The heterosexual–homosexual binary normalises heterosexuality
and marginalises homosexuality. On a continuum of orientation lesbians
and gay men would identify themselves somewhere unproblematically
towards one end. Bisexual people find themselves somewhere in the middle.
Orientation may be flexible, like identity, for there are different ways of
being lesbian or gay, and there is a sexual fluidity among lesbians that may
be more marked than in gay men (Diamond 2009). For the first time, more
young people in the UK describe themselves as bisexual than gay or lesbian
combined, recent figures from the Office for National Statistics (ONS) show
(ONS 2017). It is the latest evidence (requiring sympathetic theological
analysis) pointing to a shift in attitudes towards sexuality, with increasing
numbers viewing their own position as somewhere on a *continuum* rather
than it being a black-or-white question. A recent survey (YouGov 2016)
found that half of young people in Britain, and almost a quarter of the
population overall, define themselves as something other than 100 per cent
heterosexual. These results should cause no surprise. Alfred Kinsey published similar results in the two Kinsey Reports of 1948 and 1953.

Trans people confront an ambivalence with regard to the male–female binary, while intersex clearly find the male–female binary difficult. What sense can heterosexuality make to one who cannot identify himself or herself against the other (*hetero-*) sex? While intersex and transgender should not be conflated, Cornwall notes that

> both phenomena, and the experiences of both groups, demonstrate the limitations of theologies which assume always stable, *binary models of maleness and femaleness*. Sexual theologies … must therefore acknowledge that intersex and transgender people may face particular challenges surrounding sexuality, and that intersex and transgender themselves pose questions for sexual theologies assuming *stable, binary sex*, gender and sexuality. (Cornwall 2015: 658, emphases added)

All persons considered in this chapter have a problem with one or more of the three binaries. Lesbian and bisexual women, and gay and bisexual men need have no problem with the male–female binary. They identify as women or men. They have a problem with the heterosexual–homosexual binary, inasmuch as the binary divides not merely sexual orientation but dumps much of their personal and social lives into the morally reprehensible category. They may also have a problem with the masculine–feminine binary insofar as they are likely to reject many of the characteristics of heteronormative behaviour which prescribe what counts as properly feminine or masculine (Chapter 9).

It should not be forgotten that, in 2016, 93.4 per cent of the UK population still identified themselves as primarily heterosexual or straight (ONS 2017). This big majority has *no* problem with the male–female binary. It will be for them a default setting and a matter of self-evident intuition. Any continuum showing sexuality to be altogether more flexible and inclusive must clearly also include them. However, growing numbers of straight women and men query the masculine–feminine binary because they do not identify with many of the cultural stereotypes of the ideal man or woman, their models of perfect bodies, and their competitive behaviours based on violence. Christian practice is likely to be a refutation of many of these.

In this chapter we thought about self-knowledge and about the language of personal identity, both of which require a social framework out of which people live (what Bourdieu called a *habitus*). Since self-knowledge is always mediated to us through people around us (however much we are reflexively aware), the Christian task is to provide an alternative *habitus* wherein all participants are able to receive affirmation and encouraged to find self-acceptance. Ultimately that is because there is a God who loves them deeply and accepts all of us as we are. A language is needed that does not hurt or pathologise any of us but foregrounds that we are all the children of God who has made us with an astonishing diversity. That language requires a community of practice where there is no linguistic or symbolic violence, only the practice of love.

In Part I, I have ranged across large tracts of human experience, plotting or 'scoping' questions of gender as they arise in power relations between men and women; in the symbolic systems that encode gender bias and that authorise, directly or obliquely, violence against minorities; and in the difficulty of many individuals attempting to express deep self-knowledge by means of cognitive frameworks, some of which are deeply wounding. These early chapters are my attempt to achieve my first aim, 'to depict the relations between women and men as a pervasive human and global problem, in order to expand the range of theological thought required to address it'. The link, explored in this chapter, between epistemology and violence, makes the task of examining core beliefs surrounding gender all the more urgent. The Christian task is to love all such people as neighbours; to listen to their experiences, not simply as a duty, but in order to understand them and thereby love them more completely, and to respect and honour difference. This task, to be attempted in Parts II and III, will be facilitated by exploring the possibility of a non-binary faith that embraces women and sex/gender minorities without discrimination. That will be a faith, a 'symbolic system', in continuity with what has gone before, yet different in its agapic and unconditional acceptance of all God's children.

It takes two philosophers, sympathetic to theology, to suggest the role of theologians in relation to the issues discussed in Part I of this book. 'Given the impact on the lives of countless men, women, and children of false, overly simplistic, and unjustified gender narratives – many of which can and do cause psychological, spiritual, and relational injury', they insist, for

> theological and religious leaders to fail to take gender and gender narratives seriously is a failure not only in the realm of ethics and social justice but also a failure in love. If Christian leaders and all people of goodwill (religious or otherwise) hope to make an impact not only on the present generation but also on the generations to come, then they must be willing to engage in genuine dialogue with feminist thinkers, and when necessary and applicable, to revise some of their most cherished – but perhaps unwarranted and un-*natural* – assumptions and beliefs. (Nielsen and Norton 2015: 150, authors' emphasis)

# PART II

# Double Vision
## Catholics and Protestants on Sexual Difference

## CHAPTER 4

# The Vatican and the War on Gender

## Balthasar and the Binaries

One might reasonably expect that the Roman Catholic Church, which insists on *the recognition of the inherent, inalienable dignity of women*, the importance of women's presence, and participation in all aspects of social life, and which admires 'the genius of women' (Pope John Paul II 1995: paras 9, 10; Pope Francis 2015) everywhere, to generate a theology from which their full dignity and equal rights follows, and to seek common cause with secular organisations and academic disciplines to the extent that they too are pursuing similar ends. Instead, however, we will find in the present chapter that 'gender', a term that in secular thought picks out the arena where the struggle for dignity and equality between women and men happens, has become a multifaceted enemy the church is determined to oppose, whatever the moral and theological cost both to its own integrity and to those millions of people who are adversely affected by the firming up of its gendered teachings.

We have already noted the power of cultural and symbolic systems to express the 'androcentric unconscious'. Unfortunately, Balthasar's theology is such a system. While he might be commended for foregrounding gender in his work (Gonzalez 2004: 569), its androcentrism is more than 'unconscious'. It is often painfully explicit and metaphysically justified. As Elisabeth Vasko charges, it is one of those 'dualistic anthropologies that identify masculinity with leadership, reason, and aggressiveness and femininity with receptivity, emotion, and nurturance' (Vasko 2014: 507). They are 'particularly troubling', she continues, 'as they lift up models of dominance–submission as biologically normative for gender relations. *Such gender assumptions cloak sexual violence in invisibility, allowing perpetrators and victim-survivors to rationalize such behavior as natural and (in theological contexts) God given*' (Vasko 2014: 507, author's emphasis).

An extreme statement of sexual dimorphism, governing human biology and psychology and the human sense of self, is written into the beginning of Balthasar's account of 'Man and Woman' in his *Theo-Drama*: 'The male body is male throughout, right down to each cell of which it consists, and the female body is utterly female; and this is also true of their whole empirical experience and ego-consciousness' (Balthasar 1990: 365). How does he know this? The unbridgeable gap between men and women notwithstanding, they are said to share 'an identical human nature'. The proffered dichotomy between human sex and human nature cannot be further characterised or explained. It is 'a mystery: as a human being, man is always in communion with his counterimage, woman, and yet never reaches her. The converse is true of woman' (Balthasar 1990: 366). Part of the mystery of the human person is said to be that we can never 'possess' the other.

There are actually two mysteries running here: the conundrum how human beings can be utterly different from each other, yet share an identical nature; and the limited knowledge we can have even of others with whom we may be intimate. We cannot ever 'possess' the other of the opposite sex because 'this impossibility is "enfleshed" in the diverse and complementary constitution of the sexes' (Balthasar 1990: 366). But Balthasar never pauses to think that the mystery of the other person is unconfined to sexual difference: *no* other person can be fully known, whatever side of the apparently unbridgeable sexual gap they may be.

Balthasar turns Genesis 1–3 into a phenomenology of sexuality. While he finds the two creation accounts in Genesis 'embody much legendary wisdom … purified of mythical bias', he (and it must be said, following him, all three popes from *Theo-Drama* to the present) actually treats them as phenomenological descriptions of relations between men and women, pouncing on and magnifying details and imposing on them the sexual binary that they cannot support. Examples quickly mount. From Genesis 2, three details are isolated. Because he is *temporally* alone in the garden prior to the making of the woman, an ontological 'primacy of the man' is asserted. Second, his loneliness is 'not good', and third, 'it affirms that the woman comes from man'. The man is said to have been 'overpowered', 'robbed of part of himself, near to his heart'. This is his *kenosis*. It 'results in the God-given fulfilment whereby he recognizes himself in the gift of the "other"' (Balthasar 1990: 373). But the man retains his 'primacy': his '(persisting) priority is located within an equality of man and woman (1990: 373)'.

But no amount of prevarication can allow a pair to be equal while one exercises primacy over the other! 'Man' and 'woman' are said to need 'the archetypal image of Christ/Church' to 'first radiate the fullness of light onto the creaturely copy', and in this Platonic exemplary world there can be no question of symmetry or equality between, on the one hand, man and woman, and on the other hand, the masculine Christ and the feminine Church. In volume 3 of *Theo-Drama*, Balthasar returns to human sexual difference and projects it back on to the divine Being. Readers unfamiliar with his metaphysics may find their jaws dropping at this point. Because 'the Logos proceeds eternally from the eternal Father' (as orthodox Christian teaching insists), the question arises whether 'is he not at least quasi-feminine vis-à-vis the latter?' (Balthasar 1992: 283). The question can arise only because he has already decided that the skewed and unequal male–female binary exists transcendentally in God. The 'provisional answer' is: because, 'However the One who comes forth from the Father is designated, as a human being he must be a man if his mission is to represent the Origin, the Father, in the world' (1992: 284). The Origin is male, but just as the first woman existed primordially and potentially in the man before she was created from the side of the first man, so the divine Word exists eternally in the divine Origin. The first Adam is incomplete without the woman who comes forth from his side. But the 'Second Adam', the incarnate Christ, is also 'incomplete until God has formed the woman from his side' (1992: 283). The woman in question is of course the Church, the Bride of Christ the Bridegroom. This is the metaphysic which is presented as the church's contribution to the human understanding of sexual difference.

## The Answer to a Non-Question

The analogy in Ephesians between Christ and the church and the bridegroom and his bride (Eph. 5.28–33), with divine–human asymmetry built into it, lies at the root of John Paul II's exposition of the 'nuptial meaning' of the body. Much is made in volume 3 of *Theo-Drama*, of the characterisation of 'woman' as 'essentially an answer [Ant-Wort]' (Balthasar 1992: 284: see Crammer 2004; Muers 2000). *Ant-Wort*, it is explained, is a pun on *Ant*, with roots meaning both 'over against' and 'toward'. 'Woman' is 'over against' 'man' in the mysterious polarity of absolute difference, while Woman is 'toward' 'Man' in existing for and with him. The question–answer schema, of course, is imposed on the creation account in Genesis 2, and the logical priority of a question over an answer becomes the ontological priority of the man over the woman. It 'clearly shows us the way in which man can be primary and woman secondary, where the primary remains unfulfilled without the secondary. The primary needs a partner of equal rank and dignity for its own fulfilment' (Balthasar 1992: 284). God makes the woman from the body of the man and gives her to him as a gift. She is 'not only man's delight: she is the help, the security, the home man needs; she is the vessel of fulfilment specially designed for him. Nor is she simply the vessel of *his* fruitfulness: she is equipped with her own explicit fruitfulness' (1992: 285, author's emphasis). The woman is fruitful in bringing the man to completion. *Her* fruitfulness 'is not a primary fruitfulness: it is an answering fruitfulness, designed to receive man's fruitfulness (which, in itself, is helpless) and bring it to its "fullness". In this way she is the "glory" of the man (1 Cor. 11.7)' (1992: 285). Woman 'is actually the fruit-bearing principle in the creaturely realm'. 'She responds through reproduction' (1992: 286).

To be secondary, to be responsive, *is* to be feminine (Balthasar 1992: 287). That is why even the Word is 'quasi-feminine' in relation to the Origin or Father, for, 'Apart from receptivity and pregnancy female sexuality does not appear to have an intrinsic value of its own' (Vasko 2014: 523; see Sain 2009). There is a 'female principle in the world' that consists in being secondary and responsive. Balthasar says so explicitly: 'insofar as every creature – be it male or female in the natural order – is originally the fruit of the primary, absolute, self-giving divine love, there is a clear analogy to the female principle in the world' (Balthasar 1992: 287). Analogically all creatures including – yes – men, are 'feminine', in that they have a 'mission', that of being ready and open to receive the seed of the divine Word, to bear it and give it its 'fully developed form'. The error of the world is the refusal of receptivity in relation to God, and the error of feminism is the refusal of receptivity in relation to God and to men. So a particular version of the male–female binary is reinforced by the transcendental metaphysic. Karen Kilby's fair and fastidious reading of Balthasar's entire corpus leads her to conclude that, throughout his writings,

> To be male is to be strong, to take initiative, to be active and goal-orientated; to be woman is to be open, receptive, surrendering, passive, to be characterized by weakness and dependence, to be contemplative. And within these clusters, perhaps the most insistent, frequently mentioned, the defining contrast, is that man takes initiative and is active, while woman is receptive. (Kilby 2012: 129)

## Sex and Violence

Violence is everywhere in these metaphysical accounts. Even God's act of making the woman from the man's rib is made into an act of violence whereby the man is 'overpowered', 'robbed of part of himself', and made to empty himself in an involuntary act of kenosis. Vasko, referring to Balthasar's treatment of the Annunciation, comments, 'The Marian fiat is a highly sexualized and erotic affair that is marked by a willingness to bear fruit. Specifically, it is the "active readiness" and "complete availability" of her womb to receive the divine seed that "represents the highest act that a creature can perform in love"' (Vasko 2014: 515). Citing Balthasar's own words, she makes clear the explicit sexual reference without which the metaphysical analogies cannot work – 'Just as the man gives his seed in sexual intercourse, so Christ sows the seed of the Word and is a total outpouring of himself for his bride' (2014: 515, citing O'Donnell 1992: 120). 'Mary's virginal receptivity', Vasko explains, 'recapitulates creation's response (feminine) to the divine offer of self-gift (masculine). Throughout all of history, Mary, as the second Eve, stands in solidarity with humanity and responds obediently in our place' (Vasko 2014: 515).

Balthasar's theology, observes Tina Beattie, 'oozes sex' (Beattie 2006: 157). Elsewhere she describes its derivation 'from the copulative ontology of the pagan cosmos' (Beattie 2013: 348). But the cosmic copulation with its erection of male–female, active–passive, inseminating–receiving binaries up into the very Godhead is also violent. An associated problem arises with Balthasar's treatment of the passages in *Revelation* in which Babylon (read Rome) is characterized as the Great Whore. While he follows Scripture in identifying unbelief and heresy with harlotry, he shows no awareness of the disparagement of the female body on which the metaphor relies. On his reading, 'This is a violent defeat in which God is depicted as a zealous warrior who goes to battle with a wanton whore in order to rescue his bride' (Vasko 2014: 520). Even the final triumph of good over evil is metaphorized as masculine intervention and conquest over feminine disobedience and wantonness, the latter being assumed to justify the former. Mary's voluntary receptivity to divine intervention at the Annunciation is made into an apex of feminine holiness, but since Balthasar defines 'feminine virtue in terms of disponibility [*sic*], humility, and obedience to masculine initiative' the precedent she sets might be a fatal one. 'Could she really say no?' (2014: 522). These very emphases on 'submission, obedience and dependence' can all too easily 'play a role in the acculturation of women to accept abuse' (2014: 517).

## Divinising Difference

Critiques of Balthasar's theology abound. I find Beattie's book-length critique convincing (Beattie 2006). One more recent critic finds his thought 'gender-bending, masochistic, reckless' (Tonstad 2016: 47). Another observes the men in his thought have a hard time too, leading, dominating, and requiring feminine receptivity to balance the 'overly masculine culture' they create (Sain 2009: 85). Susannah Cornwall observes, *contra* Balthasar, that 'difference in creation is always more than binary, always more than either–or, always more than this-not-that, because it echoes the Trinitarian difference which is always at least tri-directional … and leaves no space for models of human sex which are more than binary ones' (Cornwall 2017: 90). We have noted certain well-known features of Balthasar's thought in the present section. They include his heightening of the male–female binary by lifting it into the very being of God: his defining of the masculine–feminine binary by emphasising permanent roles to the opposite sexes and lifting these too into God; his absolutising of sexual difference; his incredible use of the early chapters of Genesis as a phenomenology of sex and gender; and the pervasive androcentrism and violent characterisation of sexual relations. Sadly these features will surface repeatedly in the writings of Popes John Paul II, Benedict XVI, and even Francis. Whereas Balthasar's name will not be found in official Vatican documents, the metaphysical thinking behind some of them is unmistakeable (see e.g., Rakoczy 2008).

In our tracing of the recent origins of the war on gender, we will begin three years before the election of John Paul II in 1978. In 1975 the Congregation for the Doctrine of the Faith (CDF) published *Persona Humana*, the 'Declaration on Certain Questions concerning Sexual Ethics'. The document sought to *ally* itself with the science of sexuality in its alleged confirmation of radical sexual difference. It began,

> According to contemporary scientific research, the human person is so profoundly affected by sexuality that it must be considered as one of the factors which give to each individual's life the principal traits that distinguish it. In fact it is from sex that the human person receives the characteristics which, on the biological, psychological and spiritual levels, make that person a man or a woman, and thereby largely condition his or her progress towards maturity and insertion into society. (CDF 1975: para. 1)

Who would have thought that that relatively new neologism – 'sexuality' – could have ascended so high, so quickly, in the hierarchy of theological significance? But the reason for its extolment is the attempt to cloak with the authority of science the two-sex binary that the Vatican sought to promulgate for purposes that had little to do with biology. The science of sexuality is alleged to teach that there are 'values proper to each of the sexes' (CDF 1975: para. 1). These constitute an 'essential order' containing 'immutable laws' which have 'absolute and immutable value' and are unreasonable to deny (CDF 1975: para. 4). Primarily on the basis of these, that is, the 'objective moral order', only secondarily 'attested' by Scripture, the judgment is reached that 'homosexual acts are intrinsically disordered and can in no case be approved of' (CDF 1975: para. 8).

The supposed fact of two opposite sexes, supported by the authority of science, was enlisted against the possibility that homosexual people might find loving relationships with each other, and the might of Divine Law, interpreted by the Magisterium, was invoked to support it. A year later it became evident that the Vatican needed clearly demarcated sexes in order to deal with another problem – the ordination of women within some of the churches. The principal theological feature of *Inter Insigniores: On the Question of Admission of Women to the Ministerial Priesthood* was that 'the incarnation of the Word took place according to the male sex: this is indeed a question of fact' (CDF 1976: para. 5). The priest acts *in persona Christi*. Christ was a man: ergo, a woman cannot represent Christ. 'That is why we . . . can never ignore the fact that Christ is a man.' Catholic women called by God to the priesthood are mistaken. Their vocation is 'mere personal attraction' (CDF 1976: para. 6). Any blurring of distinctions between the sexes would render the reservation of the priesthood to men only more deeply problematic.

## Complementarity Arrives

Complementarity as a theological *term* did not appear in official documents until *Familiaris consortio* (1981), though the ideas it encompasses go back to the Catholic personalism of the 1950s (Case 2016: 156), and to Rousseau's romantic philosophy (Thatcher 2016: 66–9). In *Familiaris consortio* the 'conjugal communion' between husband and wife 'sinks its roots in the natural complementarity that exists between man and woman' (John Paul II 1981: para. 19). In 1979 John Paul II began a series of 129 weekly audiences which came to comprise his 'theology of the body'. The first 23 of these were meditations on the early chapters of Genesis. The complementarity of two sexes occurs here too in a kind of prototype of later theology. But the topic of sexual difference is already a lot more than a discussion about relations between women and men. It becomes crucial for holding a particular line about at least two other, related matters. Complementarity was thought to be crucial in defending the traditional line over maintaining an exclusive male priesthood, proscribing homosexuality, and obliterating the testimony of intersex and trans people.

For these purposes, gender essentialism was the necessary *sine qua non*, and complementarity provided it.

The growing ideological association between complementarity and the preservation of the male priesthood becomes more explicit in the Ratzinger Report (1985). The foreboding title of Chapter 7, 'Women: A Woman' proceeds by way of a defence of the priestly status quo. The first section, 'A Priesthood in Question', raises the prior question,

> Male? Female? They are questions that for some are now viewed as obsolete, senseless, if not racist. The answer of current conformism is foreseeable: 'whether one is male or female has little interest for us, we are all simply humans'. This, in reality, has grave consequences even if at first it appears very beautiful and generous. It signifies, in fact, that sexuality is no longer rooted in anthropology; it means that sex is viewed as a simple role, interchangeable at one's pleasure.

The passage is noteworthy both for its style and for its theology. As usual, opponents are anonymous. Their identity is not to be disclosed. That also makes the misrepresentation of their views easier. People who, three or four decades ago, welcomed less rigid roles for both men and women, who were pioneers in the extension of women's rights, and who were beginning to recognise the acute discomfort of people with gender dysphoria, did not think of male and female as obsolete or senseless terms. They were coming to see that excessive binarism in both religious and secular thought was harmful to both women and men. The association of criticism of Vatican teaching with racism disguises that there are strong theological arguments against that teaching that do *not* emanate from hatred and ideology. In lumping together disparagingly the Vatican's critics ('current conformism'), the smear of political correctness is used, and is now a well-known feature of official Vatican writing about gender. Ratzinger mocks the very solidarity between women and men that redeemed humanity is destined to enjoy. Theological critics do not at all deny that Christians should base their thoughts on (theological) anthropology. They have good reasons for thinking that the Vatican's 'anthropology' is deficient and itself capable of being used ideologically. It is the Vatican that reduces sex to a 'simple role'. The assumption that a person who reassigns their gender does so casually and simply for pleasurable purposes is, frankly, horrible. Even the section title is an exercise in scare-mongering. The priesthood is *not* being questioned. Only its usurpation by men. What threatens the priesthood is the exclusion of women, which, theology aside, increases the scarcity of the species.

Themes from the theology of the body found their way into John Paul II's subsequent writings, especially *Mulieris dignitatem* (1988) and his

*Letter to Women* (1994). Like his successor, he places great weight on 'theological anthropology' (by then a standard phrase). This anthropology draws heavily on Genesis 1 and 2, and especially the verse (1.27) that proclaims that God created humanity male and female, both in God's image. This contains and 'constitutes the immutable *basis of all Christian anthropology* (John Paul II 1988: section 6, author's emphasis). Perhaps John Paul II is to be congratulated for beginning here instead of with any of a range of texts which are much less egalitarian (Porter 1996). I suggest elsewhere (Thatcher 2016: 95) that a much more solid basis for theological anthropology is Jesus Christ (and not a literal interpretation of Genesis 1). It is Christ, not Adam, who is 'the image of the invisible God' (Col. 1.15). While Genesis 1–3 featured prominently in the theology of the body, their further appeal to John Paul II may have lain in pursuing other agendas.

John Paul II also needed the sexual binary to maintain the essentialism of Vatican thought. We found this just now in Benedict's use of the term 'woman', which signified not merely one half of the human race but a perplexing problem for patriarchal thought that has no equivalent in the apparently unproblematic term 'man'. There can be 'no adequate hermeneutic of man, or of what is "human", without appropriate reference to what is "feminine"' (John Paul II 1988: section 22). The Great Essence – Woman – towers above individual women. She remains a threefold mystery: 'in the perspective of our faith, the mystery of "woman": virgin–mother–spouse' (John Paul II 1988: section 22). Pope Francis speaks regularly of the 'feminine genius', cautiously surmising that by virtue of it, 'female theologians' may be able to take up 'certain unexplored aspects of the unfathomable mystery of Christ' (Francis 2014; see Mannion 2016: 4, and Francis 2015). But as Krzysztof Olaf Charamsa scathingly observes, praising women is a further way of confirming their lesser status vis-à-vis men:

> Woman becomes a 'thing' (not a subject who can describe herself) we (men) declare to be great, to be wonderful, with her special and particular genius. She becomes a special 'thing' that we can adore. Which is another way to neutralize this 'thing': the 'thing' has no possibility to open her mouth. (Paternotte 2016: 242)

John Paul II, like Benedict after him, also attempted to invoke the selective support of science in confirmation of a range of theological objectives. 'Scientific analysis' is supposed to endorse that 'the very physical constitution of women is naturally disposed to motherhood – conception, pregnancy and giving birth ... At the same time, this also corresponds to the psycho-physical structure of women' (John Paul II 1988: para. 18). But as we noted earlier, following Linda Alcoff, the possibility of conception, gestation, and lactation for some women for a part of their lives does not entail any assumption about the nature of all women, nor whether these possibilities ought to be actualised. In the *Letter to Women* sexual difference became more firmly ontological. 'Womanhood and manhood', still understood as essences, are said to be 'complementary *not only from the physical and psychological points of view*, but also from the *ontological*. It is only through the duality of the "masculine" and the "feminine" that the "human" finds full realization' (John Paul II 1995: section 7, author's emphasis).

## Gender Ideology

We turn now from the male–female binary and its codification in complementarity to the wider question of gender. Monseigneur Krzysztof Olaf Charamsa is a former member of the CDF, and a former second secretary of the International Theological Commission. In 2015 he came out as gay and was immediately suspended. His account of the inner workings of the Magisterium in a lengthy interview (Paternotte et al. 2016) is highly illuminating. Charamsa recalls how the United Nations International Conference on Population and Development in Cairo (1994), followed by a second conference in Beijing, 'Women: Action for Equality, Development and Peace', produced 'panic and disorder' in the Vatican. It reacted defensively, and (Charamsa recalls) its reaction 'marks the Vatican's relationship to gender studies, or what they call "gender ideology"' (Paternotte et al. 2016: 227; Case 2016: 156–7). Just before the Beijing Conference, the conservative American activist Dale O'Leary presented Cardinal Ratzinger with her highly polemical position paper, 'Gender: The Deconstruction of Women; Analysis of the Gender Perspective in Preparation for the Fourth World Conference on Women Beijing, China, September, 1995'. This was later revised and published as *The Gender Agenda*. Mary Anne Case records that that was the moment when Ratzinger 'cathected on the word "gender" and sent it out into the polemic generating machinery of the Vatican' (Case 2016: 165). The word gender became the umbrella term for much else that the Vatican disliked, including 'radical feminism, gay rights, abortion, reproductive rights, new family forms, even transsexuality' (Case 2016: 166).

In 2003 the Pontifical Council for the Family published its *Lexicon: Ambiguous and Debatable Terms regarding Family Life and Ethical Questions*, which appeared in English in 2006. Post-Beijing, an authoritative definition of terms was required. Three of the seventy-eight entries were about 'gender'. In the Preface, Cardinal Alfonso López Trujillo explained the need for the Church to arm itself against a global linguistic conspiracy to undermine Catholic teaching. The *Lexicon* sought 'to enlighten people on some ambiguous or confusing terms and jargon difficult to assess'. With Cairo and Beijing in mind, he explained, 'Many expressions are used in parliaments and world forums with concealment of their true content and meaning even for the politicians and members of parliament who use them, due to their weak background in philosophy, theology, law, anthropology, etc.' (Trujillo 2003: n.p.). Gender is just such an expression. In Trujillo's mind, devious feminists and agile philosophers are managing to outwit politicians. Lawyers are mistaken in operating democratically, because they 'refuse to accept natural law', and the Church must fight back by promoting 'serious and objective [scientific] information' (Trujillo 2003).

The essays on gender were republished in French in 2011 as *Gender, la controverse* (Conseil Pontifical pour la Famille 2011), in the Church's attempt 'to answer the questions raised by the introduction of the theory of gender in the biology manuals' of French schools (Généthique 2011). The last of the three essays contained a definition of gender acceptable to the Roman Catholic Church. It read,

> Transcendent dimension of human sexuality, compatible with all aspects of the human person, comprising body, thought, spirit, and soul. Gender is thus permeable to influences exerted upon the human person, be they internal or external, but it must conform to the natural order that is already given in the body. (See Fassin 2016: 179)

Set within a Thomist and personalist linguistic framework, gender is cut down to an approved size, that of 'influences' that cannot be allowed to disrupt the 'natural order'. Nature first; culture last.

In 2003 Ratzinger's *Considerations regarding Proposals to Give Legal Recognition to Unions between Homosexual Persons*, signed off by John Paul II, complementarity becomes the bulwark of the Church's condemnation of same-sex marriage. Its 'teaching on marriage and on the complementarity of the sexes reiterates a truth that is evident to right reason and recognized as such by all the major cultures of the world' (CDF 2003: para. 2). The truth of complementarity is thought to be fully rational and obvious to everyone except the ideologues who oppose the Vatican's teaching: 'No ideology can erase from the human spirit the certainty that marriage exists solely between a man and a woman, who by mutual personal gift, proper and exclusive to themselves, tend toward the communion of their persons' (CDF 2003: para. 2). That couples of the same sex can give themselves to each other and enjoy 'the communion of their persons', cannot even be thought. In proscribing 'approval of homosexual behaviour' and any 'legal recognition of homosexual unions', Ratzinger appealed to one of the most positive features of Catholic social teaching, that of the 'common good', arguing that 'Legal recognition of homosexual unions or placing them on the same level as marriage would mean not only the approval of deviant behaviour, with the consequence of making it a model in present-day society, but would also obscure basic values which belong to the common inheritance of humanity' (CDF 2003: para. 11). Fifteen years on, these warnings seem more scare-mongering than ever. If there are basic values common to humanity, presumably they can't be 'obscured'? The suggestion that same-sex marriage might threaten the 'common good' may suggest something else: that the Church itself feels threatened because it cannot countenance the good that is realised in such marriages.

## The Church's Enemies

By 2004 'gender' was joined up with homosexuality, the undermining of the family and the threat to the common good, in Ratzinger's writings. In the *Letter to the Bishops of the Catholic Church on the Collaboration of Men and Women in the Church and in the World*, a 'tendency' is announced that emphasises the 'subordination' of women to men deliberately 'in order to give rise to antagonism' (Ratzinger and Amato 2004: para. 2). Judith Butler's famous work *Gender Trouble* was anonymously associated with it. This tendency is said to stir up needless 'opposition between men and women, in which the identity and role of one are emphasized to the disadvantage of the other, leading to harmful confusion regarding the human person, which has its most immediate and lethal effects in the structure of the family'. Ratzinger seems to think that all feminists are like Butler in wanting to diminish sexual difference: 'In order to avoid the domination of one sex or the other, their differences tend to be denied, viewed as mere effects of historical and cultural conditioning'. In order to provide an explanation for the alleged denial of sexual difference, Ratzinger evokes the sex–gender distinction, linking the term 'gender' directly to the Church's supposed opponents. He writes, 'In this perspective, physical difference, termed *sex*, is minimized, while the purely cultural element, termed *gender*, is emphasized to the maximum and held to be primary' (author's emphasis). The fear of Butler's influence is linked to 'ideologies which, for example, call into question the family, in its natural two-parent structure of mother and father, and make homosexuality and heterosexuality virtually equivalent, in a new model of polymorphous sexuality' (Ratzinger and Amato 2004: para. 2). Mysteriously, the 'deeper motivation' of this tendency must be found

> in the human attempt to be freed from one's biological conditioning. According to this perspective, human nature in itself does not possess characteristics in an absolute manner: all persons can and ought to constitute themselves as they like, since they are free from every predetermination linked to their essential constitution. (Ratzinger and Amato 2004: para. 3)

That people seeking gender reassignment should be portrayed in the vanguard of the rebellion against God and nature is shocking. In 2008, Benedict even inserted into his Christmas message to Vatican staff a vitriolic comparison between gender equality and environmental destruction, finding in both a disregard of nature, a sinful declaration of human independence from the Creator, and the error of living in opposition to the truth:

> If the Church speaks of the nature of the human being as man and woman, and demands that this order of creation be respected, this is not some antiquated metaphysics. What is involved here is faith in the Creator and a readiness to listen to the 'language' of creation. To disregard this would be the self-destruction of man himself, and hence the destruction of God's own work.
>
> What is often expressed and understood by the term 'gender' ultimately ends up being man's attempt at self-emancipation from creation and the Creator. Man wants to be his own master, and alone – always and exclusively – to determine everything that concerns him. Yet in this way he lives in opposition to the truth, in opposition to the Creator Spirit.
>
> Rain forests deserve indeed to be protected, but no less so does man, as a creature having an innate 'message' which does not contradict our freedom, but is instead its very premise. (Pope Benedict XVI 2008: section 1)

This escalation of hostility towards an enemy, now named 'gender' yet still anonymous, is strengthened via an appeal to the 'order of creation', which is thought to exclude the experience of same-sex orientation, of belonging to a third sex, of being intersex, or being trans. All deviation from the male–female binary and its approval in heterosexual marriage is a sinful rebellion against the boundaries imposed by the 'order of creation', whatever the testimony of those people who are unable to conform to it. One wonders who is failing to listen. Proper attention to 'ancient metaphysics' instead of the rhetorical lip-service paid to it, will not in any case yield up the absolute binary Benedict assumes can be found there.

As Charamsa has written, from the insider's point of view, the Catholic Church 'needs an enemy'. Once communism obliged. Or Protestantism. Now a complex of enemies is solidified, and 'gender' is its name:

> The Church fails to see real people, communities or movements. It identifies something without real knowledge of it; without awareness of the human and sexual identity and life of these people, who must remain invisible. They are viewed as an object upon which hate and fear can be projected, and which can be destroyed. *'Gender' emerges as the slogan-name of a theoretical elaboration against which the Church can build its identity.* (Paternotte 2016: 227, emphasis added)

This is the legacy which Cardinal Jorge Bergoglio of Buenos Aires inherited when he became Pope Francis in 2013. How would he deal with it?

## More of the Same

The publication of Francis's remarkable Apostolic Exhortation, *Amoris Laetitia*, in March 2016, would suggest that a new era of pastoral care had opened up. Anyone reading this encomium in praise of married love, with its outpouring of papal empathy in response to human weakness and its acknowledgement of the Church's many pastoral failings, might think a new era had dawned. Chapter 8, 'Accompanying, Discerning and Integrating Weakness', and the section 'The Logic of Pastoral Mercy' (Francis 2016: paras 307–12) would seem to signal a marked shift away from the tone of the earlier works we have just considered. But a change of tone and style do not signal a change of doctrine. Two Synods had preceded the publication of *Amoris Laetitia* in 2014 and 2015, yet between them, the Pope welcomed 'an international who's who of self-described proponents of traditional marriage and opponents of same-sex marriage from diverse faith traditions and continents' (Case 2016: 155–6) to an 'International Colloquium on the Complementarity between Man and Woman'. The colloquium was sponsored by the CDF (The *Humanum* Conference), whose 'entire strategy', according to Charamsa (remember, a high-ranking Vatican insider), 'in the context of the Synod . . . was a project intended to contradict and silence the pope's intention to discuss' (Paternotte 2016: 239).

The very choice of title for the colloquium precluded *critical* discussion of complementarity. Its authority and normativity was simply assumed. Elsewhere I have used the term 'repetitive consolidation' to describe how the repeated statement of a dubious proposition, irrespective of any truth-claims the statement contains, leads to its acceptance (Thatcher 2018: 17).

The colloquium was engaging in repetitive consolidation. Francis's short opening address is noteworthy for the promise it never delivered. On the one hand it seemed to prise open the prevailing definition of complementarity and its application to marriage: 'it is a word into which many meanings are compressed' (Francis 2014). Basing his own definition of complementarity on 1 Corinthians 12 (a letter in which Paul *discourages* marriage), he informed the conference that

> Christians find its deepest meaning in the first Letter to the Corinthians where Saint Paul tells us that the Spirit has endowed each of us with different gifts so that – just as the human body's members work together for the good of the whole – everyone's gifts can work together for the benefit of each (cf. 1 Cor. 12). To reflect upon 'complementarity' is nothing less than to ponder the dynamic harmonies at the heart of all Creation. This is a big word, harmony. All complementarities were made by our Creator, so the Author of harmony achieves this harmony. (Francis 2014)

In this address, complementarity becomes a synonym for the harmony of all things in the life of God and the life of the world. When applied to marriage the Pope exhorts the conference not to

> confuse that term with the simplistic idea that all the roles and relations of the two sexes are fixed in a single, static pattern. Complementarity will take many forms as each man and woman brings his or her distinctive contributions to their marriage and to the formation of their children – his or her personal richness, personal charisma. Complementarity becomes a great wealth. (Francis 2014)

Francis seems here to acknowledge the broad polysemic possibilities of complementarity, including the abandonment of assumed roles of husband and wife. Paul's metaphor of the body is an integrated whole of many parts, not a single pair of opposites. On the other hand what might have become a thoughtful revisioning of complementarity in the service of diversity within creation, and within marriage, quickly retreats into Benedict's narrower vision of 'the family' and its enemies. Even Benedict's analogy between the crisis within the family and the crisis of ecology is invoked. Francis warns,

> The crisis in the family has produced an ecological crisis, for social environments, like natural environments, need protection. And although the human race has come to understand the need to address conditions that menace our natural environments, we have been slower to recognize that our fragile social environments are under threat as well, slower in our culture, and also in our Catholic Church. It is therefore essential that we foster a new human ecology. (Francis 2014)

Francis, then, concurs with his predecessor that there is an 'ideology of gender', and that the Church's enemies can be conveniently and collectively accused of 'ideological colonization' (Francis 2016: see Bracke and Paternotte 2016: 143). Gerard Loughlin has pointed to the irony of the Vatican's use of the term 'ideology', since, he avers, the Vatican has an ideology of its own – sexual dimorphism – which it is able to sustain only by ignoring or denying the very existence of what he calls the third bodies of the intersexed, the homosexual, and the transgendered (Loughlin 2018: 473). In sum, the ideology of gender

> operates as a frame that encapsulates a wide spectrum of issues and actors whose connection cannot be taken for granted ... [I]t brings together a number of concerns high on the agenda for conservative Catholic activists: rejection of a wide range of reproductive rights for women (notably abortion), rejection of same-sex marriage and homosexual parenting, attachment to particular roles for men and women ... sex education, and the endorsement of particular – heteronormative – norms about sexuality ... It also amalgamates potentially dissenting actors (feminists, LGBTQ activists, and gender studies scholars) under a single figure of 'the enemy' to be combated by the Church. (Bracke and Paternotte 2016: 148)

Examining Balthasar's thought on gender has at least opened up for us the appropriate level of analysis that theology can and should undertake in offering renewed reflection on gender (in all three meanings of the term adopted earlier). But it has come to a dead end. With this sober estimate of Vatican thinking about gender in the present century, and the misery it causes, we turn in the next chapter to see how Protestant thought in the same period has also exaggerated the male–female binary and also come to wage war against its various opponents. But we do so retaining the possibility that there is a much better 'theological anthropology' available to the churches, which enables them to love and serve, and engage positively with the very minorities it demonises as its opponents. That is Charamsa's view too, for whom 'gender studies' is no opponent, but

> a way of thinking that is connected to life, concrete life, to people who gain awareness of their own dignity and identity, and begin to see the possibility to be themselves. From a Christian point of view, one might say that this is a very Christian movement, a truly evangelical movement. This is the Gospel: 'work in progress' to understand our nature and our call to be and love! (Paternotte et al. 2016: 228)

CHAPTER 5

# Women, Men, and Barth

Karl Barth is perhaps the most justly famous and celebrated Reformed theologian of the twentieth century. He and Balthasar were lifelong friends, and he undoubtedly influenced Balthasar's own work (Wigley 2007). Yet his treatment of gender, and the characterisation of homosexuality that follows from it, is deeply unsatisfactory. Written over half a century ago, why bother with it at all? My answer is that there is much in contemporary worldwide Christian thought that replicates it, especially among conservative and more fundamentalist people who are inclined to take the *ipsissima verba* of Scripture as 'God's Word'. That is not to claim that millions of people have read Barth or even been directly influenced by him. But I *do* claim his views on gender are harmful to women, harmful to men who dominate women, and very harmful to gay people should they internalise his a priori understanding of them as perverse. I claim the male–female binary in Barth must be replaced with a better doctrine of human being which does not regard women as secondary to men or heterosexuality to be compulsory. That said, his writings belong to a different time, and his achievements in many other areas – theological, political, ecclesial – deserve enormous respect.

## Genesis and Gender

We will find many similarities between the writings of Barth and Balthasar, not least their attempt to treat the early chapters of Genesis as a contemporary phenomenology of sexuality. Several times Barth says the narratives have the genre of a saga, but he reads them straightforwardly as if they were historical events with permanent ontological significance. Genesis 2.18–25, says Barth, 'has only one theme – the completion of the creation of man by the adding to the male of the female' (Barth 1958: 288). The basic form of all humanity is relational. Its constitution is 'I–Thou'. The sociality of human being is more basic than its individuality.

Barth's problem, like Balthasar's, is that half of human being is a different and inferior sex from theirs', and they cannot reconcile the modern equality of the sexes with the ontological priority accorded to just one of them. 'Everything [in Genesis 1 and 2] aims at the one fact, to wit, that God did not create man alone, as a single human being, but in the *unequal duality* of male and female' (1958: 288, emphasis added).

For Barth the biblical revelation is that God has established a covenant with humankind, and humankind must also correspond with this structure, so that our covenantal relationship with each other, or rather between the sexes, is the 'internal basis' of the covenantal structure put in place by God and described by Genesis 2. So the solitary male needed a partner, not just any partner – like the other animals and birds in the garden – but a partner with particular characteristics. The partner or 'helper' must 'resemble' the man without being a copy of him. So the partner must be similar to the man and different from him. The purpose of the partner is to overcome the solitariness of the man. The partner must be sufficiently like him to be human and to overcome his loneliness. The partner must be a gift to the man, in order to anticipate the giftedness of the covenant God will make with all humankind. The man needs an I–Thou relationship with his 'helpmeet' because that is how God will be in relationship with Israel. Without his partner 'there is a gap which must be filled if man is really to be man and not in some sense to be so only potentially' (Barth 1958: 292). He welcomes her as God's gift to him, and as part of himself ('This is now bone of my bones . . .').

'Who is woman?' asks Barth rhetorically, echoing the essentialising question of the popes in the previous chapter. The answer is: Woman is the one who overcomes the man's lonely plight. The woman

> makes him what he could not be in his solitariness – a man completed by God. The simplest and most comprehensive definition of woman is that she is the being to which man, himself becoming male, can and must say in the exercise of his freedom that 'this' is now the helpmeet which otherwise he had sought in vain but which had now been fashioned and brought by God. (Barth 1958: 300–1)

Only in the presence of woman does the man recognise himself, and find his own fulfilment as a man. 'This, then, is woman – the one who is so near to the man who through her existence has become man, and is therefore so indispensable to him for his own sake.'

The man's naming of the woman ('this one shall be called Woman, [*ishshah*] for out of Man [*ish*] this one was taken' – Gen. 2.23) demonstrates that, because she was taken from the man's body, she is his property. Barth denies this ('Nor does it mean that she is man's property') only to say, two sentences later, that the man's naming her means 'that in her being and existence she belongs to him'. Is there a difference? There is more obfuscation, in the same paragraph, over the equality of the woman and the man. On the one hand, Barth rejects any notion of gender equality. On the other hand, he says the inequality explicit in Genesis makes no difference to the lives of each:

> The fact that the relationship is not one of reciprocity and equality, that man was not taken out of woman but woman out of man, that primarily he does not belong to her but she to him, and that he thus belongs to her only secondarily, must not be misunderstood. The supremacy of man is not a question of value, dignity or honour, but of order. (Barth 1958: 301)

The terms 'dignity' and 'honour', as we found in the previous chapter, are honorific only, conveying a measure of respect while at the same time conveying nothing about status or 'value'. Barth alludes to 1 Corinthians 11.7 ('a man ... is the image and glory of God: but the woman is the glory of the man' – AV) perhaps in an attempt to disguise the incompatibility of his claims. The 'glory' of the woman is precisely her availability to the man, and that is not a mere matter of order only. Barth juggles with words. The woman's glory 'in a particular and decisive respect is greater even than that of man' (Barth 1958: 301–2). She exists to bring him to completion. This is her function. If her glory is 'greater' than the glory of the man, that is because it is more important that the man is brought to fulfilment than it is for the woman. 'Because she is the glory of man and marks the completion of his creation, it is not problematical but self-evident for her to be ordained for man and to be for man in her whole existence' (1958: 303). Unless women are understood this way, claims Barth, they have not been understood at all.

And there is further obfuscation over the subsidiarity of the woman's role. Feminist critics rightly point out that the woman is set up for service and sacrifice, for devotion to the man, and for no other role. These criticisms are justified but perhaps anticipated by Barth who makes the man instead the one who sacrifices himself for the sake of the woman. First, God anaesthetises the man ('caused a deep sleep to fall upon the man, and he slept' – Gen. 2.21) in order to create the woman. There is no hint of violence in the Genesis narrative, but God's act of making the woman is read (as Balthasar does, following Barth?) as an 'attack' on the man that he is obliged to suffer in order to bring about the woman.

The man 'had to allow the infliction upon himself of a mortal wound. For one who was not a lump of dead earth but a living soul it entailed sacrifice, pain and mortal peril as God marched to this climax of His work. God spared him' (Barth 1958: 302), but 'the never-absent pain of deprivation in his relationship to woman is the constant reminder of that from which he was spared'. Really? Men can deaden the pain that women cause them by thinking of the pain of Adam (even when he was unconscious while apparently enduring it)?

Second, a man shall 'leave his father and his mother, and shall cleave unto his wife: and they shall be one flesh' (Gen. 2.24). This detail, often remarked upon, that the man and not the woman leaves the parental home in order to marry, also becomes overladen with male sacrifice. He is able to achieve his end, the possession of a wife, again through 'sacrifice, pain and mortal peril' (Barth 1958: 305). As if there was and remains an ideal of transhistorical courtship, 'Things have to happen as they do when man and woman love each other and are married; man has to be the one who seeks, desires, sacrifices.' By a tortuous reversal, the male sex is really the weaker sex after all. Why? Because it 'is utterly dependent on woman for the fulfilment of his relationship to her, so that to this extent he is the weaker half'. This 'tearing himself away from his roots' is a 'required sacrifice', the price of 'autonomy attained'. The man is really the subordinate one – subordinate to 'the arrangement' that requires of him to leave his home and seek out a partner. It is a 'humiliation' for the man that, only 'as the one who seeks, desires, sacrifices and is referred to her – he confronts the woman as the weaker partner, can he be her lord and stronger than she' (Barth 1958: 306). Even as he lords it over her, 'in practice woman need not fear this pre-eminence'. The ire that these observations rightly generate may be somewhat tempered by the realisation that they were written 70+ years ago, but how many millions of women in the last 70 years have suffered from their partners lording it over them? How many have been taught not to fear masculine pre-eminence only to fall as tragic victims to it?

## Mystery or Mystification?

Barth returns to his analysis of sexed human being in his *Dogmatics*, III.4, section 54 (1961). It is a major theme of his theology that 'man' is destined to live in covenant with God, but man is 'man and woman' (Barth 1961: 116), and that the 'first and typical sphere of fellow-humanity, the first and typical differentiation and relationship between man and man, is that between male and female' (Barth 1961: 117). The relationship between male and female 'correspond[s] to the relationship between Yahweh and His people' and that of Christ to the church. Immediately the most obvious problem arises: the relationship between God and the people of God is necessarily hierarchical; is the 'hierarchism' of this relationship to be mapped onto the relationship between men and women? Or are there other elements of the analogy that render it serviceable in a gendered context? Here Balthasar is more convincing in his attempt, however bizarre the outcome, to model sexual difference on difference within the Trinity. Sexual difference alone among human differences is, for Barth, 'structural and functional'. 'Man never exists as such, but always as the human male or the human female.' Both are human. In this their solidarity resides. But how can there be solidarity, when 'No other distinction between man and man goes so deep as that in which the human male and the human female are so utterly different from each other' (Barth 1961: 117)?

We may wonder how this utter difference is derived from divine revelation. The binary is prised open and repeatedly restated. It is a matter of 'Either-Or'. 'God his Creator requires that each should be genuinely and fully the one or the other, male or female, that he should acknowledge his sex instead of trying in some way to deny it, that he should rejoice in it rather than be ashamed of it' (Barth 1961: 149). But '"male *or* female" is immediately to be completed and transcended by the "male *and* female"' (author's emphases). Barth asks, '[H]ow is it possible to characterise man except in his distinctive relation to woman, or woman except in her distinctive relation to man? ... [I]t is so deeply a question of being in relation to the other, of duality rather than unity.'

Further inquiry into this duality is for Barth, pointless, because 'it is not a question of psychology, pedagogy, hygiene and the like' (Barth 1961: 150), but a matter of the 'command of God'. 'Male and female being is the prototype of all I and Thou', but it is impossible to define the mystery of the sexes any further. Theology can

> merely point to something which cannot be expressed, to the mystery in which man stands revealed to God and to Him alone. It is at the point where he is indefinable that he is sought and found by the divine command ... we cannot really characterise man and woman in the form of a definition, but only as we recall that in their very differentiation God has willed and made them in mutual relation ... (Barth 1961: 151)

Yes, there is a boundary between psychology and theology but might we not expect from theology more than an attempt to conceal the basis for its core assertions? Can any sense be made of revelation in this context if God reveals something only to God alone and no one else? What if, as it happens, there are people who cannot find I–Thou relationships with members of another sex? Or who are intersex? Or who are far from at ease with their sexed bodies? Suppose that much patient scientific inquiry and empathic listening showed this binary to have no application at all to substantial minorities of people, what would become of Barth's assertions then? In the end, the binary is a mystery to Barth himself and to everyone else except God, who in revealing it does so only to Godself. Barth's mysterious position is beyond investigation.

But there are yet other, theological, reasons why the 'I–Thou' relationship, despite its popularity since Martin Buber published his famous work of that title in German (*Ich und Du*) in 1923, cannot have male and female being as its prototype. Twenty years ago, Eugene Rogers noted that 'I–Thou categories fall short prima facie of likeness to the triunity of the creator. They pay too little attention to the work of the Holy Spirit' (Rogers 1999: 184). 'I–Ye', he suggests, incorporating the plural form, would be better, drawing upon Gospel stories where the encounter of Jesus with individuals is always accompanied by the mediating and facilitating presence of other people. 'I–Thou phenomenology tends to reduce co-humanity to co-individuality', he claims. 'I–Thou categories systematically *hide* the presence of third parties and ecclesial mediation: disciples, crowds, friends' (Rogers 1999: 184, author's emphasis). Barth would have done better to have used his Christology, and the notion of the church as God's family, if he had wanted a theological rationale for human relations.

What guidance then, if any, can theology give to men and women regarding how they relate to each other in the asymmetrical form that is set up by God? That question might be put in a different way: Are there models of masculinity or femininity that are pleasing to God, or (in Barth's terms) that fulfil the divine command? God, not theology, may give the appropriate advice, for 'The command of God ... will disclose to them the male or female being to which they have to remain faithful.' It may do so 'in new and surprising ways. The summons to both man and woman to be true to themselves may take completely unforeseen forms right outside the systems in which we like to think' (Barth 1961: 151).

Much of how we think about sexuality and gender now would have been 'completely unforeseen' nearly 70 years ago, but it is hard to think Barth would have found much to welcome, given his starting points, in twenty-first-century thought about each. While he writes disparagingly about 'systems' of thought it is clear that he too has a system (architectonic, in fact, given the size of his *Dogmatics*). More tellingly his strictures about systems can be turned back against his own system, for the God who works in new and surprising ways may have no use for a binary system that burdens and constricts so many of God's people. We might also wish to know how, given Barth's own system, the same people can be 'true to themselves'. Presumably, if their self-knowledge is not to be private knowledge directly disclosed to them by God, new knowledge will assist them, and if they are Christian, new ways of reading Scripture and tradition in the light of reason and experience will play their part as well.

### 'Unequal Duality'

Barth says, 'we definitely reject every phenomenology or typology of the sexes' (Barth 1961: 152). We might welcome this rejection as one that refuses the assignment of gendered characteristics like activity and passivity, rationality and emotionality, to the different sexes, yet it is hard to see how some typology is to be avoided given the system Barth himself imposes, albeit derived from apparently incontrovertible theological sources. The command of God, he says, 'lie[s] somewhere above and beyond the sphere in which such typologies are relatively possible and practicable' (Barth 1961: 153). However, the command of God cannot operate outside the 'unequal duality' which is part of it. Elements of the 'modern feminist movement' are 'a more or less express and definite desire on the part of women to occupy the position and fulfil the function of men' (Barth 1961: 155), and so are voided because they breach the divine order. 'The command of the Lord does not put anyone, man or woman, in a humiliating, dishonourable or unworthy position. It puts both man and woman in their proper place' (Barth 1961: 156). Exactly. The unequal duality may not be disturbed. 'Interpretations may vary as to where this place is, for the Lord is a living Lord and His command is ever new' (Barth 1961: 156). Here is one of many cases in Barth's writings where fluidity of interpretation seems to be allowed, only to be withdrawn in the same or the following paragraph. So, can listening to the living Lord and the Lord's command *ever* alter the subsidiary place of women within the Christian faith and church? Certainly it can, but hardly by means of or within Barth's own system.

The system closes down all attempts to live other than as a man in relation to a woman or a woman in relation to a man. Beyond the 'opposite sex', there is 'a third and supposedly higher mode of being' that some people are said to aspire to. This constitutes a 'desire to violate fidelity to one's own sex' (Barth 1961: 156). The description conveys his disparaging judgment that 'What is sought is a purely human being which in itself and properly is semi-sexual and therefore, in relation to its apparent bi-sexuality, sexless, abstractly human, and to that extent a third and distinctive being as compared with male and female' (1961: 158). Barth uses the term 'androgynous nature', which he compares to a 'neutral It' (1961: 158). Persons of variant gender are understood as wilful trans-gressors of God-given limits, bringing about their own 'dehumanisation'. '[E]ffeminacy in the male or mannishness in the female' is inconsistent with the command of God (1961: 157). In living out our masculinity or femininity there is a 'limit defined by the command of God'. But how does someone know when that limit is reached? The answer is they must be 'not merely fully aware of their sexuality, but honestly glad of it, thanking God that they are allowed to be members of their particular sex and therefore soberly and with a good conscience going the way marked out for them by this distinction'. But the answer is a cruel tautology: cruel because many people cannot be 'honestly glad of their sexuality', especially in societies and churches that – albeit unknowingly – follow Barth and 'binarise' it almost totally; tautologous, because the way is not 'marked out' for them. Far from being glad, Barth's imposed constraints lead to untold misery, prejudice, suffering, and danger.

At times Barth attempts to soften his patriarchy; indeed 'soft patriarchy' as a sociological term began to be used in the sociology of Protestantism at the beginning of the present century to refer to the 'accommodationist spirit' of patriarchal men and patriarchal institutions towards moderate feminist demands while keeping essential patriarchal structures belief systems in place (Wilcox 2004: 144). This is but one of many emphases of Barth's thinking about gender that embodies itself in Protestantism half a century later. After excoriating the paganism of Simone de Beauvoir's *The Second Sex*, he concedes,

> the description of the way in which man has made and still makes himself master of woman, the presentation of the myth with which he invests her in this process and for this purpose, and the unmasking of this myth, are all worthy of attention especially on the part of men and not least of Christian theologians. (Barth 1961: 162)

Apparently there are right and wrong ways by which men dominate women and women let themselves be dominated by men, but Barth fails to comprehend that his system legitimates the very means by which 'man ... makes himself master of woman', and assumes his superiority over 'her'. Yes, there is 'mutual orientation' within the 'polarity' of 'opposite' sexes (1961: 163), but the mutuality can no more exist simultaneously with domination than equality can exist simultaneously with hierarchy.

The 'mutual orientation' of each sex might be considered, 70 years on, to provide a belated argument for the arrival of women at all levels of the armed forces, universities, corporations, indeed almost everywhere where employment was once confined to men. But this has already happened, without help and sometimes with opposition from theology. Barth's considerable subtlety in qualifying his insistence on divine order defeats him and becomes instead equivocation. On the one hand, he recognises, as I have done (Thatcher 2016), the priority of sexual similarity over sexual difference:

> ... recognition of the reciprocity of the sexes, and therefore that which they have in common, must take absolute precedence of [*sic*] the difference in their modes of interrelation. In other words, the similarity in their interrelationship must be more important in the first instance than the illuminating and fundamental dissimilarity in which it is realised. (Barth 1961: 164)

On the other hand, the 'fundamental dissimilarity', including the hierarchical order, is emphasised to the extent that the 'mutual coordination' Barth appears to want is subverted by his own controlling ontological suppositions.

## Celibacy and Homosexuality

The two sexes are so incomplete without each other that even celibacy is ruled out along with 'clubs and ladies' circles', or any other male or female 'seclusion' or 'segregation' (Barth 1961: 165).

> [I]n obedience to the divine command there is no such thing as a self-contained and self-sufficient male life or female life. In obedience to the divine command, the life of man is ordered, related and directed to that of the woman, and that of the woman to that of the man.

Ironically, Barth is instinctually right about this, at least to the extent that single-sex institutions like public schools, seminaries, priesthoods, and church hierarchies, which are run exclusively by and for men, are liable to produce copies of themselves, misogyny, unaccountability, and theological prejudice. An argument from a different account of divine order, based on real reciprocity and not on soft and not-so-soft patriarchy would expose them and render them redundant.

What Barth regards as the created structure of human being and the reciprocity of the sexes provides his principal reason for condemning homosexuality as a 'malady', 'the physical, psychological and social sickness, the phenomenon of perversion, decadence and decay' (Barth 1961: 166). He wrote when same-sex sexual relations were illegal, and often severely punished, and medical opinion sought to explain homosexuality as a psychological disorder. It is perverse, he thought, because it countermands the man–woman relationship that is binding on absolutely everyone ('the primal form of fellow-man'). It is important to understand his contention that people who are intimate with other people of the same sex voluntarily and sinfully turn away from their natural, created heterosexual orientation. Love for someone of the same sex, he claims, summoning Romans 1 in support, is inevitably idolatry, since it places human love before the love of God and God's command. It is clear Barth has no idea about the very different subjectivities of gay, lesbian, and bisexual people. He thinks for example, that a gay man must 'despise' even the thought of a female partner, and that the act of despising is itself evidence that the universal heterosexual structure remains in place. Lesbian and gay people 'must be brought to fear, recollection and understanding' as early as possible in their lives before 'the real perversion takes place, the original decadence and disintegration begins' (1961: 166).

Barth has no difficulty finding '[m]uch that is typically masculine' is unacceptable. Fighting wars is an example. He asks, 'might not the very dubious masculine enterprise of war become intrinsically impossible if the remembrance of the confrontation with woman were suddenly to be given the normative significance which is undoubtedly its due?' (Barth 1961: 168) Most people want war to become intrinsically impossible and for peace to operate at every level of humankind. There are varieties of peacemaking for people to engage in, and there are many women who have good reason to find many men violent aggressive or violent. But men *and* women should strive to be less aggressive, even if men as a generalisation have much more to do. Naturalising war as masculine ultimately *excuses* it, and confirms peace and nurturance as exclusively feminine. Against Barth, the problem is the aggrandisement of masculinity that his system encourages and that disposes men to discharge their masculinity overaffirmatively and sometimes violently.

Barth and his contemporary followers will think this charge unfair, and he anticipates criticism by returning to the ontological order of the sexes outlined in III.4, section 54. On the one hand, 'men', that is men and women, 'are fully equal before God'. On the other hand 'there is no simple equality' (Barth 1961: 169), for man and woman are related to each other as A and B, and not as A and A. The logic is immediately spelled out. 'A precedes B, and B follows A. Order means succession. It means preceding and following. It means super- and sub-ordination.' It also means a return to equivocation, which quickly falls apart. Men and women are fully equal, except of course that they are not.

Neither can the differences in the required behaviour of each sex be guided, still less explained, by the male–female and masculine–feminine binaries that Barth presents. Having relegated women to subordination, in God's name, he quickly excoriates 'man' for his misuse of his leadership, and his exploitation of 'woman'. He can occupy his superior position 'only in humility ... taking the lead as the inspirer, leader and in initiator in their common being and action' (Barth 1961: 170). The 'strong man' is the one who obeys the divine order in service mode (1961: 176). If he does so 'he will not feel superior to woman. He will really be superior only in so far as he will primarily accept as his own a concern for the right communion of the sexes as secured by this order, and therefore for the order itself' (1961: 177). When Barth goes on to explain that 'woman' 'is in her whole existence an appeal to the kindness of man' (1961: 180–1) the analysis becomes deeply scary. What sane, free, prudent woman would act as if that statement were true?

The 'primacy of service' was to become the theory of 'servant-leadership' in much evangelical Christianity. Why should men lead at all, especially since, as Barth acknowledges, men everywhere 'exploit' the divine order and women *rightly* rebel against it. 'It is understandable that woman should protest and rebel against this exploitation', he concedes. Insisting that 'man' fulfils 'the required initiative of service in the common cause of humanity', he fails to see that men have no monopoly over service, and the bulk of it is almost certainly done by women in any case. While Barth is adept at reconciling opposites, disguising 'superordination' as service is a sleight of hand, a conceit. His admission that masculine pre-eminence messes up both men and women might have led him to abandoning the male–female binary completely instead of hanging on to it at great personal and existential cost to the subordinates it creates.

## A Harmful Legacy

Barth's now historical account of gender is not to be completely dismissed. He is clear that human being is relational, that through sociality and only through sociality we become the people we are. There is a common human nature. Surprising though it is, Barth left room for innovation in how new generations of women and men would negotiate their roles vis-à-vis each other. Women and men create their social roles (see Sonderegger 2006: 268). His warning against sexual 'systems' and his rejection of sexual 'typology' are positive. He envisages a positive contribution from theology to the understanding of gendered interaction, and does not assign particular behavioural characteristics to each sex. He says he *supports* the fight against patriarchy. He says he acknowledges the protest of women against it. He is highly critical of much that passes for acceptable masculine behaviour. Ultimately he affirms the priority of sexual similarity over sexual difference. There is much here that might be developed further, even if his own system requires a recasting in the process.

But given the esteem in which Barth's theology is still held, it is important to insist that his theological account of gender remains unremittingly harmful, and its shadow over ensuing Protestantism is long and dark. It is open to the charge levelled against Balthasar in the previous chapter – that it sanctifies violence against women – and it shares many of the features that were to appear later in Balthasar's writings. It essentialises women and men, treating them as opposites, and it is difficult to see how their unequal statuses do not result in their being assigned roles that match them. As a theological system it perpetuates the inequality of medieval thought and provides a fine example of the tendency, named by Bourdieu, of 'eternalizing the arbitrary'. To speak of 'woman' in the abstract is to ignore the diversity of real women way beyond any biological warrant, while to speak of 'man' is to intend two meanings; the male sex, and the whole of humankind, still referred to as 'man' or 'men' in Christian preaching and hymnody. Even the designations 'women' and 'men' are potentially misleading, not because they are problematic for some people (they are), but because the fundamental moral obligation in Christian ethics is to love one's *neighbour* as oneself irrespective of his or her sex, and the status of neighbour is prior, within the continuum of a common humanity, to the neighbour's contingent sexual identity. Both writers insist that men and women are 'utterly different', while sharing a common nature. Men and women relate to each other as primary–secondary, A–B. Both writers equivocate over how 'man' can have ontological primacy over 'woman' while 'woman' enjoys full equality with 'him'. Most Protestant evangelicals and Catholic cardinals agree with him here. Women have a twofold purpose: to bring the man to completion, and to be fruitful.

Both writers say they are reading Genesis 1–3 as saga or 'legendary wisdom', but their use of the text assumes a more or less straightforward factual account, not just of the creation, but of a fixed hierarchical order that is supposed to govern relations between human beings. Qualifying them as saga, that is as archetypal narratives revealing universal truths, enables them to proceed much as if they are literal and complementary accounts of real events, and as such these accounts are gratefully received by literally minded readers who assume Genesis has the last word, not the first, about sexuality and gender. They are treated as phenomenologies of sexuality – readings that sound as strange as readings of the same narratives would sound if they were treated as phenomenologies of the creation of the world. The idea, forced on the text, that the man sacrifices, or suffers, or empties himself so that the first woman can be born, is ideological, an attempt to even up the asymmetry of man and woman in Genesis 2 that Christian thought has acknowledged (and wrestled with) from 1 Corinthians to the present day. As a symbolic system, Barth's theology is open to the charge of justifying violence against women, and to the silencing of voices that protest against patriarchal churches, their dark secrets, and the dark theology on which they thrive. Despite his greatness as a theologian, 'There are undoubted shadows in Barth's work', and these include 'the quite unsustainable position on the subordination of women, and the position on homosexuality' (Gorringe 1999: 288).

The system certainly endorses the 'otherising' of all but heterosexual married people, which disrupts the solidarity between the straight majority and everyone else. Barth cannot be blamed directly for this. Even the medical profession agreed with Barth in 1961 when he categorised homosexuality as a psychological disorder, and called it a perverse malady. But he thought it perverse not on psychological or medical grounds, but because the very possibility of same-sex desire as a possible good and a basis for an enduring covenant between two people would have undermined the ontological ubiquity of the two-sex binary. For Barth that was unthinkable. So great was the theological weight that came to be placed on the binary by Catholic and by Protestant thought that it had to be defended, a priori if necessary, however much the science of sexuality and the conservative theologies of sexuality were to diverge. The system can no more cope with lesbian and gay people than it can cope with people who are bisexual, intersex, or transgender. A richer, more pluriform account of sexual difference is needed: an alternative 'theological anthropology' to the 'theology of the body' (or its Protestant equivalent) without the extrinsic reasons for adopting it.

And such an alternative is clearly available. Balthasar takes sexual difference and projects it into and onto the being of God, so there are masculine and feminine traits belonging to each of the trinitarian Persons. Barth grounds his thoughts on gender in his phenomenological/literal interpretation of the early chapters of Genesis. Yet if he had grounded his account of 'male and female' in what he had said about human persons reflecting divine Persons (III.2), the asymmetry and 'static relational order' (Stephenson 2008: 435) of the sexes in III.1 and III.4 described above would have been avoided. In III.2 he speaks of an *analogia relationis*, an analogy of relation between human persons and the divine Persons of the Trinity, so that to be created male and female in the image of God is both to be in an I–Thou human relation, and to reflect humanly the divine relations or *perichoresis* of the Persons of the Trinity. Summarising this possibility as several of Barth's critics have developed it, Lisa Stephenson writes,

> if the interpersonal relation of male and female and the Trinity are to exist as an *analogia relationis*, in light of *perichoresis* there should be mutual initiative and mutual response between the male and female. That is, there should be a correspondence to the quality and character of the relations within the Godhead to those between male and female. (Stephenson 2008: 444)

While Barth does not realise this possibility, it remains for other theologians to take up. Graham Ward has suggested that from a theological perspective, *there can be no inequality between the sexes*. One reason for this is that (as I have lamented elsewhere – Thatcher 2016) the idea of two opposite sexes is recent, and wrongly supplants 'the true understanding of creation's ontological order [that] comes from a participation in the operation of God's being' (Ward 1998: 61). A second reason is, following Ward, that once biology sets itself up 'as an independent realm of self-grounding, self-defining entities', it becomes corporeal only, and 'To handle the corporeal as if it were not also spiritual and theological is a form of idolatry; a consequence of sin, ignorance and human arrogance' (1998: 62). But there is a third reason. From a *trinitarian* perspective biological difference is 'transfigured' (as it is in Barth's treatment of the Song of Songs). As Ward explains,

> From the perspective of the revelation of the Godhead, then, it is not only orders of existence and the nature of bodies that are redefined. Sexual relations and identities are redefined also. From the point of view of revelation the difference is read in terms of a covenant constituted through reciprocal desire. It is this covenant through desire for the other that forms the nature of the Godhead itself and the economy of relations constituted through reciprocal desire within the Godhead. It is not the biology *per se*. If

you like, God does not see male and female, he sees human being in partnership, in covenantal relationships of I and Thou, One and the Other reflecting His own Triune nature. He sees the couple as human being, not male and female. (Ward 1998: 62)

After Barth, the churches have grappled with many issues in Christian ethics to do with sexuality, gender, marriage, divorce, and the presence of LGBTIQ people among and beyond them. One reason why they have equivocated over welcoming, affirming, and embracing such people is that their 'theological anthropology', Catholic and Protestant, remains stubbornly similar to the one outlined in this and the previous chapter. It equivocates over the place of women in ministry and in society. Balthasar and Barth offer a gendered system of the type Luce Irigiray dubbed 'hom (m)osexuate', that is, one which is defined entirely from the perspective of men (*hommes*). Opposition to the full rights of homosexual people and later to same-sex marriage was based on the two-sex binary, which when read as Barth and Balthasar presented it, accomplished the further marginalisation of sexual and gender minorities. The binary became more important, but for extrinsic reasons that had little to do with understanding gender, and more to do with the preservation of a hom(m)osexuality which feared the challenge that homosexuality brought to its very existence. The binary became a wall that intersex and trans people, establishing a more visible presence in church and world, ran into. It rendered their very being impossible, a mistake, a fantasy.

## Complementarity (Again)

Use of the term 'complementarity' was slower to catch on among Protestants than among Catholics. We did not find it in Barth, though we found there a lengthy description identified by that term. Stanley Grenz, the influential evangelical theologian, used the term 'supplementarity' instead. Men and women 'supplement each other' (Grenz 1990: 48) in a 'mutual relationship'. He was not the first theologian to find in the text 'Let us make man in our image', a vestige of the doctrine of the Trinity, and he found a 'supplementarity' among the *divine* Persons, 'present in a prior way'. The 'image of God' is a 'community concept', and 'As we live in love, as we live in true community, we reflect the love which characterizes the divine essence' (Grenz 1990: 51, and see Grenz 2001). But supplementarity is the reason (he thinks) why sexual love must be confined to heterosexual marriage. 'The fundamentally different outlooks toward others, life and the world that characterize males and females mean that the two sexes are supplementary' (Grenz 1990: 253). The crucial 'symbolic dimension' of heterosexual sexual intercourse (i.e., penis in vagina) is lacking in same-sex intimacy. Indeed 'there is an inherent lack of the dimension of supplementary completeness in all such relationships' (Grenz 1990: 239). From supplementarity a whole range of misconceptions is said to follow about the limits and incapacities of same-sex relationships, all far removed from the testimony of lesbian and gay Christians themselves.

Grenz's strictures about homosexuality are based primarily on his convictions about supplementarity and only secondarily on the exegesis of Scripture (see Grenz 1990: 228–31). 'Disposition', he warns, must be distinguished from action. The latter is sinful, the former not. Complementarity appeared almost incidentally in the first of three reports of Anglican Bishops on 'human sexuality' between 1991 and 2013 (House of Bishops 1991: 37, 39). In the second report, it had become one of 'a core of commonly held beliefs about human sexuality' (House of Bishops 2003: 9), based on an interpretation of Genesis 2 that was said, contrary to almost unanimous tradition, to teach '*equality* in difference', or 'complementarity' (House of Bishops 2003: 90–1). Apparently, 'the author of Genesis was enabled by God to transcend the limitations of his culture in a way that enabled him to catch a glimpse of God's original intention for the relationship between men and women' (House of Bishops 2003: 91). The Anglican document (2003) accomplishes an extraordinary but almost unspoken manoeuvre – a seamless transition from hierarchical to egalitarian complementarity. The 'correct' interpretation of Genesis 2 is said to teach this (House of Bishops 2003: 90)! This is clearly progress towards a higher valorisation of women in the Anglican Church, but the same principle was also gathering influence in the stance against same-sex marriage. By 2012 it (rather than any attempt to deploy any arguments based on biblical texts) had become the main basis of the Church of England's submission to the secular Government opposing same-sex marriage (Church of England 2012). The document recorded 'that redefining marriage to include same sex relationships will entail a dilution in the meaning of marriage for everyone by excluding the *fundamental complementarity of men and women* from the social and legal definition of marriage' (Church of England 2012, emphasis added). That position was confirmed a year later by the third Anglican report on human sexuality (House of Bishops Working Group on Human Sexuality (2013: 34)), the Pilling Report.

The manoeuvre from hierarchical to egalitarian complementarity had been made earlier by liberal evangelicals in the USA. In 1987 Christians for

Biblical Equality (now the influential CBE International) issued an uncompromising statement of faith (CBE International) that insisted that the Bible 'teaches the full equality of men and women in Creation and Redemption'; 'that both man and woman were created for full and equal partnership'; and 'that the forming of woman from man demonstrates the fundamental unity and equality of human beings'. It says 'The Bible defines the function of leadership as the empowerment of others for service rather than as the exercise of power over them', concluding, 'We believe that biblical equality as reflected in this document is true to Scripture.' The statement insists on the important distinction between inspiration and interpretation. Plentiful references to proof texts are provided, but these are likely to prove insufficient because the inegalitarians can generally find alternative texts to match them, and (as so often and over so much) interpretative stalemate results. The CBE International intervention into American evangelical politics was timely, welcome, and fruitful, but it needs a doctrine of Trinity and a theological anthropology to authenticate its vision (Chapter 7) and provide a counter-reading to the male dominance represented by Barth. Perhaps more difficult to achieve, alongside its separation of inspiration and interpretation, is the distinction that needs to be made between the Bible as the Word of God and Jesus Christ as the Word of God. Since the Person of Christ and the Bible are entirely different kinds, here a hierarchy is actually a requirement!

## Signs of Hope

The symbolic violence manifested in several provinces of the Anglican Communion towards sexuality and gender minorities is also fanned by vicious gender politics. Mark Chapman has analysed these, borrowing the idea of a 'condensation symbol' – a term describing a word or phrase associated with 'particular theological or ethical positions on a whole range of issues [that] take on far broader symbolic meaning than the presenting problem' (Chapman 2018: 197). Secular examples he gives include 'gun control' and 'family values'. 'Opposition to homosexual practice', he continues, 'has become a symbolic focus for a whole range of complex geographical, theological, and ecclesial identities', and phrases such as 'orthodox teaching on sexuality', 'biblical and faithful Anglicans', 'biblical teaching on homosexuality', and so on (my examples) have become condensation symbols in theological and ecclesial politics. 'Biblical complementarity', 'essential complementarity', and so on, belong to this genre. Parts of the Communion associate liberal teaching on sexuality with the unwelcome and pervasive dominance of Western culture and economics in the Third World, thereby harnessing their opposition to postcolonial and neocolonial narratives. More liberal people need to take this seriously, not least because the nomenclature of sexuality, homosexuality, and so on is undoubtedly Western in origin.

But there are signs of change and hope among other evangelical Protestants. Two very different appendices to the Pilling Report indicated the growing gap between 'affirming evangelicals' and their more literally minded opponents. An appendix, dissenting even from the conservative conclusions of the main report, based its opposition specifically on 'a bifocal trajectory' which the author finds 'from Genesis to Revelation' (Sinclair 2013: 160). The term signifies that binaries are written into creation and redemption alike. Heaven and earth – 'the two halves of God's creation' – are 'bifocal' even as men and women, Christ and the church, male and female are bifocal. 'Bifocality' is now a reason why the author thinks the church cannot tolerate homosexual unions. But a further appendix aligns itself with the Accepting Evangelicals organisation, which believes 'the time has come to move towards the acceptance of faithful, loving same sex partnerships at every level of church life, and the development of a positive Christian ethic for lesbian, gay, bisexual and transgender people' (Runcorn 2013: 177). Jayne Ozanne (2016) speaks for many lesbian and gay people who have been 'wounded', 'scarred', and 'silenced' by churches whose teachings render adequate pastoral care impossible, despite exhortations from the Lambeth Conference (1998) about ministering pastorally and sensitively to everyone.

The 'cognitive dissonance' between a vibrant faith and the internalisation of shame produced by it has led to mental breakdown (Ozanne 2016: xii) and even suicide (Church Times 2015). The thirteen contributors to Ozanne's book, *Journeys in Grace and Truth*, provide 'a collection of stories from leading Evangelicals ... who hold ... an affirming view' of same-sex love. Central to the spiritual reawakening of one of them is the realisation that 'binary categories of male and female' are not 'the ultimate forms of humanity' (Stowell 2016: 36–7), while another comes to see 'there are those for whom sexual identity is a much more complex issue than a simple clear-cut male/female binary divide' (Newman 2016: 57). In common with the argument of this book Newman highlights the 'sharpness' (a well-chosen cutting metaphor) of the binary divide for transgender people, observing, 'we are much more aware today of the spectrum of masculinity and femininity that lies within each one of us, and which we own and embrace with differing levels of acceptance and comfort' (Newman 2016: 58).

A more conservative evangelical writer, Andrew Sloane, urges fellow evangelicals to recognise 'male and female phenotypes exist as polar rather than binary phenomena'. He thinks, uncontroversially, that 'at either end of a spectrum of physical types lie versions of paradigmatic male and female bodies; and in between these poles there is a variety of male and female bodies, and some that are neither-nor or both-and' (Sloane 2017: 233). More controversially he characterises intersex as 'probably ... an inscription of a fallen world's brokenness on particular human bodies and therefore a *disability*' (Sloane 2017: 233–4, author's emphasis.). But he thinks 'variations of maleness and femaleness', which are incapable of procreation, are nonetheless 'complex expressions of the rich variety of God's creation', and admits the 'need to accommodate this full spectrum of bodily forms in our theology of the body as a sexed body' (Sloane 2017: 234).

Fran Porter writes that during the period of Christendom, gender was largely 'conceived of in oppositional binary terms', but these very terms – men strong, women weak, and so on – she sees not as order (as Barth does) but as 'disorder' (Porter 2015: 9). This might be unremarkable except that Porter is an Anabaptist writing for an evangelical publishing house, and her book is 'about re-thinking and re-forming our understanding and practice away from a hierarchy of power and binary opposites on the basis of sex'. She employs the term 'normative heterosexuality' (Porter 2015: 10), and laments that the 'heterosexual gender order' within Christendom 'excludes and makes illegitimate differing – lesbian, gay, bisexual and transgender (LGBT) – sexualities' (Porter 2015: 10). She 'refutes the spiritually equal yet materially differentiated argument that maintains male privilege' (Porter 2015: 82).

These three examples indicate that some traditionalist and evangelical writers are prepared to move beyond the male–female binary and its theological use to repress all but heterosexual people. But we need a further chapter on this very binary to examine its continuing hold in Christian ethics and theological thought, and to affirm what is truthful in the doctrine of complementarity, before replacing it with a doctrine of human being as an inclusive human continuum in Part III.

## CHAPTER 6

# *The Conceit of Complementarity*

## The Appeal of Complementarity

The last two chapters have identified severe problems with the emerging doctrine of complementarity. There are others, discussed later in this chapter. But its relative stability in contemporary theological thinking suggests there may be reasons for its popularity. These are not difficult to find. Primarily it confirms the experience of the great majority of people, who are, in varying degrees, straightforwardly heterosexual. In the USA 78 per cent of people say that they are completely heterosexual, against 4 per cent who say that they are completely homosexual. Of US adults, 16 per cent say that they fall somewhere in between. Of these 10 per cent say that they are more heterosexual than homosexual while 3 per cent put themselves in the middle and another 3 per cent say that they are predominantly homosexual (YouGov 2015). Among adults under 30, 31 per cent of people surveyed said they were neither completely heterosexual nor completely homosexual. A similar poll in the UK revealed a similar result. Of the British public, 72 per cent said they were completely at the heterosexual end of the scale, 4 per cent said they were completely homosexual, and 19 per cent said they were somewhere in between. YouGov noted and commented that 'With each generation, people see their sexuality as less fixed in stone' (YouGov 2015). Of adults between the ages of 18 and 24, 43 per cent place themselves in the middle of the area between 1 and 5 on the Kinsey scale and 52 per cent place themselves at one end or the other.

While this finding shows a growing impatience with the heterosexual–homosexual binary that the twentieth century took for granted, it also confirms that a very large majority of people still identify themselves as heterosexual. That result provides no justification for the view that heterosexuality is, or is supposed to be, normative for everyone. Still less does it belong to any theological critique of homosexuality, since gospel teaching embraces all kinds of minorities and never sides with majorities. But it is important to understand from the inside how majorities think, or rather, how they often do not trouble themselves to think, since the answer to a particular question appears obvious to them. In Darwin's time hierarchical complementarity was known as the doctrine of separate spheres. Darwin himself contributed to it by his account of sexual selection, which made men strong and muscular, and women fragile and alluring. His contemporaries throughout the sciences and social sciences came to believe 'that female inferiority was biologically determined' (Barton 2009: 183) and of course millions of people still believe this. Millions of people living now also remember when men having sex with men was a criminal offence (as it still is in many countries). With people from all sexual minorities in the closet or under the radar, it is understandable that unthinking heterosexual majorities, unaccustomed to any contact with 'outsiders', are slow to question what is now often called heteronormativity. When Church teaching reinforces it, it may become even harder for lay people to question. While gender diversity is increasingly taken for granted in First World countries, an older generation may be noticeably more reluctant to undergo the 'cognitive dissonance' required of it to reconsider received attitudes. Complementarity is a reassuring doctrine for them, with a well-known proof text to support it (Gen. 1.27). The text is cited by Jesus (Mk 10.6; Mt. 19.4) in an exchange with Pharisees about divorce (which he opposed). The background of the term in science and even its polysyllabic resonance subtly suggests that some authoritative weight has become attached to it.

But the 'unthinkingness' of majorities may not be entirely innocent. Church reports and sexuality education programmes are generally organised around problem cases, and in particular the case of homosexuality (Cornwall 2018). Susannah Cornwall shows that non-normative bodies and sexualities are conveniently classified as Other, requiring investigation, whereas normative bodies and sexualities escape investigation altogether. Frequently non-normative bodies and desires are portrayed as disgusting, but, as Cornwall plainly says, 'they, too, have to be made and maintained as such to shore up the idea that what is normal and natural is self-evident to everyone' (Cornwall 2018: 79). 'Heteronormativity' was coined only in 1991. The *OED* defines 'heteronormative' as 'Of, designating, or based on a world view which regards gender roles as fixed to biological sex and heterosexuality as the normal and preferred sexual orientation'. The definition is of limited value. Heterosexuality might be considered 'normative' if a large majority of people identified with it, but it can hardly be said to be 'preferred' without asking who prefers it and without denigrating alternative sexualities. A 'norm' can mean 'a model or a pattern; a type, a standard', or more specifically 'a standard or pattern of social behaviour that is accepted in or expected of a group' (*OED*). Let's distinguish between, on the one hand, the descriptive or statistical sense of 'norm', and on the other hand, the evaluative sense. If three quarters of a population say they are exclusively heterosexual then descriptively and statistically heterosexuality is normative and neutral with regard to value. But if heteronormativity carries with it additional evaluative features such as it being a model or standard or pattern that others are expected to follow, then all non-heteronormative people are stigmatised. So there is a possible non-judgmental sense that can be ascribed to heteronormativity, and there are doubtless many innocent holders of the complementarity thesis who mean nothing else than just this. But I think the term allows the cunning conflation of descriptive and evaluative meanings, and that very conflation is a reason for its popularity. Everyone ought to be how the majority of us are! How far is that from a faith that affirms the accepting, grace-filled love of God for everyone as its very *raison d'être*?

Another reason for the rise in popularity of the doctrine is its congruence with the 'procreative imperative', the command to 'Be fruitful and multiply' – found in a verse in Genesis 1 (verse 28) directly after the account of the making of male and female in the image of God. It is not widely understood either that there is no reference in the New Testament to any command to procreate, or that marriage is discouraged there as much as it is taken for granted. The propagation of *spiritual* children is the Christian version of the procreative imperative. That said, it remains obvious that procreation is one of the intentional meanings that some heterosexual couples attach to their love-making at some specific moments in their lives. Procreation is something the human *species* does (with frightening success). But it is also obvious that for the species to perpetuate itself it is far from necessary for every member of it to undertake the task of the species as a whole (as voluntarily celibate people attest).

Complementarity gives new form to an older and unsubtle interpretation of natural law. Nonetheless it is widely accepted. Having penile–vaginal penetrative sexual intercourse on this interpretation is doing what comes naturally. The meaning of sex acts can be derived purely from the purpose of the sex organs. Our very sex organs are thought to be concrete instances of (heterogenital) complementarity, designed by God to fulfil their procreative purpose. Understandable as this position is, it is open to many objections, the most obvious of which is that for significant minorities of people penile–vaginal intercourse is neither natural, nor pleasurable, nor possible, nor even thinkable. Complementarity is the new name for the old version of natural law. LGBTIQ people can now be marginalised by the use of a single word, without a single reference to Sodom or Romans 1 or other disputed texts. But Jean Porter (in several books) has proposed modifications to natural law that acknowledge the goodness of sexual desire and pleasure as found in nature. 'Once we let go of the view that sexual pleasure is itself morally problematic, we can consider the possibility that sexual activity has other purposes besides procreation' (Porter 1999: 199). Porter considers this possibility positively, arguing that while Catholic sexual morality will always stress the priority of marriage, family, and children, it may also reasonably come to hold 'that other purposes, in particular the fostering of interpersonal love, are also theologically valid aims for a sexual relationship' (Porter 1999: 222). The responsible enjoyment of our bodies, infused by virtuous love and in the absence of any intention to procreate, is already a new norm for many Christians, whatever their leaders may say.

Some Christians mean by complementarity the very inequality between women and men that has characterised the Christian tradition for most of its history. Even this, however, was capable of elevating the status of women in places where their status was yet lower. The testimony of some Korean women after they became Christians testifies to this (Choi 2009), and there are many other examples. Yes, there was a 'missionary rhetoric of gender equality' (Choi 2009: 22) among the missionaries, but also real improvement in women's lives. But past improvement still left inequality entrenched. This is the hierarchical version of complementarity, contrasted with what their opponents term 'biblical equality'. Biblical equality is the same thing as egalitarian complementarity. Christians for Biblical Equality oppose hierarchical complementarity. An important volume of 29 essays, *Discovering Biblical Equality: Complementarity without Hierarchy*, sought to combat hierarchical complementarity, which was generally called 'complementarianism' (Fee 2005). This remains a current controversy in evangelicalism, while a version of egalitarian complementarity has become adopted by Roman Catholic and many Anglican and Protestant theologians. Biblical equality also brings an improvement to women's lives when compared with its hierarchical version. But the last two chapters have shown that both versions are impossible, one because of its exclusionary heteronormative character, the other because it requires the simultaneous assertion that women are equal to men, except when they are not. Our concern in the present volume extends more widely than who is allowed to preach and lead in churches, important though that is. It is about exposing violence against women in which grand structures of religious thought are deeply implicated, and proposing revision of these in the name of God's justice.

While local arguments about complementarity continue, most versions of it serve to endorse the heteronormative order, proscribe gay marriage, bar women from the priesthood and from leadership positions, and confront contemporary understandings of gender. Pope Francis's new definition of it might have introduced a fresh, organic understanding of complementarity. Todd Salzman and Michael Lawler have proposed an alternative, *holistic* version of complementarity, founded 'not primarily on heterogenital or reproductive complementarity but on the integrated relationship between orientation, personal, and genital complementarity' (Salzman and Lawler 2008: 156). Their new definition contests the narrower, exclusive definition of the Magisterium. It

> is a multifaceted quality – orientational, physical, affective, personal, and spiritual – possessed by every person, which draws him or her into relationship with an other human being, including into the lifelong relationship of marriage, so that both may grow, individually and as a couple, into human well-being and human flourishing. (Salzman and Lawler 2008: 156)

This new definition pointedly differs from official Vatican versions in fairly obvious ways. It escapes the narrowness of heterogenital complementarity. It retains marriage as an exemplar. It allows there are loving complementary relationships that are not lifelong and are not marriages, yet which enrich the couple in their well-being and their spirituality. It intentionally includes same-sex relationships (though same-sex marriage was not on the horizon in 2008). It represents a carefully argued Catholic revisionist and inclusive position, subtly different from the versions we have considered here in Part II. The principal difficulty, I think, is that by making complementarity a 'quality ... possessed by every person', it becomes a property of individuals that characterises the drive for relationship, not the relationship itself as it embraces the participants. Complementarity becomes instead *eròs*, that propulsion towards or longing for an other. *Eròs* remains a crucial yet neglected element of human being, what James Nelson called a 'passion for connection', even as 'God's own passion for connection' energises our own passion for connection 'and hence also our own yearning for life-giving communion and our hunger for relationships of justice' (Nelson 1992: 23). One wonders whether the *eròs* tradition better expresses what the two authors intend. However, Salzman and

Lawler are seeking to nudge Catholic sexual teaching towards a more inclusive framework, and complementarity is an obvious topic to work on, just because it has become central to Vatican teaching on sexuality. The theme of the present volume is gender rather than Salzman and Lawler's focus on 'truly human sexual acts' (Salzman and Lawler 2008: 50). I'm seeking to nudge the churches towards a Christian ethic of gender that is non-binary and inclusive and I conclude that complementarity is fraught with difficulties. That said, I acknowledge the several grounds for its appeal and the opportunities for reworking that it affords.

Before taking leave of complementarity there are a couple of metaphysical issues that will enable us to move on more speedily. These are the troublesome concepts of 'difference' and 'nature'. In neoconservative theology sexual difference is absolute, and human nature is fractured by the alleged ontological difference between women and men. I will make simple, theological suggestions about each.

## What Sort of Difference Is Sexual Difference?

The first suggestion is this: the usual characterisation of sexual difference in theology is the alternative between 'functional' and 'ontological' accounts. The functional understanding is based on the need for the procreation of the single human species. The ontological account is the modern account that locates sexual difference in the very being of women and men. I suggest both accounts are finally unsatisfactory and that human difference is best understood theologically as mirroring *divine* difference, the obvious place where Christians locate individuality and diversity in a dynamic unity.

One of the most interesting criticisms of the use of the early Genesis chapters to establish (mistakenly) the absolute sexual difference between women and men has been made by Laurence Hemming. Hemming is a conservative, self-consciously Vatican-compliant theologian whose conflict with authority gives his demolition of complementarian orthodoxy an added crash factor. He has in his sights the elevation of sexual difference to an ontological principle or status, and argues this is a distortion of Scripture and tradition alike. He argues the new theology has changed the functional difference between women and men into an ontological difference. He thinks the new emphasis has changed the meaning of Genesis 1 and 2, sexualised the Church's teaching, the social sphere and even the Church itself, and (here the premises mount up) lies contrary to our angelic future state. He wants to return to a functional sexual difference.

My plea is for sexual difference to be understood in a non-binary trinitarian way, but that is to anticipate.

Hemming asks, innocently enough, 'Is society based on the family, or is the family only possible in that there already is society?' (Hemming 2010: 62, and see Hemming 2006). He answers that both Aristotle (whose question it is) and the Christian tradition have answered that society is prior to the family, until the recent turns to the proof texts of Genesis 1–3, which reverse the emphasis on the priority of society in Christian social teaching, and mistakenly sexualise it. Fierce is his charge:

> the end of Genesis chapter two and beginning of chapter three is increasingly interpreted as the revelatory description, the instantiation in fact, of sexual difference, and at the same time the basis for the disclosure of the nuptial meaning of the body. The meaning of the book of Genesis is converted from its place in Christian discourse as the inception of the history of redemption to a narrative about the inception of the meaning of sexual difference. This shift inaugurates an understanding of male and female as essentialised sexed identities subtly different from earlier discourses. (Hemming 2010: 63)

The modern conservative orthodoxy has 'the effect of *sexualising* debates about human combination, and shifting them subtly away from the reinforcement of marriage (for those with a vocation to marry – not all do) and the diagnosis and extirpation of sin (for those who, in the Church's eyes, err)' and elevating them to an 'ontological' status (Hemming 2010: 64, author's emphasis). 'Put still more sharply', he continues,

> I am concerned that in the very attempt to free us from the increasing sexualisation of the social sphere, the Church has sexualised herself, making issues of sexuality a standard of orthodoxy instead of a question of the diagnosis and avoidance of sin. This is to elevate sex to an intolerably central place in the Christian life: most lives are *not* consumed with sex, and are at most only marginally concerned with it. (Hemming 2010: 64, author's emphasis)

Hemming thinks, along with Aristotle and the Christian tradition, that sexual difference is functional, not ontological. Using the enigmatic saying of Jesus that 'they cannot die anymore, because they are like angels and are children of God, being children of the resurrection' (Lk. 20.36), he thinks sexual difference is not carried over into eternity. Rather than focusing on the beginning of alleged ontological difference (in Genesis), he thinks theology should concentrate rather on the *end* state of human beings (like angels). Christians should believe St. Paul when he taught 'that in baptism there is neither male nor female' (Hemming 2010: 65). I won't follow him into his valorisation of celibacy over marriage, or his diagnosis of sexual sin, but I give due weight to his criticisms of the sexualisation of Christian teaching about sex and gender. He explains how and why the churches have made such an enormous fuss about sexual questions, and invented new moral doctrines that have no place in the church (where, I add, they cause enormous moral damage).

The new conservatism assumes sexual difference is ontological. All the way down, women and men are thought to be different in their very being, down to every cell of our bodies, as Balthasar asserts, incomplete without each other within the divine marital economy and according to the nuptial meaning of the body. Hemming rightly sees this as an over-description, replacing the functional difference that Christian theologians in the main have been content to borrow from Aristotle. But functional difference is an incomplete account of sexual difference, and like ontological difference, it standardly allows asymmetry and inequality to flourish, unannounced and built in.

The good news is that there is an alternative to the functional–ontological duality. Ultimately our best model of difference will be found in the doctrine of Godself where Persons are equal, in relation, and different, while comprising a single mysterious Unity. Divine ontology, not the riven neoconservative version of sexual division, is best able to inform human personhood, and when it does, it infuses it with a trans-forming presence of respect and justice. Ironically, papal versions of the 'social Trinity' – the *communio personarum* – (Pope John Paul II 1979) lead away from the ontological male–female binary, towards a unity where difference is embraced. True, there are qualifications and disclaimers galore in affirming an analogy between divine and human persons, but there are advantages to persevering with it as well, not least that it provides a model for sexual difference unique to theology, and disruptive of gender binaries both in theology and elsewhere.

## Is There a Human Nature or Natures?

The second suggestion raises and answers the question, 'Is there a human nature?' Complementarity assumes a two-nature answer. The answer I propose in this book coincides easily with one-nature: a single human nature guarantees human solidarity irrespective of gender. But there are two other alternatives: that human beings *lack* a nature: and that all created beings have a *natura communis* that God intends. These alternatives repay careful consideration, for they illuminate what is at stake in speaking of human nature at all. My suggestion is similar to the suggestion about human difference. Just as theology can illuminate human difference by modelling it on divine difference, so theology can illuminate human nature by modelling it on the nature of God.

Affirming the existence of a single human nature generates the problem how we could have access to it. How could we know what it was? Wouldn't it elide over real differences between people? Wouldn't it replicate nineteenth-century notions of 'man' as a 'special creation', conveniently abstracted from other animals and created beings (with disastrous environmental consequences)? Daniel Horan names these 'the problems of knowledge, depersonalization, and ecological elitism' (Horan 2014: 98). But these difficulties apply to a two-nature theory also. Defining the nature of 'woman', for instance, is certain to overlook the many different oppressions that most women endure, as feminist theologians have consistently pointed out. One also needs to know who does the defining. Horan summarises the basic problem with neoconservative theologies of gender, Protestant and Catholic alike:

> According to this schema, men complement women (and vice versa) because each lacks qualities inherent in the other. However, the presupposed absent qualities are not of equal value or dignity. On the contrary, those characteristics identified with men are privileged as superior to and more valuable than those identified as foundational to the *nature* of women. In this case, which might be described as symptomatic of the dual-nature essentialist approach, women are inherently inferior and subordinate to men because the qualities fundamentally identified with women are hierarchically beneath those fundamentally identified with men. (Horan 2014: 101, author's emphasis)

That conclusion confirms my analysis in Part II of this book. Two sexes. Two natures. What then of a third alternative: there is no human nature at all? The lack of a human nature would seem to be a reasonable deduction from a human nature to which we have no access. Why affirm one, if we have no knowledge of it, or see little point in applying to ourselves that troublesome generalisation? 'Nature', as modern thinkers often point out, is a static, classical category with no place in modern discourses. Occam's razor (the principle that when two or more explanations are available, the simplest one is to be preferred) severs it, or at any rate it severs any understanding of it that turns out to be an elusive essence, or a static and ahistorical substance. Once we situate ourselves as individuals firmly in history and society, a more concrete relational understanding of our nature can emerge. 'A dynamic sense of relationality shifts our prioritization of subjective inherency toward a more constructive notion of the human person that recognizes that human beings are constituted, at least in part, by social institutions and practices' (Horan 2014: 105). Our relationality has several intersecting dimensions (including race, gender, class, ability, and so on). Our 'factical' and grounded historicity is yet another disrupter of the neat distinction between female and male, and the defined roles given to each.

It is impossible, then, to assert that there is a human nature that is temporally or ontologically prior to its coming to be in particular historical circumstances or in particular people. But I continue to think there *is* a human nature, and for two reasons. First we have a collective understanding of ourselves. Even to say 'we' here presupposes we are picking out creatures who are 'us', a *genus* to which we belong. There is a collective solidarity among persons that is capable of inspiring great acts of generosity and empathy. Jesus himself expressed solidarity with the poor and dispossessed of humankind (e.g., Mt. 25.31–46). Human solidarity, however, does not exclude an empathic sense of creatureliness with non-human beings. Susan Parsons has argued for this, through her idea of 'appropriate universalism' in her *Feminism and Christian Ethics*. Solidarity with co-sufferers may be a prompt to extend our sense of moral outrage towards the pointless suffering of all sentient creatures. The second reason is a theological necessity. Human beings are 'brothers and sisters' of Jesus (e.g., Mk 3.35; Heb. 2). There is a recurring sameness we share with him and he with us. We need to speak of a human nature because Jesus had one. The Christ of the Nicene Creed 'became human' (*enanthròpèsanta*). The Chalcedonian Definition records he is 'perfect in humanness' (*anthròpotèti*); he is 'of the same reality as we are ourselves' (*homoousion hèmin*); he is 'apprehended in two natures' (*duo physesin*). The boundaries between 'human' and 'non-human' are for us increasingly blurred, and may already have been made blurred in the asseveration that 'the Word became *flesh*' (Jn 1.14), not specifically human flesh – just flesh. We might build an understanding of Christ's human nature that is a lot more flexible and dynamic than the one that the Nicene Fathers ascribed to him. The point of contention is not the real humanity of Jesus or the question how human he was. It is to claim that without some concept of humanness, the humanity of Jesus (and by extension his solidarity with us) cannot be discussed at all.

The present conundrums over human nature find a place in the long-running discussion in Western philosophical and theological traditions over the relation between particulars and universals. Duns Scotus (*c*.1266–1308) grappled uniquely with this problem, and central to his solution (as Horan reminds us) is his idea of *haecceitas*, or the 'thisness' of particular things. Scotus thinks the universe is made up of unique particular entities, not universals. Universals are not denied (they make classification possible), but they are subordinated to particulars, which are primary. Things have a *natura communis* that is a real, logical but secondary existence. I find three advantages in Horan's careful recovery and deployment of Scotus' *haecceitas* in a postmodern gendered context. First, as he says, Scotus provides a framework within which the value of individual people does not depend on their belonging to a class or essence that precedes them a priori. Rather

> The uniqueness, unrepeatability, and inalienable inherency of one's *haecceitas* can be interpreted as an elevation of the particular and personal over the universal or the common. This resituating of human personhood within a theological framework, where the individual is understood as primary, and the universal is seen as concurrently present and real (yet secondary), unveils the intrinsic relationality, dignity, and value of each person over against the depersonalizing elevation of 'humanity' in a general and essentialist sense. (Horan 2014: 113)

The primacy of the individual over essences or natures that instantiate them is not to be confused with laments about the individualism of 'Western culture' at the present time. Individual persons are primary, theologically speaking, to their secondary classifications because God has made them in God's image. Second, a theological framework that emphasises particulars over universals, and values them directly in relation to God (instead of hierarchically in relation to each other) provides a further argument against complementarity. So,

> With regard to the additional problems of complementarity, Scotus's *haecceitas* avoids binary distinctions between genders and biological sexes. The value of human personhood is located within the context of the principle of individuation, which is really identical with, yet formally distinct from, a person's actual existence or being. Value and dignity, then, are not located within a given person's status as male or female ... (Horan 2014: 114)

Third, it follows, as a sort of theological corollary to the idea of *haecceitas*, that 'individuals are what God primarily intends, not the biological gender or the socialised and constructed gender shared among a certain population' (Horan 2014: 114). Difference is created by God, not measured by people with the power to divide. Within a Scotist framework it is God who 'adjudicates alterity' (Horan 2014: 115), and Christ who declares no alterity too great that it cannot be transformed by love.

I just suggested the theological problem of human nature might be resolved by grounding it in the nature of God. Again the notion of people as the *locus* and symbol of the divine image is central to the claim made here. Our human nature reflects God's own nature. What is God's nature? One might say, following Aquinas, that God's nature is to exist. On that account everything that exists does so because it participates in God's nature, whose 'essence' is to exist. But one can say more than this. The biblical revelation requires that God creates, that God loves (and of course much else besides). Our human nature, our own *natura communis*, may be thought rightly to incorporate these elements of God's nature, especially through the engagement of faith with God. Orthodoxy speaks easily of our 'deification'. Our nature, at least in part, is what we are capable of becoming (as the late John Macquarrie – my doctoral supervisor in the 1970s – influentially taught; Macquarrie 1966: 205, 213).

I have included these difficult sections about difference and nature, not to pronounce definitively, but to suggest that the endorsements of binary human nature and binary human difference, based on ontological accounts of each, are not really endorsements at all. There are better theological accounts of human nature available. We must now examine other grounds for thinking complementarity can be laid to rest.

Before turning finally away from complementarity we will note some further difficulties with it, grouped into four headings: exegetical, ideological, theological, and logical.

## Exegetical and Ideological Difficulties

### *Origins*

First the origins of the term in eighteenth-century Romanticism and in twentieth-century physics are hardly promising theologically. In *Émile* Rousseau wrote, 'Yet where sex is concerned man and woman are unlike; each is the complement of the other' (Rousseau 1762, Book V), before unveiling a mass of assumptions about 'Sophy, or Woman' that even the present Curia would find sexist. Rousseau thinks women and men are so unlike that a basis for discussing whether they could be equal does not exist. Mindful of the genetic fallacy that origin is no guide to meaning, a quick read of Rousseau nonetheless confirms the dismissive and androcentric milieu from which complementarity descends. A second line of

descent is Niels Bohr's quantum theory, which accounted for the phenomenon of light through the complementary descriptions involving
waves and particles. Theologians began to use the term very loosely to
describe the relationship between scientific and theological descriptions of
the world (see Oliver 1978), and more recently to describe complementary
religious traditions in their approach to the Real or God. Alister McGrath
traces and parallels its use in the patristic doctrine of the two natures of
Christ (McGrath 1998) where he finds it a useful heuristic device, but in
his treatment of 'Theology and Complementarity' (McGrath 1998:
195–206), he appears unaware of its growing use in (dubious) theological
theories of sexuality and gender emanating from Rome and Canterbury.
Of course it is open to theological supporters of male–female complementarity to argue that they are merely adopting and adapting a neologism to
suit their purposes, but in doing so they are introducing much more than a
mere logical principle.

## Sola Scriptura

Complementarity in its egalitarian version is based squarely on two verses
in Genesis 1 (26–7): 'Then God [*Elohim*] said, "Let us make humankind
[*adam*] in our image, according to our likeness. . ." So God created
humankind in his image, in the image of God he created them; male
and female he created them.' The egalitarian version accords priority to
Genesis 1 over Genesis 2 (since no amount of creative exegesis of Genesis
2 can suggest equality). The inegalitarian version, which reflects the
majority view among Christians throughout the centuries, has accorded
priority to Genesis 2. There are exegetical, hermeneutical, and Christological difficulties that need to be resolved prior to any attempt to base
ontological sexual difference on these verses. If Genesis 1 tells us anything
about created sexual difference it is that it is not fundamental at all. God
creates adam, 'humankind' or 'humanity'. Adam is an 'earth creature', not
a male human being with a name, and the earth creature is male and
female. As Jennifer Knust notes, 'If God/Elohim created humankind at
once, male and female, and both were made in God's image, then why did
Yhwh need to create the female a second time?' (Knust 2011: 50). The
second account of the creation of humankind (Gen. 2.4b–3.24) is noto-
riously difficult to reconcile with the first. It has been used from the New
Testament onwards to establish the ontological priority of the man on the
basis of his temporal priority over the woman; for the responsibility of the
woman for tempting the man and being the cause of his downfall, and

much else. Biblical literalists seek ingeniously to reconcile the two accounts, yet if complementarity is a non-starter there is no need to arbitrate between them. The error is to prefer *sola scriptura*, the mainly Protestant principle that matters of faith and practice must be established on the basis of Scripture alone, when read primarily in its plain or straightforward sense, instead of a theological and Christological interpretation of Scripture that gives it priority but not exclusive primacy over other theological sources. Rowan Williams thinks complementarity 'a problematic and non-scriptural theory . . . applied narrowly and crudely to physical differentiation without regard to psychological structures' (Williams 2002: 320).

## Phenomenology of Sexuality

Earlier we saw how Balthasar and Barth had used these chapters as a phenomenology of sexuality. Some details of two creation myths are fashioned into a sexual system that impinges on the being of substantial minorities of people whose bodies and desires do not fit. The first of these tells of the making of *adam* on the sixth day, before God rested. Would the neoconservatives interpret the six days of creation also as a phenomenology? Do they imagine the Elohim of Genesis 1 putting his feet up for the first Sabbath? It is not difficult to read biblical creation accounts and scientific accounts side by side and find them thoroughly congruent, but that can only be done by recognising the former as inspired myths, fabricated in a pre-scientific and pre-Christian age. And that is just what the neoconservatives do not do. The making of *adam* is still understood as the six days of creation used to be understood, that is as real events in time to which the biblical texts directly refer. It is doubtful whether even the communities who authored the myths understood them in this way. One might ask, on the same basis, why all complementarians are not vegetarian? The next verses of Genesis 1 record that 'God said, "See, I have given you every plant yielding seed that is upon the face of all the earth, and every tree with seed in its fruit; you shall have them for food"' (Gen. 1.29). While there is a compelling theological case for vegetarianism (which rests on a lot more than this text), one must ask meat-eating complementarians why they do not obey God's commanding of a plant-based diet? What are the rules for applying *sola scriptura* to some parts only of Genesis? Why do they not see the later, controlled meat consumption authorised in the Pentateuch as a post-lapsarian concession, to be withdrawn now that Christ has come and initiated God's new Kingdom?

*Advocacy Reading*

'Advocacy reading' is a term used of the type of biblical interpretation that combines *analytical* with *politically prescriptive* approaches to the text (Hendel 2009]: 7). As a reading strategy it is open to the charge of compromising academic integrity and non-partisan scholarship in a single movement. Feminism is often accused of this. But I think the theological 'mainstream' practices a covert version of advocacy reading, and nowhere is this more apparent than over the issue of sexual difference. The politics of course are not progressive. They are highly regressive, fitting perfectly with conservative social and ecclesial agendas while claiming authority variously – in the Bible, in dead scholars, in papal and magisterial pro-nouncements, and so on.

Chris Cook has provided a depressing list of Christian bodies whose advocacy reading overrides the present, though provisional, state of scien-tific knowledge, in favour of a priori assertion based in conservative ideological advocacy. Taking homosexuality as an example he notes, factually, that 'Various strands of research combined with a prevailing medical consensus, identify homosexuality as a normal variant within the spectrum of human sexual experience' (Cook 2018: 2). An appropriate theological response to contemporary scientific views might be to welcome them. 'Such major shifts in professional and scientific opinion might be taken as tribute to the good influence of science upon society and the willingness of medical professionals to change their minds on the basis of good evidence' (Cook 2018: 3). And that is what many Christian groups do not do, including the authors of the Pilling Report, who, 'having received conflicting evidence from medical authorities and conservative Christian sources, concluded that "neither the medical nor the social sciences have arrived at any firm consensus that would impact decisively on the moral arguments"' (Cook 2018: 2). But Cook points out that 'this conclusion seems contrary to the view of most medical and scientific groups, which generally assert that the sciences do impact decisively on such arguments' (Cook 2018: 2). He names journals and charities such as the Core Issues Trust, which he accuses of 'making the science fit' the prior ideological commitments.

*Covert Complementarity*

Complementarity is also an orthodoxy adopted by secular groups influ-enced by Protestant and Catholic supporters. An example is the American

College of Pediatricians. In 2017 I attended an open meeting on the topic 'gender and sexuality' at a local evangelical Anglican church near my home in Plymouth. The material reproduced was from this 'College' and was invested by the presenters with the incontrovertible authority of science. No one was told that the American College of Pediatricians is a socially conservative advocacy group of 500 members that split from the American Academy of Pediatrics (which has 64,000 members) in 2002, when the Academy supported the adoption of children by same-sex couples. A paper, 'Gender Ideology Harms Children', still available on the College website (American College of Pediatricians 2017), affirms that 'human sexuality is an objective biological binary trait', and that 'Human sexuality is binary by design.'

From this position no alternatives are admitted, and majority scientific views are dismissed as 'politically correct'. 'A person's belief that he or she is something they are not is, at best, a sign of confused thinking', while gender dysphoria is 'an objective psychological problem ... that lies in the mind not the body, and it should be treated as such'. The hope of transitioning is luridly described as 'conditioning children into believing a lifetime of chemical and surgical impersonation of the opposite sex', which is then identified as 'child abuse'. Pretending to offer scientific evidence, the covert values of 'traditional' Christianity obtrude throughout their publications, for instance in the claim there is 'sound evidence' that children with two same-sex parents (i.e., children 'exposed to the homo-sexual lifestyle') 'may be at increased risk for emotional, mental, and even physical harm' (American College of Pediatricians 2017a). Much of the output of this organisation selects and spins scientific data and filters it through the prism of pre-existing conservative ideology. The ideology is complementarian and exclusive. It is sad to see Christians cooperating in the production and distribution of these half-truths.

## Theological and Logical Difficulties

### Who Is God's Image?

Perhaps the greatest of the flaws in the complementarity idea is its margin-alisation of the Person of Christ. This suggestion is based on biblical teaching about the image of God. Christ, says St Paul, not 'Adam', is the image of God. 'The god of this world has blinded the minds of the unbelievers, to keep them from seeing the light of the gospel of the glory of Christ, who is the image of God' (2 Cor. 4.4). There's nothing exegetically tenuous about that. Christ is the image of God. Christ 'is the image of the invisible God, the firstborn of all creation', writes the author of Colossians (Col. 1.15; see Thatcher 2016: 146–9). Jesus Christ, who from Paul onwards is known as the Second Adam, is no recapitulation to an imagined prelapsarian state, but the image of God *de novo*, making all things new. There is no shortage of theological *motifs* for connecting with Jesus Christ, for the church is his Body, a metaphorical living organism that exists to embody the new state of things where differences of race, class, and gender are broken down. Churches of course are not like this. That may be why too many theological and ecclesial pronouncements about gender turn away 'from seeing the light of the gospel of the glory of Christ' because that same gospel removes the prejudices that speak domination, fear, violence, and exclusion.

## *Where Is Imagination?*

Eschatology too seems to be marginalised by complementarity. There are many difficulties associated with the various beliefs about life after death, but none of these should be allowed to stifle the eschatological imagination, which has at different times envisaged streets paved with gold and the eternal flames of hell. A grounded eschatological imagination, however, plays with simple ingredients. The next life, Christians envisage, will be unlike the present life since all the forms of sin – violence, prejudice, hatred, and so on – will have no place in its redeemed, restored state. But it will be *like* this present life to the extent that the same forms of sin have already been overcome. In 1995 the gay evangelical theologian Michael Vasey bewailed the decline of the influence of heaven in theologies of sexuality. 'The hope of heaven does not rest on fitting in with the way of the world', he wrote (with an eye on compulsory heterosexuality), 'but on the Lion and the Lamb (Rev. 5:5) – on the beauty of a king who strives for justice and the love of a gentle friend who takes to himself our pain and failure' (Vasey 1995: 248).

Vasey would have been delighted with 'the stronger eschatological awareness in the Western Church' at the present time, which 'has meant that the quest for the natural order in the beginning has no longer been as obviously necessary to the moral quest and indeed to salvation. One emphasises the new reality of the New Creation, which surpasses rather than restores the perfection of the old' (Bethmont 2018: 212). The goods of the new natural theology, of marriage, family, and heterosexuality, were not opposed or derided by Vasey in themselves. Rather it was the idolatrous elevation of these goods to the exclusion of alternative relationships and sexualities that Vasey sensed and movingly wrote about. The argument throughout the present volume is similar, both in its affirmation of the goods of marriage and family, its affirmation of non-binary relationships, and its determination to give pre-eminence to Jesus and the present and future hope of new life, over forced readings of Genesis and their alleged prescriptions for the social and moral order.

## Consistency

How is complementarity to be reconciled with other Catholic emphases that seem to be in conflict with it? What happens to celibacy if complementarity is true? Traditionally the churches have offered marriage and celibacy as the two sole institutions that receive divine approval for regulating people's sex lives. The Roman Catholic Church still holds that celibacy is better. We have just seen this is the earlier tradition that complementarity actually erodes. Complementarity must count as an innovation. Its innovatory character per se need not be a problem since innovation is constantly necessary to keep doctrine alive. The problem is one of consistency. How is complementarity compatible with the stubborn Catholic insistence on the male priesthood? The isolation of priests from women in their training and professional development (that is, the *lack* of complementarity) was partly responsible for the abuse crisis. Yes, complementarity might be adopted by Catholic advocates of the priesting of women. Liberal Anglicans used it. I'm not suggesting this, of course (there are better arguments available). I *am* suggesting that the priestly status quo is incompatible with complementarity. The vowed single life and the practice of monastic community can hardly be reconciled with the assumption that all men need women and all women need men in their growth to fulfilment. Complementarity is even incompatible with Christology. Jesus, being fully and completely human, 'yet without sin' (Heb. 4.15), presumably also required a woman or women for him to be complete, since without them (according to the new dogma), even He cannot be completely human after all.

## Sex Roles

Since complementarity requires that men and women complement each other, it follows that each must lack certain qualities that can only be provided by the other. These qualities, as we have seen, are ontological, and so extend to the psychological and emotional realms as well, resulting (so the argument runs) in same-sex marriages being a priori unable to provide the complementarity that comes with straight marriage. But, as Eric Reitan deftly points out, such a position requires that 'these "gendered" qualities *can't* cross the borders of biological sex'. Proponents 'need to hold that women, by virtue of their sex, *can't* possess the "masculine" strengths, since those are the exclusive province of men; and men *can't* possess the feminine ones' (Reitan 2017: 216, author's emphases). If appropriate 'masculine' and 'feminine' virtues are required for couples to complement one another, continues Reitan, 'it might make more sense to pair people off in terms of how they score on personality tests that measure how masculine or feminine they are, rather than pairing them off by whether they are biologically male and female' (Reitan 2017: 216).

## Fertilisation Science

We have seen in the previous chapters that some theological justifications of complementarity rely explicitly on men and women assuming active and passive roles, respectively. The man is active, the woman receptive. In Catholic versions of this, the active seed of the Word is joyfully received by the Virgin Mary. Having straight sex is clearly the experience at the basis of such imagery. As Katie Grimes summarises, 'Just as sperm finds procreative completion in the ovum, so the ovum is brought to procreative completion by the sperm. What the penis/sperm is, so is man; what the vagina/ovum is, so is woman' (Grimes 2016: 81). But the imagery is inaccurate, not to say wrong, even pruriently wrong. Men do not always initiate having sex. Women are not passive when they are enjoying sex. They may be more active than men when having sex, especially if they choose to be on top. As I pointed out in 1993, the description of having straight sex as the penetration of a vagina is already androcentric since it could equally well be described as the envelopment of a penis (Thatcher 1993: 102). But I had no idea back in a previous century that the fertilisation science that is supposed to support the idea of *active sperm striving to reach a passive womb*, does not do so. Grimes, summarising recent research, explains:

> In fact, sperm do not actively swim toward a passively waiting ovum. Nor do they penetrate the ovum. They are instead 'attracted by the egg and activated by it' .... [R]ather than swimming toward the egg, sperm are pulled toward the ovum in a process called chemotaxis. The ovum shoots out chemicals that tow the stranded sperm toward it ... '[T]he forward

thrust of sperm is extremely weak'. They do not act as 'forceful penetrators'. The sperm spend most of their energy swimming sideways, not forward; they attempt to escape any surface they encounter. Rather than penetrating the egg, they are captured by it. If anything, sperm act more cowardly than valiantly. Further undermining gender conventions, in human beings, chemotaxis does not simply direct sperm; it selects them. (Grimes 2016: 82)

Fertilisation science (at least on this persuasive reading of it) does not support the 'fairy tale' of active insemination and passive reception so beloved by John Paul II. It allows the truism that 'sperm and ovum certainly act as complementary partners in the process of conception', but nothing can be inferred from that about women and men being complementary partners to each other in social, domestic, or professional life. But there is a further twist. Grimes (mischievously?) points out that fertilisation science might equally be used to reverse the active–receptive roles that the theology of the body assigns to women and men:

> The ovum certainly is not passive. Nor is the ovum receptive. Yes, a sperm eventually is made to come inside the ovum. But the ovum acts much more like a pillaging thief than a lovingly receptive mother. The ovum takes the sperm; the ovum does not wait to be asked; the ovum does not even wait for an answer. The ovum takes the sperm inside more akin to the way a predator consumes its prey. (Grimes 2016: 82–3)

## The Conceit of Complementarity

The overall problem with complementarity lies in its elevation of absolute difference over other accounts, and its exclusionary intent, not in its confirmation of the basic intuitions of most heterosexual people. If straight cisgender people, the large majority, reflect on their *own* experience, they are likely to find the assumptions of complementarity unproblematic, and if they are theists they may uncontroversially think God has made them this way with the divine intention that we should all 'be fruitful and multiply', and 'replenish the earth and subdue it'. But within the human species not everyone is expected to carry out the procreative purpose. There is even a respected theological argument (Song 2014) to the effect that, since Christ is risen and the new order has come, there is no obligation among Christians to obey the procreative imperative at all. *Hubris* sets in, though, as soon as the lazy assumption that 'some' or 'most' must really mean 'all'. Not only is that move one of the most basic mistakes in elementary logic, it impedes the spiritual growth of the very people who affirm it, and it does so in several ways.

There is pride (one of the seven deadly sins) in thinking that one is right. The identification of groups of others (not just in the area of gender) serves to strengthen and solidify the sense of identity of the majority excluding group, yet at the price of rendering communication with the excluded groups more difficult. Homosexuality in particular has been used scandalously (see Vasey-Saunders 2015) by many evangelical Christians and lobby groups in this way, creating a stronger sense of identity among the accusers by scapegoating particular kinds of offenders. The 'otherising' of people with whom a troublesome difference of some kind has been identified, is usually a source of conflict with potential for escalation and of course violence. Sexual difference (as even some conservative commentators acknowledge) has been raised to an ontological status that has become idolatrous. Why place limits on what God can do? Why should there not be a variety of sexual differences in creation, rather than just one, just as there is variety everywhere else in the 'Book of Nature'? Why not a continuum of difference? There is a huge price that has been and is still being paid for the maintenance of complementarian orthodoxy, written on the bodies and lives of the excluded and the marginalised, by suffering and even death. When Christians discuss how God redeems us they often say, with Paul, they are 'bought with a price' (1 Cor. 6.20). But there is also a shocking price that victims of 'right belief' have had to pay and are continuing to pay in many parts of the world. The psychological havoc wreaked upon the bodies and souls of Christian lesbians (Webster 1995) and gays (Moore 2003) by the infliction of doctrinal complementarity has been, and remains, immense. Christian trans people are the latest victims (Beardsley and O'Brien 2016; Dowd and Beardsley 2018) of this cruel ideology.

We have seen the two-sex binary view is deeply rooted in contemporary Catholic and Protestant doctrine and that it impacts strongly on their ethics of sexuality and gender. There is a particular irony about assuming complementarity is supported by the witness of Scripture and tradition. Genesis 2 has always been the dominant account of the creation of people in the Christian tradition, and it has been understood to underwrite the assumption that women are subordinate. Would it not be more honest to admit this, and then mount a theological argument for revisions in the light of social and scientific understanding, rather than claim *per impossibile* that the churches have always taught complementarity? Is it too much to ask that creation be understood first in the light of the coming of Christ, as the authors of the Fourth Gospel and the Letter to the Colossians do (Jn 1.1–18; Col. 1.15–20)? The Catholic Church universally and stubbornly retains the structures of patriarchy with the corollary that women must remain in second place, for that is both what patriarchy is and does. The low valorisation of women is essential for the Catholic and (many) evangelical churches to maintain while patriarchy crumbles all around them. 'Traditionalists' have even been known to celebrate such prejudice as a holy and costly alternative to the ways of the world. But the world is not fooled.

We have seen that one of the marks of systemic violence is the defining by powerful groups of less powerful groups in such a way that the power of the former over the latter is maintained and naturalised. The link between hierarchical complementarity and domestic violence in conservative Christian households has been made repeatedly (Marsden 2018). Harmful doctrines lead to harmful practices. *Lex orandi lex credendi*, that is, how the church worships expresses what it believes. But I have used the strong word 'conceit' in the title of this chapter because of the excessively high status of complementarity in the churches and a corresponding reluctance to criticise it. There is even a case for the stronger word '*deceit*' in relation to it. There is a case for saying that the pursuit of the gender agenda is more than a particular kind of religious advocacy. Theology will always include a kind of religious advocacy, since it will seek in its service to the churches, to commend the faith as a joyful life-giving option for people to embrace, even as God as the object of faith embraces them. But advocacy that involves the misrepresentation of science, or that conceals evidence that counts against it, can never be a companion to theology.

The question arises why a doctrine that sits so uneasily with the very ethos of Catholicism should be defended by its hierarchy with such vehemence. The answer has little to do with, say, the defence of marriage, and more to do with the continued exclusion of women from priesthood, and the replacing of the worn-out biblical passages that are purported to declaim homosexuality with a new strategy for marginalising gays. Worse, the rendering invisible of intersex people and the wilful misrepresentation of the testimony of trans people (and particularly the witness of the trans Christian community) represent a failure of love and of agapic understanding that reaches tragic proportions. It is another case (remember the Euthyphro Dilemma) when believers have wrongly concluded that God legitimises unjust actions. As Robert Song remarks, not only do the traditionalists 'have to begin to show why this is the way of love, there are exceptionally problematic, not to say disastrous consequences of conservative positions' (Song 2014: 79).

The present chapter completes Part II of the book, and also the first part of its second aim, 'to critique naïve and harmful theological accounts of the relations between women and men as binary opposites'. It is time to attend to the second part of that aim – 'to replace them, and the exclusions they engender, with what will be called 'the human continuum'. This is the task of Part III.

# The Human Continuum
## A Place for Everyone

## CHAPTER 7

# The Continuum and the Doctrine of God

## The 'Shared and Common Spectrum'

There are some potentially troublesome conceptual problems with the very idea of a continuum that I need to address. It has been pointed out to me that a gender continuum with male and female as opposite poles may not, after all, avoid the problems associated with binary assumptions about gender. First, the idea of a continuum might not be sufficient to undo the asymmetrical valuing of one of the poles over the other. Men and women might be related in a continuum instead of a binary, this objection runs, yet the continuum would provide no insurance against the downwards slide into inequality. For the continuum idea to work, each point along the continuum would have to be equally valuable in the first place. The gender hierarchy may remain, then, even within the continuum. Second, the idea of a human continuum still retains the binary terms, but as poles, if not polar opposites. 'Male' and 'female' then, are still retained as 'contrastive sites', far apart. Third, since the gender binary functions as a social-symbolic system below the level of consciousness, the idea of a continuum is unlikely to affect it. In other words, tinkering around with concepts doesn't touch the alienating power of a skewed symbolic system. Finally, the continuum might be found incompatible with gender realism, or with the experience of the majority of human beings who identify themselves within a binary system almost without thought that it could be otherwise.

I hope this chapter resolves these problems. I have critiqued gender hierarchy throughout Part II. Given the fluidity of concepts and their varying uses, there is no a priori method of securing in advance that the continuum excludes binary understandings of it. The meaning of the term signals, without obvious difficulty, an end to binary thinking. In the previous chapter I dismissed the functional account of sexual difference, suggesting that for a theological understanding of human difference, *divine* difference counts supremely, for in it there can be no slide into inequality among the divine Persons. Belief in a single human nature leaves no room for different degrees of humanity, differently valuable to God. My (standard) treatment of Paul's statement, 'there is no longer male and female', illustrates that sexual and gender differences *remain*, yet without them causing the violence and inequality that infect many real relations between women and men throughout the world. These considerations are obviously theological, and are allowed a determining influence in the flow of argument.

So the 'human continuum' is a conscious attempt to replace oppositional thinking with a unifying alternative. When applied to humanity, 'continuum' (like countless other concepts in science) lies somewhere between literal and metaphorical meanings, so I have no qualms about calling it a metaphor or a symbol. Since I acknowledge sexual difference I acknowledge that there are creatures who are male and female, but these do not need to be placed opposite each other. Characteristics usually associated with male and female in any case overlap substantially. If a linear model of the continuum leaves the impression that 'male' is at one end and 'female' at the other end, a more circular model should modify such difficulties. The difficulty that inequitable symbolic systems are so entrenched in human societies and groups that revisionary conceptual proposals are impotent against them, is defeatist. Of course, if they operate entirely at the level of the subconscious, no one would be aware of the need to defeat them. The difficulty that the continuum is incompatible with unreflective (and binary) thought about personal identity is blatantly majoritarian, a sentiment that should find no place in any Christian theology concerned for the stranger and the oppressed. Finally I noted earlier that the continuum operates in three related areas (male–female, straight–gay, masculine–feminine), so there will inevitably be some overlap between them.

'The Seventeenth- and Eighteenth-Century Sexuality Hypothesis' (McKeon 2012) provides a useful introduction to the entrenched character of the modern sex binary. At a conference entitled 'Before Sex', held 'in order to make explicit and available a major breakthrough in research on the history of gender and sexuality', Michael McKeon explained the hypothesis by saying,

> People have always understood the disparity between men and women as essential to their experience of the world. But the customary distinction between the genders *along a shared and common spectrum* was replaced over the course of this period by the tendency to view men and women as basically different from each other, separate ways of being whose difference

is crucially marked by a preference for the other sex and crucially mediated by the existence of a category of people who, on the contrary, prefer the same sex. (McKeon 2012: 791–2, emphasis added)

The 'shared and common spectrum' is *not* an invention of modernity. Rather modernity has supplanted it with a different view. The common spectrum was the single human body that accommodated sexual difference as a variation along a spectrum, not as a binary. Being non-binary, the spectrum accounted for people who in a binary system would have found themselves marginalised and stigmatised, even if it did not always accommodate them. This 'traditional one-sex model of anatomy', continues McKeon,

> was incompletely challenged and replaced by the modern two-sex model, according to which the difference between men and women is not a matter of distinction along a common gradient but a radical separation based on fundamental physiological differences. Women are not an underdeveloped and inferior version of men; they are biologically and naturally different from them – the opposite sex. (McKeon 2012: 793)

For our present purposes, three features (from several others that the hypothesis generates) will be noted. The first (to change the metaphor) is that the common spectrum was no level playing field offering a basis for sex equality. It always was a 'gradient' with men at the top. The downwards slide was always a dangerous possibility for men, whereas the upwards climb was a Sisyphean task for women. Second, the new opposite-sex binary was cemented by the fact of same-sex desire. The medical identification of a particular class of people as 'homosexual', and therefore as deviant, allowed heterosexuality to become normative and exclusive. And third, the late modern concept of gender was itself premised on a binary view of human sexuality.

These three features of the hypothesis correspond to the three binaries outlined in Chapter 1. What is needed is a continuum or spectrum that replaces them: in the first case, a continuum but without the gender gradient; in the second case, a continuum of human sexual diversity where difference is understood and welcomed (without being subjected to the binary that judges it); and in the third case a set of moral practices based on common human virtue that steadfastly refuses to sexualise moral actions by deeming them exclusively masculine or feminine. Secular thought has already moved a long way in this direction, whereas theology has remained far behind. The function of gender theology is neither to catch up with secular thought nor to reinscribe it in theological language, but to make contributions to it from its own unique perspectives. The very categories modern thought brings to our human identities and desires are themselves based on binary thinking. We are a lot more variable than our binary cultural schemes allow. The charge increasingly made by some African church leaders that homosexuality is a Western phenomenon is, unfortunately, partly right. Men having sexual relations with men is universal, but the particular classification of them (what Foucault called the *scientia sexualis*) as 'homosexual' is definitely of European origin. But it is only *partly* right. Those same leaders may need to acknowledge that the moral disgust evinced by homosexuality and imparted by the Christian missionaries is of European origin also.

## Biology and the Continuum

Biologists already view human sex as existing along a 'spectrum' rather than a binary (Ainsworth 2015). The validity of the very idea of the 'dimorphism of the human organism' is at stake (Heinamäa 2012: 226). The default account of sex difference posits the presence or absence of a Y chromosome as the decisive factor: with it, you are male, and without it, you are female. But some people straddle the boundary thereby causing huge problems for social institutions and legal frameworks that assume the binary as a given, and much inconvenience and *angst* for the people themselves. Susannah Cornwall has helpfully described (in several places, e.g., Cornwall 2010, 2015, 2015a) the quite different conditions of being intersex or transgender, and the major revisions that are necessary for theology to make if it is to remain truthful and capable of sourcing hope and practical pastoral care for people whose bodies or gender identities differ from the usual binary norms. Churches of course, as we have seen, have extrinsic motivations for maintaining the binaries, whatever biologists are saying. Joan Roughgarden explains,

> The XX/XY system determination is widely believed to define [the] biological basis for a gender binary. Yet this system allows for both a gender binary and great overlap between XX and XY bodies, as well as gender crossing. The details of what's actually on the X and Y chromosomes, and which tissues respond to the products of these genes, determine the degree of male/female difference at the whole-body level, as well as allowing for transgendered bodies. (Roughgarden 2013: 199)

Roughgarden advocates a spectral understanding of human biology but she is not *rejecting* the gender binary altogether. The binary remains unproblematic for substantial majorities of people, but not all. The spectrum does not render the binary null. It modifies it, allowing and expecting variation.

Sexual differentiation takes place within the first eight weeks of pregnancy. Claire Ainsworth, explaining the 'sex spectrum', observes that 'Gene mutations affecting gonad development can result in a person with XY chromosomes developing typically female characteristics, whereas alterations in hormone signalling can cause XX individuals to develop along male lines' (Ainsworth 2015: 289). The gene that switches on male development in the gonads was identified as *SRY* in 1990, so that XX individuals who carry a fragment of the Y chromosome that contains *SRY* develop as males. A decade later the genes that 'actively promote ovarian development and suppress the testicular programme – such as one called *WNT4*' were identified (Ainsworth 2015: 289). These and other important discoveries

> have pointed to a complex process of sex determination, in which the identity of the gonad emerges from a contest between two opposing networks of gene activity. Changes in the activity or amounts of molecules (such as WNT4) in the networks can tip the balance towards or away from the sex seemingly spelled out by the chromosomes. (Ainsworth 2015: 289)

A typical male has XY chromosomes, and a typical female has XX. For 'typical' women and men, a biological binary at the chromosomal level remains. But owing to genetic variation or chance events in development, some people do not fit into either category. The label DSD (disorder of sex development) is attached to some of these people, but because this term is discriminatory, VSC (variations of sex characteristics) is now gaining traction. Their sex chromosomes do not match their sexual anatomy (Ainsworth 2015: 290). Are there male and female brains? Not exactly, writes Robin Henig, 'But at least a few brain characteristics, such as density of the gray matter or size of the hypothalamus, do tend to differ between genders. It turns out transgender people's brains may more closely resemble brains of their self-identified gender than those of the gender assigned at birth' (Henig 2017: 56). But research on brain characteristics is still at an early stage. 'Non-binary' has itself become a genuine identity word, and, as Kristina Olson explains, non-binary people are recognised and studied as a distinct group of people. 'Put simply, these are individuals who do not feel as if they are boys or girls, men or women, nor do they feel fully masculine or feminine. Instead many *nonbinary* people fall somewhere in the middle of a *spectrum* from masculine to feminine' (Olson 2017, emphases added).

## The Spectrum of Desire

Denis Alexander, a recent Gifford lecturer, confirms the long-established view held by Kinsey, that sexual attraction also exists along a continuum from exclusively heterosexual to exclusively homosexual. (He uses the abbreviation SSA – 'same-sex attraction' – which itself is controversial, since it is used by some homosexual people who do not identify as homosexual and sometimes preface the term with the adjective 'unwanted'. I use the term only in this section.) SSA, he writes, 'is not a discrete variable and exists *along a continuum*, from attraction exclusively toward the opposite sex (OSA) to attraction exclusively toward the same sex, with attraction to both sexes equally in the middle' (Alexander 2017: 214, emphasis added). He acknowledges the difficulties surrounding the definition and measurement of SSA, and examines its putative causes – environmental, biological, and freedom of choice. '[I]t is very likely that many different causes are operating in tandem and that causes are operating in different ways across the cohort of same-sex attracted individuals, in ways that are likely to be gender – and culture – specific' (Alexander 2017: 213). Of SSA people, 80–90 per cent have a stable attraction, though 10 to 20 per cent change their orientation. This happens in both directions, from gay to straight and straight to gay.

SSA, he continues, usually begins around the age of puberty. Female SSA is 'much more labile than in men' (Alexander 2017: 215). Personal freedom as a cause is almost ruled out. Choice may be a causal factor for a 'small – possibly very small – minority of male SSA individuals, if it can be a matter of choice at all, whereas the scope for choice in females may be somewhat greater' (2017: 217). There is no evidence that SSA is caused by abnormal parental relationships (2017: 219), and very little evidence for the 'socialisation hypothesis', i.e., 'the hypothesis that pre-pubertal children are "blank slates" with regard to sexual attraction and that attraction is acquired or learned from sociocultural cues and interactions with parents, siblings, peers, mentors, role models and the wider culture' (2017: 220). Although there is 'no single genetic mutation [that] is causally responsible for SSA by itself, multiple variants, potentially several hundreds or thousands, could be influencing SSA in combination' (2017: 223). In conclusion,

> The social and cultural environment in which people live is constantly changing, including friends and partners, together with personal motivations and aspirations, creating a complex system in which biological

make-up is integrated with multiple environmental, social and cultural factors. Thus, there is no point in looking for *the* cause of same-sex attraction – it does not exist. (2017: 232, author's emphasis)

We have just observed how the continuum works in the cases of human sex and human sex attraction. I next make a case for reading 'male and female' in key biblical texts as a continuum too, both in their historical contexts and in their contributions to a theology of gender, full of promise for the present time.

## The Continuum and God's Image

Genesis 1.27 is a founding text for supporters of a sex binary, Catholic and Protestant. In suggesting a different non-binary interpretation, I plead no privileged access to original meanings. I suggest only that a non-binary interpretation is at least as plausible as a binary one.

> God created the human [*ha'adam*] in his image [*salmo*]; in God's image he created him [*'oto*]; male and female he created them [*'otam*]. (See Hendel, Kronfeld, and Pardes 2011: 76)

In order to appreciate the possible meaning(s) of this verse, it is necessary to appreciate that in the Hebrew the verse is a 'poetic triplet', that the poem produces 'parallelistic effects', an 'expressive use of rhyme', and 'shifting chiasms and word order in each line, which are the biblical poem's stock in trade' (Hendel et al. 2010: 76). This stylistic interweaving of God, the human, and male and female, already 'call[s] into being and partially erase[s] the sharp distinctions' between them. As Hendel et al. explain, 'the human' is 'grammatically masculine singular but is specified as "male and female" and plural'. Within 'the human' there is therefore both an 'ontological singularity and plurality' that is 'mirrored in God', while God, who 'says' in the previous verse 'Let us make a human [*adam*] in our image, after our likeness' is 'morphologically plural but grammatically masculine singular' (Hendel et al. 2010: 76). *ha'adam* refers to the 'human species', to humanity as a collective noun (Hess 2005: 146).

The human then, like God, is both singular and plural; the image of God is both male and female and the absolute difference between God and the human is already queried by the ocular and substantial use of the metaphor 'image'. The poem therefore 'complicates, intensifies, and reorients the duality of male/female in its very moment of linguistic origin'. Hendel et al. observe that in the passage 'The first human(s) is thus called into being as a composite equality in which male, female, and God are related to one another.' They conclude,

> A reading of the first Creation story inspired by contemporary gender theory would thus argue that gender and sexuality are inaugurated as physical and metaphysical qualities *in a continuum* rather than as purely dichotomous essences or types. This poem unpacks the seemingly natural binaries – human/God and male/female – into a highly nuanced and reflective theory of gender and self. (Hendel et al. 2011: 76, emphasis added)

This interpretation fairly obviously weakens and problematises the modern confidence that God created opposite sexes, or that human beings must be straightforwardly one or the other. That God is plural in Genesis 1, not just specifically two, and that the human images God, might also suggest textually what is true theologically, that whatever our sex, we belong to the species *'adam* first and foremost. Is this modest claim about humanity as a continuum 'presentist'? In part, Yes. Hendel et al. admit to being inspired by contemporary gender theory, so to some extent present concerns may govern the questions put to the text. But presentism already exists in the dominant view that there are only two sexes.

The history of interpretation of these verses includes the supposition of a sequential gap between God's creation of 'the human' or 'the earthling', and God's subsequent creation of the human as male and female, giving rise to the suggestion that 'the first human was not a man at all: he (or it) was simply an earth creature, an *adam* without a discernible gender, until we learn that "male (*ish*) and female (*ishah*), God created them"' (Knust 2011: 50). The suggestion cannot be pressed further without assuming a chronological sequence, but one can still claim the text assumes, narratively, that the creation of humanity precedes its division into sexes. Genesis 2 of course assumes the man was created first, and there is no doubt that the chronological priority of the man over the woman and her creation from him, has been interpreted as the ontological priority of the man over the woman, in all respects. It was articulated early in the New Testament by Paul (1 Cor. 11.7–12) and later by the Pauline school (1 Tim. 2.8–15). Genesis 1 contains no such assumption.

In Islam too there is a common assumption that male and female are binaries, and that God, gendered masculine, legitimises male superiority. But that assumption may be as improbable as the binary in Genesis 1. Asma Barlas, the notable Islamic theologian, finds the assumption groundless. She argues, 'not only does the Qur'an not define women and men in terms of binary oppositions . . . it also does not portray women as lesser or defective men, or the two sexes as incompatible, incommensurable, or unequal, in the tradition of Western/ized patriarchal thought' (Barlas 2002: 130). Drawing on the verse 'reverence [God] who created you from a single Person' (Qur'an 4.1) and many others, she concludes, 'Male and female thus are not only inseparable in the Qur'an but they also are ontologically the same, hence equal' (Barlas 2002: 134). Again a plausible non-binary theological anthropology is adduced that confronts the dominant reading, with its inevitable valorisation of masculinity. The problem, thinks Barlas, is not the text, but the masculinist projections onto it.

But there is another element of Genesis 1.26–7 that usually and unjustifiably escapes notice. We have already observed that God is plural in Genesis 1.26 (with all its attendant difficulties for monotheism). Since *ha'adam*, the human, is created in God's image, and the human is created male and female, it follows that both the male and the female image God. Hendel et al. think the poem breaks down the separation between divine and human being. Students have sometimes told me, 'God is beyond gender – He is neither male nor female', inviting the comment that their use of the male pronoun indicates the persistence of the male image of God at the expense of the near elimination of its counterbalancing female counterpart. Standard ways of speaking of God theoretically and formally concede that God is 'beyond gender' (not least because sex is an attribute of creatureliness and God is Creator), whereas theological, liturgical, and vernacular talk of God continues to replicate, at a very deep level, male hegemony. One way of analysing the masculine imbalance in thinking about God is to compare it with thinking about gender at the human level. Complementarity asserts equality at some (murky) level while simultaneously requiring the ontological priority of the male. The history of complementarity as an effective epistemological device contributes to, even as it derives from, the unbalanced male God of Christian iconography and private devotion. Fifty years of feminist theology have not unseated him.

The peculiarity of this impasse has recently been exposed by the philosopher of religion, Michael Rea. After noting that the God who is understood to have no body can hardly be thought of as masculine, he asserts, against the 'traditional' view, that to say 'one way of characterizing God is more accurate than another is just to say that it comes closer to telling the straightforward, literal truth about what God is really like (intrinsically or extrinsically, essentially or contingently)' (Rea 2016: 100). That has a real consequence for women. Directly echoing Mary Daly, he observes, 'masculine characterizations of God obscure (or perhaps even tacitly deny) that traits definitive or stereotypical of womanhood reflect the image of God' (2016: 102). The consequence of this is harm to women (and to the men who think, arrogantly, their representation of God's image is superior). '[I]f God is (exclusively or predominantly) masculine, then the traits that are definitive or stereotypical of masculinity are more divine than those definitive or stereotypical of femininity' (2016: 102). Traditionalists might argue (or just passively assume) that since God *is* more truthfully depicted as masculine, then the consequences for women are – well – just too bad. They should get over it and stop whingeing. But the position of the 'masculinists' is intolerable.

The 'equality thesis', as Rea states it, is that

> All human beings are created equally in the image of God; and if mental and behavioural characteristics contribute at all to gender membership, then the ones that contribute to making someone a woman are no more or less relevant to her bearing the image of God than those that contribute to making someone a man. (Rea 2016: 103)

Elizabeth Johnson used the *imago Dei* doctrine, back in 1984, to argue for a similar position. She contended that 'Normative conceptualization of God in analogy with male reality alone is the equivalent of the graven image, a finite representation being taken for and worshiped as the whole' (Johnson 1984: 443, and see Johnson 1993). 'If women are created in the image of God, then God can be spoken of in female metaphors in as full and limited a way as God is imaged in male ones' (1993: 54). I argue the idea that the image of God offers no ground or shelter for the assumption of a human binary. We have just seen there are textual and theological reasons for thinking God made *ha'adam* 'male and female', not male *or* female. The conjunction 'and' is inclusive: the disjunction 'or' is exclusive. An inclusive understanding of humanity as male and female also provides a basis for recognising intersex and trans people as included within the spectrum that is human being, to the same extent as everyone else. The reason is obvious. There is

> one human nature celebrated in an interdependence of multiple differences. Not a binary view of two forever predetermined male and female natures, nor abbreviation to a single ideal, but a diversity of ways of being human: a multipolar set of combinations of essential human elements, of which sexuality is but one. (Johnson 2002: 155–6)

## The Image and the Medievals

Earlier in the book we noted how in medieval theology a good case can be made for the understanding of women and men as already a continuum, but one in which the gender slide operated from male to female. I argued for a reclamation of the continuum without the slide. We will now revisit medieval thought to pursue how women were believed to be less in the image of God than men. Philip Reynolds explains how attempts to reconcile egalitarian and inegalitarian visions of God's image in this period perpetuated ambiguity about women as full bearers of God's image. This ambiguity has allowed discrimination and prejudice to thrive. Actually, the case for an unambiguous and affirmative doctrine of equality in the period was strong and well known, writes Reynolds, but the attempted incorporation of the vexatious contrary case resulted in compromise. There were five elements to the egalitarian case. Since the medievals thought that the image of God lay in the soul or the mind, the sex of bodies should have been irrelevant to the possession of God's image by all embodied human beings. The Vulgate's use of *homo* at Genesis 1.27 was understood to refer collectively to humankind, prior to sexual division. Mary's position among the saints guaranteed that women could not be spiritually inferior to men. Augustine 'is entirely clear: both man and woman are made in God's image, for the image exists in a part of human nature that is independent of gender' (Reynolds 1988: 173). And a contribution to the egalitarian case was found in the difficult notion of humankind as an *infima species* – important for the continuum idea in this book.

Reynolds defines an *infima species* as one 'that cannot be related as genus to an inferior differentiation of species' (Reynolds 1988: 173). Sexual difference is a difference that humans share with animals and so it cannot be a difference that applies specifically to humans only. It cannot be a 'specifying attribute' of the species defining what the species is. 'It is difficult to see how gender could be specifying, for it affects all animals and apparently in the same way; therefore, if gender were specifying it would differentiate the genus animal, with the result that a ewe would be more closely related to a cow than to a ram' (1988: 173). A human being may differ from another human being in countless material ways while sharing the essence of human being in common. But these material differences do not 'specify' human being as such. The statement 'God created the human' (Gen. 1.27) was (rightly) understood to imply that humankind is the genus, and since 'the human species ... is made in God's image, then the image must be prior to sexual difference and be unaffected by it' (1988: 173).

All these points could be marshalled together for a positive theological account of gender. The problem, however, is that they do not tell the whole biblical story (or rather stories). Genesis 2.4b–5 has the man made first, and the woman deriving from him. Parts of the New Testament seized on the temporal priority of the man in this narrative to justify his ontological male superiority and the requirement of female obedience. 1 Corinthians 11.7–8 was particularly influential – 'For a man ought not to have his head veiled, since he is the image and reflection of God; but woman is the reflection of man. Indeed, man was not made from woman, but woman from man.' These verses of course are from an early Pauline letter, and generally the tradition took this line. Compromises were ingenious. Augustine grappled openly with the problem. He surmised that since the image of God is in the mind (that part of the human being that is capable of knowing God), women and men are both made in the image of God, but since men are more rational, the instantiation of the divine image is greater in men. 'In Augustine's view ... Eve represents the mind in its inferior mode of operation' (Reynolds 1988: 178–9). Hugh of St. Victor and Lombard (both twelfth century) developed the asymmetrical analogy between God as the *principium* or source of all things, and Adam (the named individual man, *vir*) as the *principium* of humankind, because the first man 'gave birth' to the woman. Albert (thirteenth century) thought that 'all men are in God's image, but women only imperfectly, since man dominates woman' (1988: 182).

Bonaventure's solution made use of 'the distinction between what is essential to the image and what may be regarded as additional perfections', so while the being or *esse* of women and men is equally in God's image, there is a *bene esse* of the image, a 'clearer expression' (Reynolds 1988: 184) that belongs to men only. What began as a compromise ends in contradiction: his view is that 'there is no "feminine face" of God ... God is entirely beyond gender, but he [*sic*] is thought of as having gender, and only the masculine gender is applicable. Indeed in Bonaventure's sexual symbolism the woman represents precisely that which is other than God and receives him' (1988: 189). For Aquinas, 'The male is more in God's image according to certain exterior attributes, such as his status as *principium* of the entire human race. But he is also more in God's image according to his interior nature, for his rational powers are greater than those of the female' (1988: 186).

Reynolds's survey illustrates the legacy of ambiguity attaching to attempts to reconcile parallel strands of Scripture: on the one hand, the strand linking Genesis 1.26–7 and Galatians 3.28; on the other hand, the strand linking Genesis 2.4b–5, 1 Corinthians 11, and some other passages in the New Testament Letters. The dominance of the latter strand reached its nadir in the appalling *Malleus Maleficarum* (1486)(see Thatcher 2008:

100–7). Androcentrism easily spills over into misogyny. Helen Kraus's balanced and detailed study of the Hebrew text of Genesis 1–4 and its subsequent translations concludes the text is responsible for the belief, 'held by some women as well as men, that they are biologically and therefore socially subordinate to men' (Kraus 2011: 192). There is no doubt

> that this mind set has its roots in the story of Genesis 1–4 and is somehow sanctified by it. The Hebrew account of the Creation and Fall and its intrinsic androcentricity cannot escape a 'guilty' verdict, even if the translations have played their part in perpetuating the gender inequality. In mitigation, the translators might claim that they retained as much of the original meaning as possible and therefore it is the Hebrew text that must be ultimately responsible for any influence upon the faith communities that adopted the translations. (2011: 192–3)

## 'No Longer Male and Female'

While we have spent some time considering what the 'image of God' might mean for relations of gender (admittedly only a fragment of wider historical and contemporary discussion), it should be insisted upon that in considering the image of God, Genesis 1 should always be secondary in the Christian mind (Thatcher 2016: 146–9: and see Barton 2009). Why? The answer is simple: in the New Testament it is Christ who is the image of God, not Adam, whether conceived as 'human being' or as the name of the first male progenitor (Gen. 5.3). Once it is understood that the image of God is ontologically and primarily Christ, and only secondarily, the humankind of Genesis 1.27, a crucial element of interpretation is added. That is what happens in Paul's Letter to the Galatians.

In order to prevent 'no longer male and female' being used merely as a proof text endorsing modern gender equality, it will be necessary to set Paul's vision of the new humanity established in Christ in the wider context of the letter. I take the NRSV translation of Galatians 3.28 as the more accurate one: 'There is no longer Jew or Greek, there is no longer slave or free, there is no longer male and female [*arsen kai thelu*]; for all of you are one in Christ Jesus.' The abolition of three binaries appears to be announced in this verse. The first two are joined by the disjunction 'or' (*oude*), but the third is joined by the conjunction 'and' (*kai*). '. . . male *and* female' (*arsen kai thèlu*) is also embedded in the Septuagint text of Genesis 1.27. Since Paul probably had this verse in mind as he wrote, he may not have read 'male and female' as a binary at all. 'And' and 'or' are logical connectives but one joins two (or more) nouns or clauses, etc., while the other divides. The Vulgate ('There is neither Jew nor Greek: there is neither bond nor free: there is neither male nor female') uses the same connective (*neque*) in all three pairs of terms (*non est Iudaeus neque Graecus non est servus neque liber non est masculus neque femina*). Both the Authorized Version (Protestant) and the Douay–Rheims Version (Catholic) of the Bible follow the Vulgate, so the illusion that the three pairs are alike has been perpetuated from Jerome onwards, in Catholic and Protestant thought, down to the end of the last century.

Remarkably the context – the Galatia of Paul's day – reveals an argument that at root is about the theology of gender. Why else would circumcision be the big issue? Men, the male organ, and the menace of sanctified masculinity, are prominent in the Letter, to a degree usually unrecognized or avoided. Historically the issue of gender has been one about the place and value of women in a world run by men. In Galatia women are no problem at all. They are not asking for their bodies to be marked as a sign of God's favour. The problem for Paul is one about the place of men's bodies and the practice of masculinity in the new creation where neither counts for anything anymore, and the men don't like it. Brigitte Kahl notes 'the male body-language of the letter', finding twenty-two penile references to 'foreskin', 'circumcision', 'circumcise', and 'sperm' (and the notorious reference to castration (5.12)), while 'Even the gospel itself is linked to male anatomy, with Paul coining the two rather striking phrases "gospel of the foreskin" and "gospel of the circumcision" (2.7), which are repeated nowhere else in the New Testament' (Kahl 2000: 40).

Who and what counts as Abraham's *sperma* (variously translated as 'seed' 'offspring', 'issue') is an early point of controversy in the Letter. For Paul it no longer depends on male *sperma* or the male line of descent, marked on the male body by circumcision. It is marked instead by faith (3.6–7). Commenting on the phrase 'Abraham and his seed' (quoted in 3.16), he seizes on the singular noun 'seed' and applies it not to the physical descendants of Abraham but to the single 'one person, who is Christ' (3.16, NRSV). The conclusion of the argument in Galatians 3 is that the former 'children of Abraham' are now 'in Christ' (3.28) and so no longer need to define themselves with reference to historic physical fatherhood. Being in Christ is a 'radical decentering of maleness' that 'could be seen as one of the most "natural" reasons why physical maleness (*arsen*) cannot any longer bear the identity marker of circumcision for those who enter into the messianic communities from the Gentile side' (Kahl 2000: 41).

Kahl shows that while maleness is 'decentred', femaleness is 'recentred' by means of the two mothers, Hagar and Sarah (4.21–31) (even Paul thinks of himself metaphorically as a mother in birthing the Galatian communities – 4.19). All his readers knew that Hagar was Abraham's slave, and Sarah his wife (Gen. 16). But they were unprepared for Paul's allegorical take on their relationship to these women:

> Now this is an allegory: these women are two covenants. One woman, in fact, is Hagar, from Mount Sinai, bearing children for slavery. Now Hagar is Mount Sinai in Arabia and corresponds to the present Jerusalem, for she is in slavery with her children. But the other woman corresponds to the Jerusalem above; she is free, and she is our mother. (4.24–6)

The Jewish Christians insisting on circumcision are identified as the 'children' of the slave-girl. The real inheritors of God's promises (who followed Paul) are the children of Sarah. Their true identity is not from Abraham but from Sarah. Abraham's fatherhood is replaced by Sarah's motherhood, the free, faithful, and genuine ancestor. The male line has become redundant.

There are two further points from Kahl's fine essay that advance the case being made in this book: one about the deconstruction of the old masculinity; the other about the binary nature of what is superseded. No true male Jew possessed a foreskin: no female Jew possessed a foreskin to lose. The women are *de natura* uncircumcised. The difficulty among the male converts to Paul's gospel was that if they remained uncircumcised they would be regarded as similar to women in a crucial respect. Their masculinity would be compromised. Circumcision appears in Bourdieu's account of the institutionalisation of masculinity among the Berbers. It distinguishes 'between those whose manliness it consecrates and those who cannot undergo the initiation and who cannot fail to see themselves as lacking' (Bourdieu 2001: 25). Paul's ethical teaching may have further compromised the masculinity of the male Galatian Christians. Exhortations to bear one another's burdens, to serve one another, and indeed Paul's own example in boasting of weakness and suffering, all provide signs of a different non-hierarchical, non-binary form of community life where being a man required a different performance of masculinity than the one sought after by the circumcised converts.

Second, there are two references to the 'elemental spirits of the universe' (*ta stoicheia*) in Galatians 4 (vv. 3, 9). In the first the spirits represent the enslavement of the people of God awaiting their redemption. In the second the spirits represent both the pagan gods of Gentile worship and the return of circumcised Christians to the enslavement of the Jewish law. According to a suggestion of J. Louis Martyn (cited in Kahl 2000: 44), the elemental spirits may be

> the universal polarities that the Greeks and others thought to be the basis of the cosmos, structuring reality in binary oppositional pairs like air vs. earth, fire vs. water, but also Law vs. non-Law, circumcision vs. non-circumcision, slave vs. free and female vs. male and so on. Paul presupposes that this bi-polar order of the 'world' (*kosmos*) has been broken down through the cross.

I have suggested that Paul did not regard the phrase 'male and female' as indicating a binary. I have tried to avoid using Galatians 3.28 as a proof text that then requires a tortuous balancing act with other texts where masculine superiority is assumed. I have tried to follow the profound theological argument of the Letter instead. The presenting issue is much more than a matter of circumcision. Those who returned to the old male hegemony were said to be returning to the elemental spirits that govern the world. They were attempting to arrogate to themselves the male superiority that circumcision formerly accorded them. But Paul is adamant that the Christian community is one where the binaries of race, gender, and class are overcome by Jesus Christ and the 'oneness' of believers of every kind through the new humanity he inaugurates. Galatians 3.28 forms the apex of a profound theological argument running through previous chapters. It is a genuinely intersectional conclusion, causing the binaries to fall away. Thinking Christologically is what drives Paul's thoughts. That is what drives his allegorical interpretation of Hagar and Sarah. He does not treat the Hebrew Bible as law! Indeed that type of exegesis was largely responsible for his problem.

It is important to stress that this reading of Paul, and indeed the argument of this book, does not require the erasure of sexual difference, only the binaries that constitute sexual difference in harmful and exploitative ways. Why follow Paul at all, here? I acknowledge the contrary emphases elsewhere in the Pauline corpus, and that when he uses the baptismal formula of Galatians 3.28 in 1 Corinthians (12.13), he omits the crucial 'no longer male and female' clause. Paul had opponents at Corinth and elsewhere. He records he opposed Peter 'to his face, because he was clearly in the wrong' (Gal. 2.11). In 1 Corinthians (11.7–8) he not only leaves the gender hierarchy intact: he uses the metaphor of the image of God, read through the 'events' described in Genesis 2 and 3, to justify it ('For a man ought not to have his head veiled, since he is the image and reflection of God; but woman is the reflection of man. Indeed, man was not made from woman, but woman from man'). Writers in the Pauline school (who were probably the authors of the later Letters attributed to him) clearly did not see Christian communities as non-hierarchical organisations.

Paul should be followed because he wins the argument with his opponents. To the extent that his thoughts about gender are inconsistent across his Letters, his lengthy, complex, and subtle argument against his opponents in Galatia is superior to, say, his argument in favour of veil wearing in Corinth (1 Cor. 11). Outside the Gospels I urge priority be given to the teaching on gender in Galatians on the grounds of method, of theology, and of the Euthyphro Dilemma. The method is Christological. Reflection on the meaning of the death and resurrection of Christ leads to his vision for a unified humanity in which everyone has a place and that is already proleptically present in the Christian communities. Paul does not simply assert, basing his teaching on his apostolic authority. He digs deeply into the Hebrew Bible and interprets it creatively in the attempt to convince other Christians that his account of the faith makes better sense than theirs. The theology is radically inclusive. My reading of the resolution of the Euthyphro Dilemma clearly tips the balance in favour of his argument in Galatians. The latter view harms women directly, and men indirectly. It is a prime example of the symbolic violence Bourdieu describes. People of all faiths need to stop blaming God for the harm their teachings cause.

## The Trinity and the Continuum

In what senses, if any, does the doctrine of the Trinity contribute to the overcoming of binary thinking on the human level? The distinguished medievalist Anglican theologian, the late Marilyn McCord Adams, observes, 'Way back in the twelfth century, Richard of St. Victor made centuries-old trends explicit, when he represented *the Holy Trinity as a paradigm of "same-sex" friendship*' (Adams 1992: 325, author's emphasis). 'How could we have missed it?' she asks. 'Father, Son, and Holy Spirit, an intimate community of lovers, the center of Christian worship for over 1,600 years!' (1992: 325). Hugo Quero and Joseph Goh suggest that 'If the divine community, the Trinity, has the number three as the starting point for relationalities, their very imagery disrupts the pre-eminence of binary relationships as the hegemonic ones' (Quero and Goh 2018: 304). Well, if God is One and God is Three, that God is Two is ruled out absolutely. Three, however, makes God more than a 'binity' or a duality. God is plural, just as God is singular. No one is suggesting that there are binaries in God. The very lack of binaries is an additional reason for 'doing' the theology of gender from God's own being.

Nonetheless Quero and Goh (2018) move easily from the Trinity to the affirmation of sexual relations beyond human pairing, i.e., to polyamory. My inclination is more modest. I have noticed that in academic and popular writing about gender a range of basic concepts emerges: *persons* and *relations*; *identity* and *difference*; and *equality* and *diversity* (e.g., Thatcher 1993: 52–60; 2011: 118–27; 2016: 177–86). It has been exhilarating to point out time and again to startled and sceptical audiences that these concepts have been in play for many centuries as Christians have struggled to say, in the least inadequate way they can think of, what must be said about God. The Athanasian Creed, or *Quicunque vult* (probably early sixth century), declares, 'And the Catholick Faith is this: That we worship one God in Trinity, and Trinity in Unity; Neither confounding the Persons: nor dividing the Substance' (Book of Common Prayer 1662). The Creed requires two positions to be held concurrently. God is to be worshipped as One, without mixing up the Persons. And God is to be worshipped as Three without there being three gods. The divine Mystery is such that both affirmations are required (a case where the principle of complementarity may be justified!).

The Creed almost labours to say that the three *Persons* are *distinct* ('For there is one Person of the Father, another of the Son: and another of the Holy Ghost'), yet their *relations* to each other are such that their overall unity is unimpaired ('But the Godhead of the Father, of the Son, and of the Holy Ghost, is all one'). The *identity* of each Person is ultimately unfathomable ('The Father incomprehensible, the Son incomprehensible; and the Holy Ghost incomprehensible') yet each Person is known *differently* in the divine economy. Difference is no barrier to unity. The Creed is adamant that the Persons are *equal* – 'None is afore, or after other: none is greater, or less than another; But the whole three Persons are co-eternal together: and co-equal.' Yet the Persons are also *diverse* ('the Father is Almighty, the Son Almighty: and the Holy Ghost Almighty. And yet they are not three Almighties: but one Almighty'). A community of co-equal Persons has to be one of mutuality and reciprocity, a clearly vital feature of human personal relationships.

We may have qualms about the diversity of the persons being further marked by relations of origin within the Creed, but that difficulty must be laid aside (along with several more internal difficulties, including the viability of the so-called 'social doctrine of the Trinity'). I think the Trinity provides a set of fine analogies about the relations between *human* persons.

Persons are necessarily and inevitably in relation with other persons, and these relations are exposed, individually and socially, to exploitation and violence. When they are restored, i.e., when they reflect the image of the Triune God, human personal relations inhabit the very being of God by whose grace they reflect and embody the divine love and justice. The problem of identity versus difference was also Paul's problem in Galatia. No, a shorn penis was no longer necessary for men to identify as God's chosen ones. The grounds of identity had shifted. A new identity (the body of Christ) becomes primary, and within that identity, differences are affirmed, but non-violently, not abolished or reduced to 'the Same'. In God, identity and difference reside side by side. The equality of the divine Persons speaks volumes about the requirement for equality on the human level.

Immediately there are objections. Hasn't the social doctrine of the Trinity suffered already from overexposure, invoked to justify the functioning of most things plural, including democratic societies, ecclesiastical committees, and (as we have just seen) polyamorous arrangements? Patrick Cheng too thinks the Trinity 'can be a model for individuals who are polyamorous'. Linn Tonstad's apt name for this is 'corrective projectionism' (Tonstad 2016: 13), and she is particularly pained by theologians like Cheng writing about sexual difference and illicitly (in her view) modelling idealised human difference on the difference between the divine Persons. But she overstates her case. The very similarity of concepts in the case both of divine and human persons is more than coincidental or serendipitous. *Some* trinitarian language (person, relation, difference, substance, unity, being, and so on) is strikingly gender-neutral and may yet shed important light on the redemption of sinful and gendered human relations. Tonstad's placing of divine difference so far above human sexual difference might seem to introduce a disconnection between the divine and the human, whereas a timely warning about pressing analogies too far might have been sufficient.

The very overlap between talk of divine Persons and human persons indicates the appropriateness of the cluster of analogies they generate. Talk of (human) persons inevitably leads to talk about their relations, about identity and difference, and about equality and diversity. Yet these were and are the very issues that emerge whenever the church has tried to talk about faith in God. The author of Genesis 1 could have had no trinitarian faith. We who do should be able to acknowledge the *imago Dei* in relations of communion and justice between people. We should expect these relations to be embodied in the Body of Christ.

Duality and opposition therefore have no place in God. There are no polarities in God (despite Böhme's and Schelling's speculations), so 'male and female' can't replicate any. There are only Persons in living, vibrant, creative, loving, reciprocal relation, sometimes referred to by the (ambivalently derived) term *perichòrèsis*. That many of us are able to reproduce and therefore find ourselves male or female doesn't say anything about God since God does not and does not need to reproduce. But that we are persons reflects very much our being in the image of God because it makes possible our capacity to give and receive love, whether that love is manifested in marriage, gay or straight, or in various models of friendship (including of course celibacy: perhaps even in polyamory). God is beyond sex (and so beyond male and female) but not beyond relationship. Rather God *is* relationship, both in Godself and in the redeemed community.

Neither can a God who is a Communion of co-equal Persons be thought to authorise analogies (such as Aquinas') that begin with a single *principium* or origin and move downwards to an authorising human male who is the *princeps* of the human and biological worlds over whom he exercises dominion. Jürgen Moltmann has gamely attempted to 'feminise' God the Father by drawing from the metaphor that the Father 'gives birth to his Son', asserting 'He [*sic*] is a motherly Father. He cannot be understood to have a single sex, masculine, but must be understood to be bisexual or transsexual' (Moltmann 1992: 22). Moltmann has in mind the edict of the Council of Toledo (675) that the Son comes 'from the womb of the Father'. True, Moltmann is alert to the idolatrous position of masculine names in speaking of God, and to birthing metaphors providing one way of modifying them. His suggestion, though, is open to the obvious objection that 'motherly Father' preserves God's fatherhood by usurping that activity that is necessarily feminine and assigning it to the Father. Relations of origin have always had limited, speculative value once they are accepted, as it must be that since God is eternal, all the persons must be eternal too. Whether it is pastorally useful to speak of God as 'bisexual or transsexual' in any more than a speculative and abstract sense is an issue that must be postponed to the next chapter.

In the present chapter I have made good the promise to replace binary opposites and 'the exclusions they engender, with what will be called the human continuum' (the second part of aim 2 of the book). I have done this by considering and combining afresh elements of the core Christian doctrines of God, of Christ, of the divine image, and of the divine Trinity. I invite readers to assess the plausibility of the theological framework or 'theological anthropology' I have suggested. It is based on solid biblical, theological, doctrinal, and traditional considerations; arrives at a non-binary, 'spectral' understanding of the human being; and expresses itself through the idea of the human continuum. Having reached this point, the next task is 'To demonstrate how the human continuum enables a more inclusive theological understanding not only of relations between women and men, but also among LGBTIQ people' (the third aim of the book). That will be done in the next two chapters.

## CHAPTER 8

# The Human Continuum:
## A Place for Everyone

### Intersex and the Continuum

This chapter begins the third aim of the book, to demonstrate how the human continuum enables a more inclusive theological understanding not only of relations between women and men, but also among LGBTIQ people. It begins with intersex. Intersex is an umbrella term that covers a range of human bodies deemed unusual. It is

> used for a variety of conditions in which a person is born with a reproductive or sexual anatomy that doesn't seem to fit the typical definitions of female or male. For example, a person might be born appearing to be female on the outside, but having mostly male-typical anatomy on the inside. Or a person may be born with genitals that seem to be in-between the usual male and female types – for example, a girl may be born with a noticeably large clitoris, or lacking a vaginal opening, or a boy may be born with a notably small penis, or with a scrotum that is divided so that it has formed more like labia. Or a person may be born with mosaic genetics, so that some of her cells have XX chromosomes and some of them have XY. (Intersex Society of North America [ISNA], undated)

These bodies are known by the medical names given to them. Once known as hermaphrodites, the term 'intersex' is generally preferred by the people under the umbrella. Some intersex people dislike the term because it defines them by a medical condition, preferring instead the medical term, Disordered Sexual Development (DSD), which defines the condition rather than the person. The issue is controversial and unresolved (see Cornwall 2015b), and there is growing support for the more neutral 'Intersex and Variations of Sex Characteristics' (IVSC)(Monro et al. 2017: 1). But behind and beyond the medical names are people made in the image of God, made to love, made for love, always more than the names identifying them or their medical conditions. These names include

Androgen Insensitivity Syndrome (AIS),[1] Congenital Adrenal Hyperplasia (CAH),[2] Ovo-Testes,[3] Turner Syndrome,[4] and Klinefelter's Syndrome. Of CAH, Susannah Cornwall writes,

> In XX foetuses with 'classic' (prenatal-onset) CAH, the excess in testosterone can cause unusual genital development before birth – a large clitoris and, sometimes, fused labia ... It is the surgery on infants' genitals that is the contentious issue ... Surgery to create a vaginal opening *is* sometimes necessary, and must occur before menstruation begins ... (Cornwall 2010: 239, author's emphasis)

About 1 in 660 boys and men has Klinefelter's Syndrome, an extra XX chromosome (NHS undated). They may be unaware of it, though they will be infertile in later life. About 1 in 770 boys has Hypospadias (ISNA, undated).

How many people have an intersex condition? ISNA states, 'If you ask experts at medical centers how often a child is born so noticeably atypical

---

[1] The website of the British National Health Service states, 'A child born with AIS is genetically male, but the external appearance of their genitals may be female or somewhere between male and female ... Most people born with the condition are unable to have children, but they'll otherwise be perfectly healthy and able to lead a normal life... AIS is caused by a genetic fault that's usually passed on to a child by their mother. This genetic fault means that, despite being genetically male, the body doesn't respond to testosterone (the male sex hormone) properly and male sexual development doesn't happen as normal. This means the penis doesn't form or is underdeveloped. The child's genitals may appear female, or between male and female, but they don't have a womb or ovaries and have fully or partially undescended testicles' (National Health Service 2018) [www.nhs .uk/conditions/androgen-insensitivity-syndrome/]. Note that the genetic difference is still described as a 'fault'.

[2] The British National Health Service states, 'Congenital adrenal hyperplasia (CAH) is a group of inherited disorders that result in impaired hormone production from the adrenal glands' (National Health Service 2015) [www.genomicseducation.hee.nhs.uk/resources/genetic-conditions-factsheets/ item/73-congenital-adrenal-hyperplasia-21/].

[3] Ovotestes, once called 'true hermaphroditism' are 'gonads (sex glands) containing both ovarian and testicular tissue. These are sometimes present in place of one or both ovaries or testes. ... Testicular tissue in ovotestes involves an increased risk of gonadal cancer' (Intersex Society of North America, undated) [www.isna.org/faq/conditions/ovo-testes].

[4] 'Turner syndrome is a female-only genetic disorder that affects about 1 in every 2,000 baby girls. A girl with Turner syndrome only has one normal X sex chromosome, rather than the usual two. This chromosome variation happens randomly when the baby is conceived in the womb ... 90% of girls with Turner syndrome don't produce enough of these sex hormones, which means:
- they may not begin sexual development or fully develop breasts without female hormone replacement therapy (HRT)
- they may begin sexual development but not complete it
- they may not start their monthly periods naturally
- it's likely they'll be unable to have a baby without assistance (infertile).

Even though many women with Turner syndrome have undeveloped ovaries and are infertile, their vagina and womb develop normally. This means they're able to have a normal sex life following treatment with female hormones' (NHS undated) [www.nhs.uk/conditions/turner-syndrome/].

in terms of genitalia that a specialist in sex differentiation is called in, the number comes out to about 1 in 1500 to 1 in 2000 births.' Cornwall puts it at 1:2,500 (Cornwall 2013: 220) but also warns against concentrating too much on numbers. That is because it becomes too easy for sceptics to accuse advocates for intersex people of overinflating the statistics, and it distracts from the potential significance of *any* difference, however rare (Cornwall, private correspondence). John Hare, a former consultant obstetrician and gynaecologist, states that up to 2 per cent of people, 'when all the usual determinants of maleness and femaleness are put together ... cannot be clearly assigned to a male or female gender' (Hare 2007: 98, citing Preves 2003). It is nearly as common as having red hair. Indeed Hare thinks 'the concept of the "pure" or unambiguous female or male becomes invalid; we are all variants' (Hare 2015: 93). Mosaicism to some extent may be common to all of us. 'To a greater or lesser degree we are all intersex. The human race is a rainbow, not simply two blocks, one of pink and one of blue. That is the principle on which we need to learn to relate to one another and to God' (Hare 2015: 93).

There have always been people who today would be classed as intersex. Connection is sometimes made with the 'eunuchs who have been so from birth' (Matt. 19.12) (e.g., DeFranza 2015: 68–106). Hare finds four classes of people between male and female (*saris khama, aylonith, androginos,* and *tumtum*) named by the rabbis of the biblical and Talmudic periods (Hare 2015: 83–90). In this, he thinks, 'the early rabbis developed a code that was, in some ways, more liberal than that which governs society today' (2015: 88). We have already noted 'the shared and common spectrum' of sexed bodies widely believed to have existed prior to the nineteenth century. There is a good case for saying that the first half of the nineteenth century was more open about intersex conditions than the last half of the twentieth century. Indeed, the attitude of the medical profession towards them in the nineteenth century proves the increasing influence of the male–female binary and its deleterious consequences for them. There were 110 reports of 'hermaphroditism' published in the medical journals of the United States between 1808 and 1904. The reports show that treatment in the early part of the period was more social than medical, for example telling patients to wear trousers instead of skirts, or vice versa, and get on with their lives (Matta 2005). Only as the modern sexual binary took hold of the medical profession later in the century and coincided with advances in surgical techniques such as 'more effective anaesthetics and the introduction of antiseptic and aseptic methods' and 'the rise of gynecology and urology as medical specialties' (Matta 2005: 78) did the prospect of 'corrective' surgery arise. But that is only half the story. The same binary medicalised same-sex love (calling it, for the first time, 'homosexuality'), and hermaphrodites and homosexuals were linked together in the medical mind. Whereas

> early 19th-century physicians had regarded hermaphrodites as a curious and disturbing anatomical puzzle to be solved (and often explained by causes such as conception on a state line or startling a pregnant woman), intro-ducing the language of development redefined hermaphroditism and homosexuality as the results of a biological process gone horribly wrong. Both hermaphrodites and homosexuals, therefore, were *biological deviants from a dimorphic, heterosexual norm*; treating their condition consisted of normalizing the outward behavioral and anatomical effects of that process. (Matta 2005: 79, emphasis added)

Homosexual people came to be known as 'psychic hermaphrodites'. 'How else', asks Christina Matta, 'to accurately describe patients who looked like one sex but behaved like the other in their sexual lives than to claim their bodies were of one sex and their minds of the other?' (Matta 2005: 79). In the USA especially, fear that hermaphrodites might engage in sexual activity regarded as unnatural or homosexual led to the attempt to prevent this by medical means. The binary not only provided strong social pressure for intersex people to conform to male–female norms. It associated them with homosexuality and the growing moral horror afforded to non-procreative sexual activity. Thus did social, moral, medi-cal, and religious assumptions cause secrecy, shame, and the internalisation of vicious and unthinking judgements about the being of intersex people.

Medical practice is changing fast. Roughly up to the 1980s, young children with unusual genitalia were given corrective surgery. As Cornwall explains, 'this sometimes involved reducing or entirely removing large clitorises and small penises, with more emphasis placed on appearance than sensation' (Cornwall 2015: 658). But from the mid-1990s, she continues, 'many intersex people who had had surgery as children argued that this intervention, coupled with the secrecy surrounding their condi-tions, had caused them more problems than having unusual genitals would have done'. The enjoyment of sex as adults was impaired or lost because of 'physical and psychological scarring caused by early surgery' (2015: 659). Currently 'treatments for intersex are likely to include delayed or less invasive surgery, along with support for children and families as they consider the implications of early, delayed, or no surgery' (2015: 659; 2013: 221). But the aim of any surgery remains controversial. A current report recommends 'A legal moratorium should be put in place to prevent unnecessary surgeries and other irreversible harmful procedures being carried out on infants and children too young to give informed consent' (Monro 2017: 1).

What do intersex people want? They want to be heard, to be allowed to speak for themselves. They want their experience to count. They want to be accepted for who they are and how they are. They want their differences to be recognised, so that 'intersex' (and DSD) does not become a stigma-bearing objectification that reduces them to a single condition in the eyes of a majority. When they are heard, they want their experience to precede any theory their listeners may hold about them, especially theory that converts difference into weirdness and seeks to normalise it. Increasingly parents of intersex children do not seek 'corrective' surgery for their children, and many adults who have had surgery have complained of unsatisfactory and demeaning outcomes such as the need for further operations, and the impossibility of pleasurable sexual experience.

It could hardly be more obvious that the male–female binary has potentially disastrous consequences for intersex people. They confront the binary by showing it to be fallible, inadequate, and exclusive, but the binary has confronted intersex people with the expectation of normal-isation or secrecy and silence. Back in Chapter 1 I described a continuum as 'a continuous sequence in which adjacent elements are not perceptibly different from each other, but the extremes are quite distinct'. A biological continuum finds intersexed bodies statistically unusual but otherwise unremarkable. Their difference from other bodies is accounted for by a particular pattern of 'adjacent elements' across the continuum of male and female that is sometimes fuzzy and complicated. Since the intersex condi-tions are a recurring fact of nature, their presence within humanity should rather occasion no surprise at all, and that is what most intersex people want.

When we considered gender as a symbolic system we noted its propen-sity towards the creation of violence. While ideological assumptions may be unspoken and tacit, challenging them may evoke intense reactions. Intersex people unwittingly challenge binary ecclesiastical and theological thought. Male-only ministry requires exact determinations to be available about who is a man. The treatment of the late Sally Gross illustrates the point. Ordained a Dominican priest as the man Selwyn Gross, her intersex condition subsequently became known, and when she was classified as female, she was stripped of her clerical status. The resounding 'No' to same-sex marriage requires unambiguous bodies (and desires). But the theological anthropology of the last chapter does not support the theory or the practice of what I called earlier 'divinising difference'. The collapse, under interrogation, of complementarity (above, Part II) requires an alternative theological anthropology, and in Chapter 7 I laid out a skeletal view of one. God makes humanity male *and* female, not male *or* female.

Elyse Raby has grouped theological analyses of intersex into three types: the pathological, the benign, and the good. The first type assumes 'human perfection' to be 'expressed in two dichotomous sexes', so that intersex occurs 'as a "result of fallen nature" and contrary to the divine will' (Raby 2018: 98). We met the idea of the Fall as an aetiological curse in relation to homosexuality earlier. This type is pastorally disastrous since it requires particular people to believe themselves to be direct, passive, and unwilling victims of original sin and of God's curse upon it. It also provides a frightening rationale and incentive for corrective surgery. The second type 'acknowledges that intersex is one possible form of human embodiment but does not conclude that it is necessarily part of God's intention for creation' (2018: 99). The third type (Cornwall is identified as the principal exemplar) assumes that intersex is unremarkably good, just as any and every human being is made in God's image. As the intersex writer Michelle O'Brien puts it, 'We reflect G*d, and exist between male and female; as an intersex person, I am more a mixture of both than usual, and just as reflective of the God who is both male *and* female' (O'Brien 2016: 48). But Raby seeks (and finds) further justification for the assumption of goodness, and finds it in the action of God throughout creation as a whole. 'Intersex', she says, 'is not a deviation from a divinely intended norm because genetic variation and diversity are constitutive aspects of how God formed creation and enables its freedom' (Raby 2018: 105). Neither is it merely benign, since 'God is continually present to and active within creation as primary cause and sustaining Spirit of Love, willing all things into being' (2018: 105). There is diversity throughout nature. There is diversity within God and within humanity, and human diversity extends to biological sex.

Another example of the third type is Megan DeFranza's compelling *Sex Difference in Christian Theology*. However, after a spirited defence of the goodness of intersex, she finally pulls back from modifying the male–female binary that her arguments have rightly called into question. Intersex, she says, 'certainly requires an alteration of the binary model. It necessitates opening up space in between the categories of male and female. Instead of two discrete categories, intersex shows how these overlap in various ways' (DeFranza 2015: 270). Cornwall's work on intersex is said not merely to challenge 'the binary framework' but to eliminate it (2015: 260), and that is a bridge too far. Should the binary ever be dissolved, heteronormativity would be dissolved along with it, and Christian sexual ethics would collapse. While 'the simplistic binary model and its naïve repetition in theological anthropologies' is inadequate (2015: 268), the Christian life requires a certain retention of heteronormativity along with 'sexual chastity – monogamous chastity within marriage and celibate chastity outside of marriage. This kind of holiness has value for the community and the individual' (2015: 282–3).

When we thought about the neologism 'heteronormativity' we noted the difference between the descriptive and evaluative senses of it. Heteronormativity is not one thing that has to be eliminated, modified, or transcended. In the descriptive or statistical sense it points to the social fact that the majority of men and women have no difficulty identifying themselves as heterosexual, and discovering their desire for union with the other (*heteros, hetera*) sex. Heteronormativity in this sense is not going to be undone, removed, collapsed, or dissolved, however much minorities may rail against it. However, the accompanying expectation that all people should find themselves this way is of course evaluative and deeply damaging. I think the understanding of sexuality as a continuum should relieve DeFranza's anxieties. The call for 'space between the sexes' for intersex people is welcome but perhaps needs to be more structurally based. It is akin to similar calls for homosexual people to be 'accommodated' within an otherwise heterosexual framework. A continuum is more obviously inclusive. It acknowledges the need for the lines, boundaries, and demarcations between men and women to be relaxed, and the fluidity of sexual difference to be recognised. The social need for a continuum exists for the sake of non-intersexed people too, so that we come to relinquish the arrogant assumption that everyone is like us. We have good reason to be thankful for the intersexed for laying the issue bare, and teaching us the need for proper respect for minorities.

The social and theological adoption of a continuum approach to sexuality is unlikely to lead to a collapse of Christian sexual ethics, as DeFranza fears. But since the fear is widespread that any sexual activity of or between people within or between sexual and gender minorities is unchaste and unholy, it is important to lay it to rest. Heterosexual marriage may be an unhelpful recommendation to intersex people, many of whom may be unable to participate in the sexual routines of marriage in any case. I have defended and commended Christian marriage, in its non-hierarchical and non-patriarchal forms, for many years (e.g. Thatcher 1993, 1999, 2002, 2007, 2011, 2012), but I can't yet see how the human continuum threatens it. The arrival of same-sex marriage was thought to threaten heterosexual marriage, while it actually distributes the benefits of marriage yet more widely.

## Transgender and the Continuum

Transgender, like intersex, is also an 'umbrella term'. It 'includes people who are described as "transsexual"; it describes the expression of, or identification with, gender in a way that differs from the sex assigned at birth, and which in some cases may be affirmed through "transition"' (Beardsley and O'Brien 2016: 195). It also includes 'people who do not identify with a gender ("non-binary"), people who identify as "third gender", and people who cross-dress, amongst others' (2016: 195). The term 'transsexual' is different, and problematic. It is used of someone who identifies with the

> opposite sex to that which they were assigned at birth, wishes to perma-
> nently live as a member of that sex, which usually involves some form of
> 'transition', and can include surgical reassignment and/or sex-hormone
> replacement, both of which alter sex characteristics so they match gender
> identity, and aid living in that gender. (2016: 195)

Already, then, we have met five terms within the transgender 'umbrella', implying a continuum among particular identities. Indeed a recent report on trans people identified four continua among trans people ('sex', 'gender identity', 'gender expression', and 'sexual orientation' (Girschik (2008) in Bong 2018: 40). Gilchrist (2013) shows how from an initially fragmented development process, these schema are created, but I shall remain with the basic human continuum in order to indicate that everyone standing beneath the umbrella term 'transgender' has an unqualified and ultimately unremarkable place within it.

The binary impacts differently on trans people when compared with the intersexed, but again the human continuum provides a better framework for inclusion. Trans people are not one. 'The experiences of trans people have few common threads across the categories within the transgender spectrum, with transvestite and transsexual people having very different experiences' (Woolley 2016: 40). Nonetheless, a spectrum they remain, and there is even doubt among trans people whether their aspirations for themselves assert or deny the wider sexual binary. Jasmine Woolley presents an example of this doubt when she asks, 'Does transsexualism challenge the gender binary, or does it reinforce it? Opinion within the trans world is divided' (2016: 42, 44).

What do Christian trans people want? Fortunately two recent books detailing the experience and theology of Christians who are themselves transgender, provide some answers. Like all trans people they want to be listened to, and not regarded through polarised lenses (O'Brien, 2016: 50). They want non-transgender majorities to understand the traumatic conditions under which trans people, prior to and sometimes even after transition (if one is made), generally live their lives. They generally dislike the medical terminology used to describe them – 'there is a mixed response to the intervention of the medical profession. On the one hand many transsexual people want medical intervention in order to bring their bodies into line with their social expression, but there is disagreement on classifying gender dysphoria as a medical condition' (Woolley 2016: 43). On the other hand, 'the journey that trans people undertake is primarily a social, spiritual and psychological one, and while the physical changes are important milestones they are only one aspect of a complex journey' (Dowd and Beardsley 2018: 115). Christian trans people are weary of their misrepresentation in, or being ignored by, church documents. Often they are judged and found deviant, in accordance with the very binary their existence is calling into question, whereas Roman Catholic trans people suffer the full force of Vatican polemic against them, finding them guilty of the sin of hubris in attempting to choose the sex other than that which God intended for them.

In opposition to current Catholic teaching, the independent researcher, Susan Gilchrist, asks 'the crucial question . . . whether gender and sexually variant identities are intrinsic elements of personality, or the outcomes of a lifestyle choice?' (Gilchrist 2017: 3; and see Gilchrist 2016). This question, she says, displays a fatal confusion between neurophysiological and psychological aspects of the developing person, and wrongly attributes the exercise of moral freedom to behavioural outcomes that are not exactly predetermined, but that are the results of the interaction between early brain development in the infant and the developing moral choices of the adult. She holds 'that gender and sexually variant identities and behaviour are naturally expected variations of the human condition which are intrinsic to the personality created, that arise very early in development, and which cannot be changed by the individual concerned or by the actions of others in subsequent life' (Gilchrist 2017: 1). '[T]he development of identity and personality is expressed in a continuing struggle where the primarily unconscious and adventurous forces of neurophysiology remain pitted against the more conscious restraining and controlling forces of cognitive thought' (2017: 5). She draws on research that shows that the gender identification of gender-variant children is unchangeably fixed by the age of three. As the child grows into the adult, 'the physiological, neurological and psychological aspects of brain development act together to form a finely tuned system in which the maximum amount of individuality, possessiveness, intelligence and inquisitiveness, together with the minimum degree of energy expenditure is generated' (2017: 9).

Gilchrist positions herself well within the orbit of current scientific research, even though conclusions are tentative and (like all good science) open to new discoveries. There is a growing number of scientists who think that early brain development plays a large part in the arrival of variant gender conditions (also known as 'gender incongruence'). Terry Reed, co-founder of the Gender Identity Research and Education Society (GIRES), holds that the life-developing outcomes of surgical operations on intersex children provide good evidence for this hypothesis. 'Their gender identity resolved independently of genital appearance and the imposed gender role, in spite of the persuasive power of these two factors' (Reed 2016: 98). Included among the other evidence she cites are post-mortem studies on the brains of three people who in their lives were gender incongruent. 'In these individuals, unlike the control subjects, small nuclei in the brain, known to be sex-dimorphic, have been shown to have neural differentiation to genital and gonadal characteristics' (2016: 99). Gender incongruent people are likely to be 'intersexed at brain level' (2016: 99). Scans of the white matter of the brains of 'untreated' trans men indicate that the 'neural patterns' of these men 'are feminised', while scans of the brains of untreated trans women are reported to be 'masculinised'.

So there is growing evidence that gender incongruence is rooted in biology, and that biological causes, together with social and environmental influences, produce individuals who occupy different points along a gender spectrum. There must be wariness regarding the continuing medicalisation and objectification of people, identifying the person with the condition. Some of the causes remain unknown. But as a theologian I want to ask, in the light of previous arguments in earlier chapters, why the male–female binary should remain the default position at all. I have no wish to back an a priori theological claim about the way we are made with the authority of science, selectively understood. I prefer instead to release the ontological and theological understanding of every sort of person that the broad tradition of Christian theology actually provides. The two-sex hypothesis is the dubious one and science increasingly doesn't support it. Once the continuum replaces the binary in medical, social, and theological thought, the forceful expectation that a person should exemplify one or the other sex loses its hold. But there are clear theological pointers towards a non-binary of God, of the image of God among us, of the redeemed humanity that Christ constitutes, and of the body of Christ symbolised and enacted in the church. Ultimately it remains a bizarre state of affairs that churches should incorporate into official doctrine a theological anthropology that not only sits at odds with history and the core components of the doctrine of God: it causes immense pastoral damage and suffering.

## The Continuum and Creation

The very arrival of the modern medical nomenclature for classifying our bodies and our desires indicates that the human understanding of itself is not static, but evolutionary. Its unfolding character might be taken as God's providential care in placing us within an epistemological framework in which the world becomes increasingly knowable, while remaining ever mysterious. Gerard Loughlin notices the dynamic character of social and medical discourses actually *accords* with 'the deepest insights of the Christian tradition when it affirms the human as that creature which is called to – which finds its *telos* in – the infinite' (Loughlin 2018, no pagination). We are all becoming – on our way to our home in God, and we can expect to be changed en route.

The task of theology is to speak knowingly of the mystery of God while allowing God ever to be mysterious. Being in God's image, humans too remain mysterious. Heteronormative theology knows too much. Loughlin contrasts it with an alternative theological vision, one in which

> Theology does not think that people can be captured by such terms as heterosexual or homosexual, gay or straight. It sees people as called to become other than they think themselves, to find themselves beyond what and where they think they are, and to do so by venturing on the beyond from whence they come. (Loughlin 2018)

An alternative path for the theological mainstream is to query the ideologies that assume a fixed form for human life, attribute an almost divine status to biology in our self-determination, and 'injure' those who do not conform to it. Theology instead, he writes, is resolutely 'unconvinced by the certainties of the secular, and undermines secured identities by calling them to account in the face of the world's unknowability' (2018). It might strive for 'an unfixing of Christian complicity in the regime of heterosexuality' (2018), instead of propping it up.

Loughlin has a particular theologian in mind (Oliver O'Donovan), but his analysis applies equally to more recent evangelical accounts of homosexuality and transgender, and to the Catholic theology that dubs all deviation from heteronormativity as 'gender ideology'. Elsewhere he rightly calls out much opposition to gender ideology as itself an ideology (Loughlin 2018a: 12), but it would be wrong to think we are left in a cognitive stalemate where different theologies fling accusations of ideology at each other. There is no stalemate here because the binarists 'suppose nature dichotomous, structured by a series of dualities, such that what does not conform must be deemed "unnatural" or "unhealthy" rather than suppose nature more fluid and various' (Loughlin 2018). Why should nature not be more fluid and various? Both sides are committed to 'the real', but as Loughlin points out, '[T]he real is just what is in question, and the degree to which it comes into view through our looking, which is never less than interpretive' (Loughlin 2018).

Loughlin's essay confirms the argument of the present volume, which has found the male–female binary inadequate and injurious. He also exposes the harm that the binary inflicts on trans people in particular. No, it is not they who are Manichean (as O'Donovan suggests), who look on nature 'as something to be overcome rather than as a gift from God' (Loughlin 2018). Instead it is O'Donovan himself (and the conservative theologies that co-opt him)

> who refuses to accept nature as it comes to us, since he often refers to what nature gives as a defect, a departure from what he imagines to be a natural default, namely heterosexual dimorphism, whereby each one is either male or female and desirous of the sex one is not. But in point of fact nature is abundantly more diverse than this, and O'Donovan's default derives not from nature but from a certain reading of the Bible that leads him – at least in thought – to reject what nature gives. (2018)

The harmful assumption that gays, or intersex or trans people, are the result of a biological malfunction, is based on a binary that neither science nor nature supports. 'But instead we may say that the appearance of other forms tells us that nature is not heterosexually dimorphic, that it is more diverse than the logic of either/or suggests.'

Raby's distinctions regarding the theological appraisal of intersex people confirms this analysis. On the assumption that it is 'good' that there are intersex people, justification for that verdict was found in the action of God throughout creation as a whole and because genetic variation and diversity are constitutive aspects of how God formed creation and enables its freedom. Loughlin would agree with this, I think, reminding us that the doctrine of creation is not principally a narrative about cosmic origins but a metaphysical claim that creation as a whole and everything in it are sustained at every moment by the Creator who wills it to be and to become. 'This more metaphysical construal of creation may encompass the mythological story of beginnings, but the latter remains exactly that: a story about the meaning of the present rather than events in the past' (Loughlin 2018). We have many times in this book met the appeal to Genesis 1 to authorise the male–female binary. Not only is the appeal based on a misunderstanding of the actual text. It is a misunderstanding of the import of the doctrine of creation and the dynamic character of creation itself. Once the human continuum is allowed to replace the binary, the opportunity to disparage unusual bodies or same-sex desires falls away, for diversity is to be expected, not deplored. That said, many of us, however we identify or are identified by others, are going to need social, medical, and psychological support in our lives in order to live them fully and joyfully.

## Homosexuality and the Continuum

Much has been written about the theological legitimacy of same-sex relationships (and I have contributed to it; see Thatcher 2008, 2011). Here I confine myself to the grip that the heterosexual–homosexual binary appears to have upon many Christians and societies around the world. The binary is a subset of the male–female binary. We have already met the designation of homosexual people as 'psychic hermaphrodites'. By the beginning of the nineteenth century the male–female binary had taken such a hold that it seemed to follow that for a man even to desire another man was to behave like a woman, since – according to the binary – only women may licitly desire men. Like gender incongruence, we may believe that homosexuality too is rooted in biology, and that there are biological reasons, together with social and environmental influences, why individuals occupy different points along a spectrum of orientation. 'Gay affections', writes Gerard Loughlin, 'are indeed a modality of human nature, like the differences of sex: male, female, and intersex' (Loughlin 2015: 608). The binary has been read back into history by means of a pervasive 'presentism' – the 'tendency to introduce present-day assumptions and ideas into analyses and interpretations of the past' (Thatcher 2016: 84). There have always been intimate relations between men and men, and women and women, and social and theological attitudes to these have varied (see Vasey 1995), from the incorporation of 'the making of brothers' into liturgy (Boswell 1995), to capital punishment by drowning and 'burning without benefit of strangulation' (MacCulloch 2004: 623).

Remaining for a moment with the medical (and stigmatising) term 'homosexual', a medical and scientific narrative overlapping with that of the 'hermaphrodite' is now told, in which, once again, deviation from the binary is being replaced by the acceptance of a continuum. The statement of the Royal College of Psychiatrists (2018) (in a submission to the Church of England) may be taken as an example of current orthodox scientific opinion:

> Opposition to homosexuality in Europe reached a crescendo in the Nineteenth Century. What had earlier been regarded as a vice, evolved into a perversion or psychological illness … This unfortunate history demonstrates how marginalisation of a group of people who have a particular personality feature (in this case homosexuality) can lead to harmful medical practice and a basis for discrimination in society.

The statement continues, 'It would appear that sexual orientation is biological in nature, determined by genetic factors and/or the early uterine environment. Sexual orientation is therefore not a choice, though sexual behaviour clearly is.'

We recall 'a binary is a system or relation between two poles or opposites … a … system of classification … by which each group and sub-group is perpetually divided into two, the one with a positive and the other with a negative character'. The maintenance of the heterosexual–homosexual binary, guarantees the assumed negative character of lesbian and gay people and their relationships, and authorises the violence against them throughout the world. The sad story of Lizzie Lowe, the British teenager who committed suicide because she could not reconcile being Christian and gay (Church Times 2015), is testimony to the lethality of the binary when it is reproduced in the doctrine and practice of local churches in many denominations. 'I have personally known at least three young people who have killed themselves for similar reasons', writes a correspondent three years later, noting that the bishop who confirmed him killed himself a week later when the story of his having had sex with a rent boy became known (Church Times 2018). The binary has authorised the useless and immoral practice of conversion therapy, which severely damages the mental health of the persons who (voluntarily?) submit themselves to it. It is responsible for a serious breach of the human rights of lesbian and gay people throughout the world. Yet, as I hope this book by now has shown, it is based on theological mistakes that, however understandable, have disastrous consequences for victims. Once again the Euthyphro Dilemma helps to explain why holders of a dominant ideology are able to shrug off responsibility for the personal outcomes of their beliefs.

Consider next the continuum. The continuum has a right relation to science. It is partly a product of it, a product that, as Chris Cook noted, might be welcomed by Christians as a fine contribution to society. The growing view that homosexuality is 'a normal variant within the spectrum of human sexual experience' (Cook 2018: 2) should not generate yet another battle between science and faith. Rather, it illustrates the diversity of God's good creation, and by dissolving the negativity associated with homosexuality, it enables God's overflowing love to be more widely shared. The human continuum provides a plausible and believable theological anthropology with none of the deleterious outcomes of the binary, not least the 'scandalous' scapegoating of sexual minorities in the interests of religious party unity.

It is another mistake of the majority to think of homosexual people as all the same, just because they are not straight. They will actualise their freedom in different ways. Even Cardinal Ratzinger, in his notorious 1986 *Letter to the Bishops of the Catholic Church on the Pastoral Care of Homosexual Persons*, proclaimed that homosexual persons are persons. However, while 'the particular inclination of the homosexual person is not a sin', he continued, 'it is a more or less strong tendency ordered toward an intrinsic moral evil' and 'an objective disorder', so that 'the living out of this orientation in homosexual activity' cannot be 'a morally acceptable option' (Ratzinger 1986: para. 3). Since homosexual persons are persons, they have freedom, but cannot exercise it in 'homosexual activity'. They are indeed, then, in need of 'pastoral care', as the title of the letter makes clear, yet the only sort that can be provided is sympathy for the persons whose suffering, self-loathing, and repression the Letter helps to foster. 'Fundamentally, they are called to enact the will of God in their life by joining whatever sufferings and difficulties they experience in virtue of their condition to the sacrifice of the Lord's Cross' (1986: 12).

There are Catholics who are obedient to this teaching, as they are able. There are priests who are able to pour out the love that they might have shared with a beloved partner in the service of the Church of God and/or the congregations they serve, and remain fulfilled. There are priests and lay folk too who may boldly seek to redirect their love for a beloved other towards their love for Christ, and some, those who are sometimes brusquely named 'asexual' or who have low levels of *libido*, may shoulder the burden of celibacy without feeling its weight unduly. One can only think that as a voluntary offering their lives have a high value for God and for the people among whom they live. However, there are also many who set out to shoulder the burden believing it to be the will of God for them, and find that its weight is impossible to carry. Their sexuality may become distorted; they may seek refuge in clandestine and furtive liaisons. Their lives too have a high value for God, but for the church and the people around them, their contributions may be blighted, sour, and toxic as they become crushed by the weight they carry, and their mental and spiritual health is damaged. Then there are those who abandon their faith altogether because they know they cannot survive the cognitive and psychological dissonance it creates, or who remain within it, risking excommunication. The senses of isolation, loneliness, guilt, defeat, and failure are never far away. Is this what being a follower of Jesus is all about?

The theme of sacrifice is well known to Christians, who may find themselves in different circumstances called to suffer for their faith, and on occasion lay down their lives as their Saviour did for them. But that is no theodicy, or compensation for unnecessary suffering such as the binary teaching of conservative Christianity imposes upon its followers. The faith is there to enrich lives, not to ruin them; to bring joy, not pain.

## Bisexuality and the Continuum

Bisexuality is often considered a third sexual orientation occupying a midpoint on the gender continuum between gay and straight, but some bisexuals worry lest this way of categorising them preserves the binary, and along with it, the sense of fixity and lack of fluidity that comes with terms of identification. 'To deal with these issues', writes one bi theologian, 'my definition of a bisexual is someone for whom gender is not a barrier to sexual relations' (Lingwood 2010: 33). Between 4 and 10 per cent of men and 4 and 24 per cent of women report bisexual *attraction*, but they may not always act on it, or identify as bi. If the bisexual classification is by *behaviour* rather than attraction (i.e. by having same-sex and other-sex partners), then within the USA, 'around 1 per cent of men and 2.9 per cent of women fit this definition', though Kinsey placed it much higher (Robinson 2015: 641). We noticed earlier that more young people in the UK describe themselves as bisexual than gay or lesbian combined. Bi people 'cannot clearly signal our identity by our gender presentation or the sex of our partner – those of us in same-sex relationships, for example, are assumed to be gay or lesbian' (2015: 642–3). While bi people are stereotyped as promiscuous, most of them are in long-term monogamous relationships (2015: 643). Martha Daniels laments that bi Christians are 'Not Even on the Page' (the title of Daniels's essay, 2010), drawing attention to the hiatus in theological writing about bisexual people.

'[W]e are still barely acknowledged, and often simply another letter in the alphabet soup of inclusion' (Daniels 2010: 48).

The few theologians who write from a bi perspective agree the very existence of bi people challenges, and indeed falsifies, the heteronormative binary.

> Bisexual theologians view hierarchical binaries as separating us from one another, and ultimately, from God ... A theology that subverts hierarchical binaries such as man/woman, or heterosexual/homosexual is not easily folded into either mainstream, or gay/lesbian theologies. Indeed, for many, these categories are ontological and symbolic, created by God and reflective of God's likeness. (Robinson 2015: 651)

That 'mainstream' theology is inhospitable to bi people and their experience is a hard fact in the lives of bi Christians. Until recently the mainstream could ignore bi people, perhaps sensing the threat they pose to heteronormativity, and hoping that they would keep quiet or go away. But that isn't going to happen. The mainstream must quickly change its direction, or, to develop the metaphor, it must allow other rivulets and streams to flow into it so that its waters are richer and more diverse. We have seen in this book that there are no good theological reasons why the mainstream should resist bi people and their experience. Yes, the mainstream uses 'ontological' and 'symbolic' categories, but these can equally and plausibly be retained to give voice and expression to the human continuum to which bi people, being people, necessarily belong. Bi theology sees itself as rightly transgressive in opposing one of the binaries bi people cross. I'm hoping for a time when a more theologically inclusive, affirming, and – frankly – charitable, theological mainstream flows more broadly, and unblocks the narrower channels that would otherwise flow into it and enhance the quality of its living water.

Straight people, like this author, may be initially aghast at the claim that 'The bisexual person, whose sexual love is not limited by gender boundaries, is more open to an understanding that God's love is not limited to any one particular group. Indeed, to the extent that God's love extends to men and women, God can be called bisexual' (Lingwood 2010: 39). Yet reflection on this statement may equally evoke a sense of awe at the spiritual insight that has been given to those very bi people, who at the deepest level of their being, see themselves as existing beyond the particular limitations of gender. No, such persons are far removed from the objects of Vatican polemic who are engaged in sinful rebellion against the boundaries imposed by the 'order of creation'. This is the honest testimony of people speaking about themselves in the light of Christian self-understanding. That God might be thought of as bisexual may also elicit incredulity, but this too is misplaced as our study of the *imago Dei* has shown. God is imaged in 'male and female', not in 'male or female'. God's love, unlike our own, is not 'limited by the human boundaries that so concern humanity. God's love flows freely over our systems of limitation' (2010: 39). Of course God is above all gendered distinctions, including bisexuality, but there should be no shock at the thought of a bisexual God (symbolically of course) when the language of theology and liturgy provides a deluge of masculinist and heterosexual assumptions that go unnoticed and unremarked. As another bi theologian wrote, 'My theological claim, then, is that in the absence of a binary, either/or structure, God may be imaged in any way that is consistent with God's essential being, as much as we humans are able to know what God is and is not' (Daniels 2010: 51). Yet even as bi theologians speak for themselves, there is also caution about the aetiology of all sexual identities, including bisexuality. Margaret Robinson reminds her readers that 'identities such as lesbian, gay, and bisexual are heavily shaped by white supremacy' (Robinson 2015: 653), and we may also need to remind ourselves again that the very discourse(s) of sexuality is shaped by particular European circumstances that may not translate well (or even at all) into different cultures.

The mainstream must do better in embracing bi people. It is becoming less easy to ignore them, to pass over them in silence in the hope that dealing with the difficult questions they pose can be deferred a little longer. The misrepresentation of them, like that of trans people, as enemies of the church, is morally deficient, bearing false witness against the neighbour. The suggestion that their desires, in their 'misdirection' away from compulsory heterosexual norms, are evidence of cosmic disorder (i.e., the 'Fall') has no ground in Scripture or tradition, and is pastorally damaging if it is taken seriously. The assumption that bi people are promiscuous remains an assumption. The idea of the human continuum, the theological anthropology that gives rise to it, and the trinitarian God in whom we can all find ourselves, enables a new beginning.

## Public Spaces and the Continuum

The subtitle of the chapter is 'A Place for Everyone'. In this final section we consider some pressing questions about gender in *public* places and institutions – public toilets/restrooms; hospitals; sport and the armed services.

There is no better concrete representation of the male–female binary than segregated toilet facilities, and the semiotics that guide us into the 'right' ones. They are a creation of modernity, first appearing in Paris in the 1700s, and not until 1887 in the USA (Rhodan 2016). As the ideology of 'separate spheres' for men and women took hold – the public sphere for men, the private sphere for women – separate private spaces for women when and where they emerged into the public worlds of factory work and transport were gradually provided. Now, after the ideology of separate spheres has become weaker, the reasons for retaining separate rest rooms are said to be fourfold: the physical protection of women; the provision of sanitary facilities that only a single sex needs; privacy; and the protection of public morality (Kogan 2007). Increasingly public buildings such as churches, schools, and universities have unsegregated water closets for both sexes with a consequence that urinal basins and troughs that men in segregated conveniences are accustomed to use when urinating are lost. In many public buildings and on public transport where there are single closets, women and men share the same facilities.

The first of these grounds remains strong, not just in restrooms but everywhere else. It is necessary to understand the extent to which public lavatories still express and extend the male–female binary. It is the background to a more recent and ugly sociopolitical 'debate' about whether trans women should be legally permitted to use restrooms that are for the exclusive use of women, and trans men should be permitted to use men's facilities for the exclusive use of biological men. The obvious corollary of any prohibition is that trans women and men are not real women and men. In 2016 the 'Bathroom Bill' (as it became known) in North Carolina was passed, forbidding trans people to use facilities for people of their new gender, and several other states quickly followed suit. The very possibility of trans people using toilets that correspond to their new gender identity becomes the touchstone for anger about any perceived social weakening of the sexual binary. It becomes easy for conservative media to prey upon and contribute to fears about trans people, for example their supposed mental instability (Barnett, Nesbit, and Sorrentino 2018: 234), or about the greater likelihood of biological men impersonating trans women in women-only restrooms, in order to commit sex-related crimes or outrages of public decency. There is no evidence that 'granting transgender individuals access to gender-corresponding rest rooms results in an increase in sexual offenses' (2018: 238). It should be obvious that the segregated toilets, and not the trans people who use them, constitute the major part of the problem.

Within hospitals of the National Health Service in Britain, the binary line has been strengthened and enforced, due in part to negative publicity and fear attaching to any reported mixing of sexes in otherwise segregated accommodation. In 2010 it was felt necessary to monitor all 'breaches' of the same-sex accommodation rule, and while clinical reasons for exceptions remain, segregation has been further enforced. The policy is based on the right of every patient 'to receive high quality care that is safe and effective and respects their privacy and dignity' (NHS 2019: 1). There is to be 'a zero-tolerance approach to mixed-sex accommodation, except where it is in the overall best interest of all patients affected' (2019: 5). Trans people must be accommodated according to their presentation, whether or not they have undergone transition. 'Different genital or breast sex appearance is *not* a bar to this, since sufficient privacy can usually be ensured through the use of curtains or by accommodation in a single side room adjacent to a gender appropriate ward' (2019: 12–13). The policy strains to respect the diverse wishes of trans people faced with the binary choice of sleeping in a male or female ward.

Politicians and NHS managers have little choice but to respond to the public dislike of the mixing of the sexes in hospital wards, while at the same time respecting the rights of all patients, including trans patients. But this public dislike, and the fears that fan it, are not addressed. Key words in the present policy are safety, privacy, and dignity. Is the suggestion that mixed-sex wards are more likely to constitute dangers to women? There are undoubtedly female patients who will be horrified by the presence of men on their ward, especially if they have just been beaten up by one. While fear must be recognised, it also must not be exaggerated. The same reservation may attach itself to privacy and dignity as well. In the case of trans patients, curtains and side rooms are thought to provide some protection of privacy and dignity. Why then, should not curtains and side rooms protect the privacy and dignity to which all patients are entitled, if mixed-sex wards were instead to become commonplace? The unspoken issue here is likely to be extra-medical but deep-seated body shame that manifests itself in the fear of bodily, and especially genital, exposure. Christian ethics needs to address body shame, but hospitals – places of extraordinary vulnerability – do not provide the public space or the experimental conditions for confronting gendered social norms.

Trans prisoners face similar difficulties upon detention in British prisons. In 2018 there were 139 trans prisoners in prisons in the UK (HMPPS 2019: 2.1), and the evolving policy for the management and care of trans people includes intersex and non-binary people as well. On the one hand trans prisoners 'are able to self-declare that they are transgender and are supported to express the gender (or non-gender) with which they identify, with staff using correct pronouns' (HMPPS 2019: 3.4). On the other hand they 'must be initially allocated to part of the estate which matches their legally recognised gender' (HMPPS 2019: 4), and to wear the required clothing for that gender. There are exceptional circumstances where the initial requirement allocation can be waived. Prisoners who possess a Gender Recognition Certificate are legally required to be accommodated in facilities reserved for people with whom they share their new gender. Provision exists for Complex Case Boards to be convened when deciding further allocation or assessing risk both to the trans prisoner and the prisoners who share their facilities. The balanced assessment of risk is the central policy objective.

Christians have a big stake in the care of prisoners and in the entire reform of the prison system. Jesus himself identified with prisoners and taught that a visit to them was equivalent to a visit to him (Matt. 25.31–46). But, for the present, the custodial system is a binary one, and, as we shall see in the case of sport the system itself cannot cope adequately with non-binary people. In these circumstances the recognition of trans people and their particular needs is welcome. Adequate prison resources to secure the safety of all prisoners, and long-term education about the changing of the binary landscape inside and outside prisons, are clearly necessary.

## Sport, the Military, and the Continuum

Trans people, like many lesbian and gay people, undergo distress and discrimination in sport. Their participation in sport has been much scrutinised of late, but it must not be forgotten that lesbian and gay people remain in a similar position. Homophobia is rife in men's soccer, which explains why in the Association Football World Cup of 2018 there were no openly gay players, whereas in the Women's World Cup a year later there were at least 41 female players who were openly gay or bisexual. The heterosexual–homosexual binary is completely irrelevant to the performance of women and men in sport, and the disparity between openly gay men and women in the two competitions is probably due to the greater diversity in the fan base, less tribalism, and a more open and diversity-embracing atmosphere (ITV 2019). Racial abuse also remains common in association football.

The participation of trans women in sport organised for cis-gender women is the subject of much polarised controversy. Central to all competitive sports is the principle of *fairness*, considered as the absence of advantage, and it is widely held that trans women in particular, have a biological advantage over cis-gender women because 'high endogenous testosterone levels, are perceived to hold an advantage in sport (when testosterone has not been blocked to a cisgender female level)' (Jones et al. 2017: 702). In 2004 the International Olympic Committee (IOC) allowed trans women to take part in Olympic events if they had had gender-confirming surgery, could provide legal recognition of their gender, had been prescribed cross-sex hormone treatment for at least two years, and had lived in their experienced gender for the same time. The question arose in what respects the surgery was necessary, since having a penis conferred no physiological advantage (just as having one confers no sacramental advantage in the celebration of the Eucharist). In 2016, just prior to the Olympics in Rio de Janeiro, the IOC relaxed the rules for male-to-female trans athletes, leaving no restriction for trans men, removing the requirement for gender-confirming surgery, but retaining the regulation that trans women must have declared their gender as female for at least four years and have had their blood testosterone levels below a certain level (the figure given was 10 nmol/L) for at least a year before the competition.

More radically, Bethany Jones (et al.) argue there is *no* advantage to transgender women over cis-gender women in women's sport. They say 'men perform better than women in sport; however, no empirical research has identified the specific reason(s) why' (Jones et al. 2017: 713). While it is 'commonly believed' that high testosterone levels confer advantage, even here 'there is variation in how bodies make and respond' to it. Jones et al. confront the two-sex binary that lies at the basis of the organisation of many sports, and applaud the IOC for the limited steps they have taken in making it easier for trans people to take part. However, since there is no final set of definitions or characteristics that will settle the matter, it may never be resolved. Trans athletes expose the binary around which global sport is organised, advertised, and performed. The practice of fairness in sport is essential to its success, so it is right to struggle towards the fairest, or least unfair, procedures for sport to thrive, even if binary lines should prove variable and finally illusive to specify. Given what I have said about the human continuum I am not optimistic. It is necessary to raise awareness about who trans people are and the problems they encounter, including in sport, and the IOC has to some extent done this. In less competitive and more recreational sport, the admission of trans people, whether or not they have had surgery, should cause less or no controversy. Understanding difference is the key to living with it creatively. Strict adherence to the sporting binary can cause transphobia and needless discrimination. The theological framework developed around the single human continuum leaves no room for the dichotomy, while recognising that the global organisation of sport is based on it.

The Armed Forces, in Britain at least, have made great strides in dismantling the sex binary and the discrimination associated with it. All combat roles in the Armed forces are now open to women. The ban on LGBT personnel serving in the military was lifted in the year 2000. At the level of policy the UK Ministry of Defence professes a highly positive vision of diversity that 'harnesses the power of difference to deliver capability that safeguards our nation's security and stability' (MOD 2018: 2). Diversity and inclusion (D&I) are to be affirmed. Diversity is understood to be

> The ways in which we all differ including (but not limited to) our race, ethnicity, religion, beliefs, physical attributes, disabilities, sex, gender identity, sexual orientation, age, socio-economic background, life experiences (including marriage, civil partnership, pregnancy and maternity), skills and the way we think and do things. (MOD 2019: 10)

Inclusion is said to be 'the action of embracing these differences. Inclusion is about valuing and harnessing people's unique backgrounds, talents, perspectives and insights for the benefit of individuals and the organisation' (MOD 2019: 10). There is a moral case and a business case for D&I. The moral case is that it is 'absolutely right that our Armed Forces and Civil Service should appropriately reflect the society we exist to defend' (MOD 2019: 10). D&I 'is not just the right thing to do from a moral perspective, there is a clear business imperative for acting: diversity and inclusion contributes directly to operational effectiveness'. That is because

> a diverse and inclusive organisation is a stronger, healthier, more cohesive and resilient organisation. D&I drives performance, increases creative thinking and reduces the risks of group think – all of which are mission critical to meeting today's security challenges and threats. (MOD 2019: 11)

The military provides an example for the churches to follow. How sad that it were not the other way round! The theological analysis in Part III of this book is remarkably congruent with the changes that are happening here. There is little awareness of the striking congruity between a Christian ethic of gender and the attempts being made in the Armed Forces to formulate and implement an overall D&I policy, even – it must be said – among some of the chaplains who have a key role to play in its implementation. The moral perspectives behind the policy are self-consciously secular (however much there may be indebtedness to older religious values). The references to healthier organisations and to the dangers of 'group think' could hardly be more timely in the churches, still reeling over the abuse scandals and their attempted cover-up. An organisation confident in its diversity generates creativity. Even in the admission of continuing bullying, harassment, and discrimination within the Armed Forces, there is repentance, and in the determination to measure the success of the D&I policy against demanding objectives there exists faith and hope. Not only can the churches learn from the military, they have yet to become themselves a veritable 'Ministry of Defence', protecting us from exclusion and injustice, and keeping us safe from the damaging effects of homophobia, transphobia, misogyny, and heterosexism.

The continuum described in this and the previous chapter indicates that the persistence of the male–female binary is unnecessary for the maintenance of fidelity to the traditions of Christian theology. The binary harms people and does great damage. The continuum embraces everyone. In the next chapter we will examine the presence of the third binary in the book, and its baleful influence on both secular and religious thought.

CHAPTER 9

# *The Masculine–Feminine Binary and the Theological Critique of Culture*

## Problems with Masculine and Feminine Spiritualities

This chapter addresses the third binary of our inquiry, that between masculine and feminine. Remaining with the third aim of the book, 'to demonstrate how the human continuum enables a more inclusive theological understanding ... of relations between women and men', our probe of masculinity begins with two attempts to outline a practical spirituality based on male gendered characteristics. The first of these is Matthew Fox's *The Hidden Spirituality of Men*. The work opens with a comprehensive list of ills afflicting men in the 'dualistic patriarchy' of 'Western culture' (Fox 2008: xii). They are not in tune with their feelings; they work too hard; are often homophobic; and often believe in a male God who behaves in toxic – that is, in masculine – ways. The 'spiritual life' of men is 'in trouble' (2008: xiii) and their spirituality has become hidden (if not extinguished altogether). But Fox knows the cure. There is a 'Divine Feminine' and a 'Sacred Masculine'. Note the nominal form of the adjectives 'feminine' and 'masculine', reifying them. At times, the terms convey little more than one of the themes of this book, that God transcends all gendered characteristics. If we 'cannot receive a balanced sense of the gender of God (any statement on God is always a metaphor), then it follows that we are not living with a balanced gender sense *of ourselves*' (Fox 2008: xix, author's emphasis). But at other times, the divine Feminine is variously identified; with the rise of feminism, or the appearance of the Goddess Gaia, and so on. She has made 'a grand comeback' (Fox 2008: xviii), whereas the 'Sacred Masculine' is much less evident and can only be evinced by looking within.

Aiding men in their recovery of their true selves and their hidden spirituality is an extraordinary list of ten archetypes (including 'Father Sky: The Cosmos Lives!', 'The Green Man', 'The Blue Man', and 'The Earth Father: The Fatherly Heart'). Archetypes are eternal, whereas our

166

temporal appreciation of them falters. They are like energy fields which spark or ignite us into harmony with our most authentic selves. Within each of us (male or female) there is both a masculine and a feminine 'side'. The archetypes help us to achieve a 'sacred marriage' of our masculine and feminine sides. 'When the Sacred Masculine is combined with the sacred feminine inside each of us, we create the "sacred marriage" of compassion and passion in ourselves' (Fox 2008: xx). There are male and female archetypes. Fox explains 'A male archetype is not about men, nor are female archetypes about women, but all archetypes describe aspects of being human' (2008: xxi). They are 'stories' or 'images' by which 'men and boys, women and girls can relate to the masculine inside themselves' (2008: xxi). His female readers are asked, '[H]ow healthy are your masculine archetypes? Do you tell yourself stories that respect your own masculinity?' (2008: xxii).

Fox's use of the masculine–feminine binary is doubtless an extreme example of gendered spirituality, but I have chosen to refer to it in order to highlight some of the consequences that are likely to follow once one begins to outline a theological worldview that is actually built on exaggerated sexual difference. There is a casual essentialism about his use of 'men' as a class, but as his description of men as spiritually damaged is a recognisable stereotype of at least some men, I am inclined to let the charge of essentialism pass. There are more serious problems, for example, with the cosmic dualism that is endorsed by the 'Divine Feminine' and 'Sacred Masculine'. Cosmic dualism is arrived at by dividing up all commendable human qualities by means of sexual difference, and then projecting that difference onto the cosmos, so mirroring and exaggerating sexual difference instead of attending to the harmful effects of its exaggeration. The mediation (or even the existence) of archetypes (with deference to Carl Gustav Jung) must surely count as problematic, like the division of them into separate masculine and feminine categories. There is of course a well-known perception, almost universalised by popular psychology, of each human being having a masculine and a feminine side. This perception assumes and extends the male–female binary by intensifying it; by compressing it so that it is found within every human being. Whether a person is biologically male or female, on this view he or she is psychologically both. The key to the authentic self is the 'sacred marriage' of our masculine and feminine sides, mirroring the cosmic Divine Feminine and Sacred Masculine. Perhaps even worse, by looking within ourselves (instead of, say, right relation with other people or with the environment) the understanding of people as individuals, isolated from each other, remains too uncomfortably close to the modern, autonomous subject beloved by capitalism and consumerism alike.

Gendered ministry also intensifies sexual difference. Whereas the creation of safe spaces for particular ministries may require that the minister belongs to a particular sex (for example in ministry to victims of sexual abuse), the proliferation of 'Men's Ministries' in the United States is said to be a powerful signal to men 'to live up to the expectations of a dominant and cis-heteronormative masculinity that perpetuates patriarchal norms in family and civic life' (Berra 2018: 28). The late James Nelson (who died in 2015) was very aware of the damage that dominant and heteronormative masculinity did to men as well as women. He was a pioneer in what he called 'sexual theology', writing movingly and originally about the spirituality of the male body (and much else in the area of sexuality). I admire his work and have learned much from it, but, in pursuing the continuum idea, I want to persist with the question raised by Nelson, particularly in his work *The Intimate Connection*, whether there is a 'body theology' that can be based on the sexed body rather than on the human body. Nelson thinks there is. Is there, as Fox also thinks, a distinctive masculine spirituality? Nelson critiques the notion of 'generic man'. This is the historical 'doctrine of man', which is not only constructed by men, its abstract character means it operates above both masculine and feminine bodily experience. 'When we have assumed the stance of "generic man"', he writes, 'the stance in which male lives are presumed to be the norm for *human* lives, we have not only lost understanding of women's experience, we have also lost knowledge of men's experience insofar as it is specifically *men's*' (Nelson 1992: 18, author's emphasis). Thirty years on (the first edition was published in 1988), the time may have come to continue to appreciate Nelson's work historically while querying some of his assumptions. The notion of generic man *is* the creation of men and the bracketing out of experience is what almost all male theologians have done in historical discussion of the sources of revelation. But the claim Nelson makes (remember he writes for men here while sympathetic to feminism) is that there is gendered human experience derivable from our sexed bodies that gives rise to a 'masculine spirituality' that the generic idea of 'man' or 'men' excludes. There is also a feminine spirituality deriving from the female body, which he (wisely) makes no attempt to describe.

Necessarily, if there are spiritualities based on biological difference, then sexual organs are at the root of both, and here Nelson has original insights about penises, or specifically about the difference between the phallus (the erect penis) and the penis when soft. 'Phallus' though, easily becomes a synonym for any old masculine behaviour where power and domination are emphasised. An intercontinental missile or a sky-scraper building is straight and erect, but they are not phalluses, even if a phallic character is assigned to them on the basis that they are exemplars of male power, of the domination of nature, or of potent destruction. Men 'tend to undervalue penis and overvalue phallus' (Nelson 1992: 94). The vitality, energy, and power of the phallus can be rightly celebrated, he thinks, but it is over-celebrated against the penis. That men also have testicles provides them with salutary reminders of their vulnerability:

> Phallus bears intimations of life and vigor, while penis bears intimations of mortality. Fearing mortality, men tend to reject the qualities of penis and project them upon women who are then seen to be small, soft, and vulnerable, qualities inferior to the phallic standard. Wrinkles, so typical of penis, are not permitted in women if they are to retain their womanly attraction. (Nelson 1992: 95)

There is a point at which, I think, the phallus–penis contrast is psycho-logised into improbability. That point happens when death and resurrec-tion are associated, respectively, with the penis and the phallus, and the woman after heterosexual coupling is 'somehow associated with the "reducing" the phallus [*sic*] to flaccidity' (Nelson 1992: 103). However, Nelson insists there is power in the penis as well as the phallus, and the integration of both constitutes masculine spirituality:

> ... the penis has a different kind of power ... What was once hard and imperious is now soft and gentle. In both dimensions the man is experienc-ing his masculine power, and both are aspects of relational power. True power is mutuality, making claims and absorbing influence. It is different from the "mutuality" of external relatedness, which trades in force, com-promise, and accommodation. (Nelson 1992: 103)

There are some minor issues here along with some major ones. There are two kinds of mutuality, for instance, one of which is the amalgamation of phallic and penile qualities within the individual man. Does it not take at least two people for mutuality to occur? The connection between the phallus and resurrection, and the penis with death, while commonly asserted, is subliminal, and so unlikely to feature in conscious thought. Are the 'soft' qualities of the penis consciously projected onto women? But among the major difficulties are these. Women generally lack power in relation to men. Is this lack of power now to be understood as a lack of a penis (as their sexed bodies would seem to confirm)? Is this a new use for the antiquated term 'penis-envy'? *Sharing* power is the issue, not 'phallicising' it. Another difficulty is that the phallus and the penis, while different modes of the same male organ, become constructs at some distance from the male genitals and the experience of them. When my penis is soft, I am not valuing it at all because I am unaware of it (unless I'm using it as the excretory organ that it is). Yes, it is essential that men generally learn to become more gentle, irrespective of the angle of their penises. When their penises are hard, they should still be gentle, appropriately, with them.

References to genitalia are crude, but unavoidable if there is to be a distinct spirituality based exclusively on the sexed body. What seems to be needed is the redemption of all human bodies from patriarchal constructions that reduce them to roles or functions, or which fail to conceive them as necessarily related (albeit differently) to other bodies. Back in Chapter 6 we noted the criticism of Katie Grimes regarding the theological construction of bodies, summarised in the statement that, 'What the penis/sperm is, so is man; what the vagina/ovum is, so is woman.' It is possible to link the very idea of natality to the being of women (and mortality to the being of men)(Jantzen 1998). Different constructs are needed that avoid assumptions of superiority and the cloaking of inevitable violence. In particular the basic dualism that men are active and women receptive must be removed. If we are going to have a genital theology, it may be possible to theorise the vagina as a place of welcome, a gentle enveloper, an active embracer, a paradigm of openness to the other, as the very gateway to life (and not 'the Devil's gateway' as Tertullian referred, to women), and so on. My worry, however, is that these are romantic masculine and feminine constructs, which, while challenging sexist ideology, cause the same ideology to reappear in a new guise. If women are to flourish, they also need some of the qualities associated with the phallus – they too need power, to be firm and up for it, especially when protecting themselves from patriarchal violence. There is much they need to penetrate. And men need qualities associated with the vagina, to be able to welcome what is other, to envelop (e.g. to hug) their comrades, to be soft and receptive (most of the time), to affirm their natality (but with a difference), and so on. Not even Jesus qualifies as a model of masculinity, since it is his humanity, not his masculinity, that guarantees his solidarity with all of us (and so, in accordance with Christian doctrine, saves us).

To think, then, of masculinity and femininity as a continuum avoids stereotypes. It also affirms particularity and avoids androgyny. In the end 'masculine' and 'feminine' are morally useless terms. There is no need to classify behaviour or appearance in this way. The terms become redundant. Too often, they perpetuate stereotypes and make no contribution to gender justice. For all its situatedness in an African tribe, Bourdieu's contempt for the very idea of femininity still rings true. Women, he wrote,

> exist first through and for the gaze of others, that, as welcoming, attractive and available *objects*. They are expected to be 'feminine', that is to say, smiling, friendly, attentive, submissive, demure, restrained, self-effacing. And what is called 'femininity' is often nothing other than a form of indulgence towards real or supposed male expectations, particularly as regards the aggrandizement of the ego. (Bourdieu 2001: 66)

No one is expected to embody all the different ways of being a man and a woman. Everyone might reasonably be expected to live out their relations by embodying human virtues. A *human* spirituality is required, and differently lived. Even as we attempt it, it will already be a product of social, cultural, racial, intellectual, and religious facticities which have gone into the shaping of each of us.

## Secular Culture and Femininity

The discussion of femininity here will not be based on, for example, the role of Mary in the life of Catholic women, or on alleged roles for women deemed to be biblical. Adrienne Evans and Sarah Riley's *Technologies of Sexiness* (2015) analyses the cultural conditions within which at least some women in the West arrive at some sense of their gendered selves. Theirs is a secular work, by women, about women, and for women, which has no mention of religion, theology, or spirituality in its pages. I think their sociological analysis is more useful to theology than peering inwards, fastening on to archetypes, or getting to grips with our opposite psychological sex supposedly within ourselves. Women, they say, develop their sexual selves 'through a process in which individuals navigate and negotiate master narratives of sexual minority identity', and 'these master narratives are apparent in discourse that is publicly available' (Evans and Riley 2015: viii). There are said to be three distinct but well-integrated master narratives that problematise women's sexuality – neoliberalism, consumerism, and post-feminism. The first of these 'is a form of governance that argues that market forces, rather than state intervention, should be allowed to drive the economy' (2015: 3). It requires citizens 'to think of themselves as autonomous individuals responsible for their own welfare: a standpoint that requires them to engage in self-surveillance in order to implement necessary acts of transformation' (2015: 3).

Aiding neoliberalism are the 'psy-disciplines' or the 'psy-complex'. They 'make sense in the context of a neoliberal project because they allow us to define ourselves in individualistic, self-governing ways. From the language of psychology, the social context in which a person lives is reduced to the immediate context of interpersonal relations, locating any personal, social, or health problems, and their attendant solutions, within the individual' (Evans and Riley 2015: 9). Consumption was promoted 'as a means by which individuals could exercise the autonomy and freedom of neoliberal subjectivity and develop their own "choiceful biography", creating a life narrative articulated through the possession of goods' (2015: 9). Neoliberalism and consumerism are said (following Zygmunt Bauman and others) to combine to heighten certain freedoms, 'but these freedoms are primarily exercised through consumption, either of goods or of less tangible resources, such as gym memberships and other entertainment and leisure practices' (2015: 10). In the realm of sexuality, the latest vibrators and the public availability of Viagra, without prescription, demonstrate the process well. The first offers the (ultimately false) hope of intense 'autonomously created pleasure' (2015: 10) without the inconvenience of relationship, while the second offers the dubious possibility of renewed orgasmic experience without the inconvenience of attending to the likely relational causes of erectile difficulty.

Into this cultural and political context 'post-feminism' arrives as a trivialisation and corruption of the achievements of earlier feminists. Evans and Riley characterise it more as a 'form of sense-making that incorporates neoliberal constructs of subjectivity and the centrality of consumerism in individual biographies to articulate a particular form of contemporary femininity' (Evans and Riley 2015: 13). The female body now becomes 'a marker of successful femininity' as never before. 'Consumer practices and products oriented around beauty have increased exponentially, requiring time, effort, money, and skill' (2015: 14). In this consumption-driven market, hyper-femininity is highly prized yet never achieved, not least because what was called (since 1975) 'the male gaze' – in which women present themselves as objects of male pleasure – is partly replaced by the *female* gaze, by which women assess their appearance, often cruelly, in relation to other women. For feminism, sexualised culture remains 'a cultural space for resisting objectification', whereas for post-feminism it is a space 'for both reproducing the male gaze and producing a narcissistic neoliberal self-policing gaze' (2015: 32). The discourse of feminism emphasising freedom, empowerment, and agency is stolen by neoliberalism and consumerism, and re-presented through popular media into an

irresistible rhetoric that markets endless products for individuals to pur-
chase in order to achieve hyper-femininity. But more subtly it taps into
and heightens neoliberalism as a master narrative, as a dominant form of
'sense-making', even as the same narrative offers shrunken opportunity for
meaningful freedom at all. The 'rebranding' of Brazilian waxes makes the
point well, 'implying that the practice of genital hair removal is a personal
choice rather than a culturally defined notion of beauty and sexiness'
(2015: 33), doubtless aided by the ubiquity of shaven pubes in internet
pornography. Other examples include breast augmentation, vaginal cos-
metic surgery, and other 'doing-it-for-me' choices that instead invite
alternative analyses of false-consciousness, or the uncritical internalisation
of shifting cultural norms. In conclusion the authors assert,

> Taking up neoliberal subjectivities that require people to create a sense of
> self through consumerism and lifestyle thus sets people up to fail, while
> encouraging them to locate these failures as their own individual failures (to
> consume appropriately) rather than as failures of the social structure, or in
> the logic of neoliberalism itself. (2015: 133)

## Perverse Holiness

*Technologies of Sexiness* is most helpful to theology, since it is an example of
a compelling analysis of the powerful and detrimental cultural influences
on people generally and women in particular in First World societies. It
interprets, in general and obviously controversial terms, the social realities
within which at least some women live their lives. This is the sort of social
criticism that theology can gratefully accept because it offers a different
form of sense-making to that of neoliberalism in all its guises. It can
welcome these distressing accounts of the lived realities of some women
yet interpret them very differently. There is a belief system (or at least an
authentic version of it) that addresses this cultural situation directly, and a
society of justice-seeking members (the church!), part of whose *raison d'être*
is to provide an attractive counter-culture to the one just outlined. In *Sex,
Gender and Christian Ethics*, Lisa Cahill, sympathetic to many of the
feminist criticisms of the Christian tradition, observed that 'Christian
morality can fund strong criticism of sexual and reproductive behaviour,
gender expectations, and family forms which dominate women' (Cahill
1996: 1). Strong theological and ethical criticism of secular culture is long
overdue, 'funded' by the very academic capital that the Christian tradition
actually provides. It is high time the churches went on the offensive against
the ideologies of the body that in First World societies perpetuate injustice

and often cause both physical and mental suffering. Sadly, few people want to hear the churches say anything about sexuality and gender, because of the content and the tone of what they have already heard and seen.

Feminism sought to enhance the freedom and agency of women, and to empower them to overcome the constraints of a patriarchal era. But the secular, neoliberal culture, does not honour the achievements of feminism. It steals them. It co-opts freedom, empowerment, and agency for its own ends. In this it becomes a 'pseudo-patriarchy', uncomfortably similar to earlier thought-worlds that achieved the subservience of women by other means. The neoliberal person is highly autonomous. Whereas the Cartesian subject was essentially a mind contingently attached to a body, the neoliberal subject is essentially a body contingently attached to a mind. Both are dualist. One is a reversal of the other. The female subject explored in *Technologies of Sexiness* is permanently anxious about her appearance and self-image, and this anxiety is not confined to women. I see this as a *reversal of holiness*, a perverse mirror-image of an authentic Christian spirituality that honours all bodies and just relations between them. A good case can be made for saying the neoliberal culture is a perverse continuation of Christian spirituality by its reversal of several characteristics of the latter. In the latter, there is a tempered seeking of completeness of the person (for example, in the 'Be perfect' injunction of Jesus in Mt. 5.48): in the former, there is a perverse seeking of perfection in the most perfect body, defined by cruel and unstable stereotypes of feminine beauty, requiring intense effort and expense. The stereotypes normally require their adoring followers to be white, young, thin, firm, smooth, and affluent (and frequently, partially naked when in public view). Since most women are not like this, and those who are, are not like it for long, the club of beauty is fiercely exclusive.

Here are three more characteristics of Christian spirituality, perversely continued and remodelled by the secular culture. Second, the club of beauty *excludes*. It has many aspirants but few members. The club invites comparison with certain religious groups, whose identity is secured at the price of excluding most people as 'other'. Their boundary walls are high, even though their posters proclaim 'a warm welcome awaits you'. Third, a stronger comparison may be made between the women who internalise the male gaze in post-feminism, and women who internalise the male understanding of women as women in most of the history of Christianity. The female gaze, as post-feminism explains it, leading to self-surveillance and further internalisation of stereotypes, is more than an echo of earlier thought-worlds in which women understood themselves through the master narratives of men. There are uncomfortable parallels between the self-surveillance required by post-feminism and the self-surveillance once required of women within a masculine Christian culture. But, fourth, *the strongest parallel is to be found in the very masculine–feminine binary itself.* The public world of consumerism exploits sexual difference relentlessly. It constantly exaggerates it, rebrands it, and plays with it. The sale of its myriad products depends on the continuous renewal and exaggeration of sexual difference, of ever-shifting icons of femininity and masculinity. The binary is very deeply rooted in the socio-cultural worlds it describes. The ideal types of both femininity and masculinity it generates are harmful. They invite counter-cultural analysis and an experience of the body that offers real freedom, empowerment, and agency.

### Sexualisation, Schooling, and Parenthood

We now know that the early sexualisation of girls can cause real harm to them. The American Psychological Association (APA) says the sexualisation of girls occurs when any of the following indicators are present: when 'a person's value comes only from his or her sexual appeal or behavior, to the exclusion of other characteristics'; when 'a person is held to a standard that equates physical attractiveness (narrowly defined) with being sexy'; when 'a person is sexually objectified – that is, made into a thing for others' sexual use, rather than seen as a person with the capacity for independent action and decision making'; and when 'sexuality is inappropriately imposed upon a person' (APA 2006: 1). The APA reported that 'virtually every media form studied provides ample evidence of the sexualization of women, including television, music videos, music lyrics, movies, magazines, sports media, video games, the Internet, and advertising' (2007: 1).

A feature of sexualisation, the report continues, is the 'narrow (and unrealistic) standard of physical beauty', while 'the models of femininity presented for young girls to study and emulate' are deeply unsatisfactory. Parents may 'convey the message that maintaining an attractive physical appearance is the most important goal for girls. Some may allow or encourage plastic surgery to help girls meet that goal' (ASA 2006: 2). A sinister consequence of sexualisation is that when girls 'think of themselves in objectified terms', they 'sexualize themselves'. We have already met this process when noting the reversal of the male gaze. 'Self-objectification', continues the report, is 'a key process whereby girls learn to think of and treat their own bodies as objects of others' desires' (2006: 2). The 'negative effects' of sexualisation have been amply demonstrated 'in a variety of domains, including cognitive functioning, physical and mental health, sexuality, and attitudes and beliefs'. 'Frequent exposure to media images that sexualize girls and women affects how girls conceptualize femininity and sexuality. Girls and young women who more frequently consume or engage with mainstream media content offer stronger endorsement of sexual stereotypes that depict women as sexual objects' (2006: 3).

Once again the devastating impact of exaggerated sexual difference is demonstrated. The damage to boys is also likely to be considerable. They may be socialised into competitive, aggressive, and violent behaviour endlessly repeated in video games and violent sports. Their respect for the full humanity of women is likely to be impaired. Once girls conform to culturally manufactured models of femininity, boys are able to differentiate more readily between what masculinity is and is not – that is, it is the opposite of femininity (as opposite-sex theory dictates). The more girls are objectified the less respect they receive, while to be 'truly masculine' is to dominate all supposedly inferior beings – women, gays, people of colour, aliens, trans people, and so on. A perverse kaleidoscope of images and a perverse cacophony of voices combine to create a toxic environment that causes acute difficulties for adolescents, unsure of their newly forming selves and culturally prompted by destructive images to guide them. The culture appears to prefer the sexualisation of girls to their full humanisation.

The subtle origins of the exaggeration of sexual difference begin at birth, or in the case of selective abortion even before it. My next example of exaggerated sexual difference is less lurid but more subtle. Javid Abdelmoneim has demonstrated how sexual difference and its intensification are encouraged in primary schools. Working for five weeks on a television documentary for the British Broadcasting Corporation, with a supportive, self-critical, gifted, male teacher in a mixed class of seven-year-old children in an English school, he found out for himself that boys believe themselves to be better than girls, stronger, cleverer, and better at being in charge and at sports. All this, of course, is well known. Less well known is that the girls also believe these things, massively underestimating themselves and in particular their physical strength. Psychometric tests showed the boys had more self-esteem and self-confidence than girls. Girls were better at resisting impulses to act (i.e., to be aggressive). Boys were more lacking than girls in the ability to express empathy and emotion (and even to provide a vocabulary for it). Boys were better at spatial awareness. Boys and girls had gendered expectations about masculine and feminine careers. They expressed joyful surprise to meet a male dancer and a female car mechanic. There were features of the teacher's interaction with the children, of the class library, and even the classroom furniture that subtly reinforced gender difference. The teacher addressed boys with 'Mate' and 'Fella', and girls with 'Love' and 'Sweetpea'. In observation the teacher was found to have endeared himself to girls twice as much as to boys. The books in the 'gender-based bookcase' mainly celebrated male superheroes, made so by their competitive and aggressive behaviour, though there were also some books about passive princesses. Boys and girls hung their outdoor clothing in separate cupboards.

Similar scenarios can be expected in countless junior classrooms throughout the world, and the scenarios themselves are constructions with damaging consequences for the girls and the boys. Girls have the same amount of muscle mass and physical strength as boys (and a simple strength test demonstrated this, to some boys' distress). Neuroimaging of the brains of boys and girls aged seven, it was explained, revealed *no* observational differences, despite the popular belief that their brains are different. Rather, brains are more plastic and 'mouldable' than previously thought. They are not fixed and variant but are 'entangled with society' even as they try to accommodate the 'tsunami of pink and blue' that confronts them daily. Boys are directed to play more with toys like Lego which may account for their greater spatial awareness. A related experiment showed adults' selection of children's toys depended strongly on the adults' preconceptions of what boys and girls preferred.

Parenthood is a supremely important and potentially rewarding task, even vocation, for the people who are capable of, and who desire it. I suggest the insistence of different roles for fathers and mothers has done huge damage to parenthood as an institution. There is a bonding between mother and child during pregnancy and breast-feeding that remains a mystery to men. And herein lies the danger: that of assuming that nurture of the young is something that women do – a mystery, like being pregnant. Insofar as mothers play a role in child care and nurture that men cannot play, it is easy to assume that child care and nurture are activities that can be gendered feminine. But this allows too many fathers to ignore their responsibilities to their children, to justify minimal or no involvement with their children's upbringing and the much-needed support their mothers need. It wrongly justifies the lack of progress in Western societies of restructuring work so that fathers have more time for their families and mothers have more time and opportunity to seek meaningful work outside the home. While there is good evidence that some men are taking more responsibility for child care and home maintenance, there are also millions of biological fathers who have little or no interest in the mothers of the children they co-produce, or in the children themselves. While this is morally deplorable, the assumption that having and caring for children is gendered feminine actually gives credence to paternal indifference. Everyone loses, including fathers, since being an active loving father can be one of the most exciting and humanising long-term activities with which a man can engage.

## An Alternative Theological Culture

Four times in the previous section I have consciously stepped outside my familiar theological comfort zone in considering, all to briefly, the socialisation of women in neoliberalism, the 'sexualisation' of girls, the gendering of classrooms, and the feminisation of parenthood. I am strongly suggesting that the exaggeration of sexual difference is still causing havoc, even in societies that pride themselves on having achieved full equal rights for minorities and gender equality. Humanisation matters: masculinisation and feminisation do not. Gender is not merely a problem for churches to postpone. It is a menace throughout the world and cannot be dumped on the Third World as a problem 'not our own'.

The female subjects of *Technologies of Sexiness* find late modern notions of femininity an undoubted burden. Heather Widdows speaks of a devastating 'epidemic of body-image anxiety' among young people that stops them going out, speaking up, exercising in public, and so on, adding, 'If there was a recreational drug or a video game that had the same effect, we would be banning it' (Widdows, cited in McDonald 2018). The 'failure in beauty', she says, causes shame, which in turn affects 'the whole of one's sense of self'. The arrival of the internet, the smart phone, and the proliferation of social media networks has led inevitably to a heightening of the visual culture. Since materialism is inevitably visual, physical appearance becomes overvalued and failure in appearance becomes stultifying. The Children's Society (in the UK) found 'deeply worrying' (in 2018) that 'at age 14, 1 in 5 girls – and almost half of children saying that they have been attracted to the same or both genders – have self-harmed'. Children, they say, 'should not be expected just to "brush off" criticism that is related to being different. This does not need to be part of growing up' (Children's Society 2018: 22).

Thankfully there are occasional Christian initiatives that address the problem. Rachel Treweek, a Church of England bishop, launched her widely reported 'Liedentity' campaign (*#liedentity* on Twitter) in February

2018. Treweek was galvanised into action by the finding that 60 per cent of girls opt-out of everyday activities because of how they think they look, and around half of adolescent boys are unhappy with their bodies (Diocese of Gloucester 2018). She explained, 'Increasingly, many young people are sourcing their identities from social media and advertising, and in the process losing their self-esteem, which is one of the reasons why our campaign is called *#liedentity*.' Addressing the problem of low self-esteem directly, participants are encouraged to use social media to post a picture of their friends or family on social media, sharing one thing they value about that person, using the hashtag *#say1thing*. Treweek introduced the campaign with the simple words,

> I long for every young person to discover their worth as a unique individual created in the image of God and to find happiness as they go on becoming who they have been created to be.
>
> We are bombarded with messages of what the 'perfect body image' is, and for many this undermines true identity. We know that for these young people having negative thoughts about how they look can impact on their entire life, causing deep unhappiness and contributing to poor mental health. (Diocese of Gloucester 2018)

Liedentity provides a fine example of micro-resistance to the harmful effects of consumerism and sexualisation on young persons, their bodies and souls. 'Barefaced Breakfasts' is another initiative that aims at helping women to overcome the 'beauty myth'. Chine McDonald invites church-women to breakfasts with no make-up on (a gendered ministry with real justification). She notes how make-up is often worn as a mask: 'time and again', she writes, 'I have seen women enter these breakfasts trying to hide themselves away, and leave with their heads held high. It is because they have been part of a community of women ready to fight the beauty myth together' (Church Times 2018).

All the arguments in this book regarding the image of God, and about what constitutes identity provide strong support for Treweek's introduction. Indeed the Christian faith offers a vision of life so sharply at odds with the consumerism just described that it mirrors Paul's lurid accounts of wrestling with principalities and powers, and his depiction of the opposition of flesh and spirit. The body, then, is central to the neoliberal culture. That is a further similarity with Christianity, both in this life and also in the next. But is there a stable vision of God's future for us in the next life, one sufficiently concrete to be inspirational and teleological at the same time, and that gives direction to our bodily, and so our gendered, living in the present? That seems a hopelessly abstract question after the concrete realities of the previous section, but Patricia Beattie Jung answers it positively and relevantly. Writing about 'sex on earth as it is in heaven' (the title of her latest book) she provides a sustained argument that there *will* be sex in heaven. She assembles a list of well-known theologians who agree that 'bodily pleasures could characterise our life to come', and that

> Those in sacramental partnerships on occasion even now may taste of such graces. Sexuality may not be annihilated, but rather 'newly clothed' . . . The relational and creative ends for which sexuality is designed will be gloriously fulfilled and sanctified. This vision of the great communion with God and each other that is to come – far from increasing the risk that sex will be idolized – constantly upholds our earthly passions to this holy standard. (Jung 2017: 67)

Since procreation is no longer needed, our bodies, including our genitals, might still be able to express the intimacy, tenderness, and oneness that we known fleetingly on earth. The hope expressed by the 'no longer male and female' phrase of Galatians 3.28 may be realised by the absence of all gender binaries, where 'Neither intersex nor transgender would be presumed to be embodied expressions of sin; neither would they be left behind, untransformed by grace' (Jung 2017: 114). Still more tentatively, 'There might well be among the saints some kind of holy polyamory imitative God's own radically inclusive, yet absolutely steadfast and fully attentive, way of loving' (2017: 116). '[W]e may taste and glimpse now, through God's grace, in some of our experiences of sexual desire and delight, what we will enjoy in full in the life of the world to come' (2017: 117).

This is an attractive vision with a clear ethical obligation: love now as you will love hereafter. Our concern in this book is with gender rather than with sexuality, but the depiction of sexed bodies in the afterlife may well have gendered implications for life in the present. The chapter began with a discussion of the difficulties involved in seeking to establish a way of Christian living that was appropriately masculine or feminine, suggesting instead a *human* spirituality freed up from a binary understanding of the human. Here, I think, Jung's vision of heaven, of an eschatological community, begins the task of picturing what Christians should be striving for in relation to gender. She gently observes that while the depiction of a future life that includes sexual love is a theological construction, so is the traditional, sexless one. One advantage of her vision of sex in heaven is that it folds convincingly into several doctrinal themes (that have been restated here in earlier chapters). She thinks the sexless view of eternity rests on 'inadequate accounts of the way God has designed humans for communion in and through the body, in all its parts', so it is for 'deeply theological reasons' that 'the denial of a transformed experience of sexual desire and delight in the life to come is inconsistent with the heart of the Christian gospel' (Jung 2017: 100).

In particular, the basic conviction about God, that God is Love, surely suggests that communion with God includes love for one another, and since we have transformed bodies in the next life, why should our loving not be transformed there too? There will be desire in the next life, but it will be desire purified of the urge to objectify and dominate, willing instead one's own good and the good of the beloved 'other'. The further conviction that God is a Trinity of co-equal Persons must be allowed to suggest that human persons, when they are transformed beyond this life, may relate to one another in a manner dimly analogous to the relations within God, called in the tradition *perichoresis* or *circumincession* (and sometimes traced back to the Greek root meaning 'dance'). As we noted earlier there is diversity within God, just as there is full equality. The heavenly fulfilment of God's love may be mimetically present wherever autonomy and relationality are in balance; where we no longer need to measure our happiness through consumption; where our bodies will no longer be required to shape up to the latest images of masculine and feminine beauty, reduced to objects or exploited. There will be no male gaze (and no female gaze as its reversal) since gazing on bodies will instead inspire admiration and delight. The determining gaze will be the loving gaze of God upon all God's creatures, affirming and rejoicing in them. There will be no need to resist objectification, since we will be in communion with each other. Sex in heaven is sex without the inequalities and imbalances of power accompanying sex on earth. All this constitutes further reflection on Paul's contention that the work of God in Christ entails a new beginning in inter-human relations now, and in particular that 'there is no longer male and female'.

## Gender Justice and Christian Virtue

Whether in heaven or on earth, there must be community for gender justice to be practised. 'Gender justice refers to the ending of inequalities between men and women, and the provision of redress to overcome these inequalities.' It requires three things in order to exist: 'recognition of the equality of women and men'; 'representation of women in institutions and decision-making positions'; and 'redistribution of economic wealth so that women can overcome the economic structures that prevent them from full participation in social life' (Hodgson 2017: 338). It is to be distinguished from *gendered* justice, when issues of gender are already viewed through 'gendered lenses' that 'reinforce patriarchal gender stereotypes, and may hinder attempts to facilitate gender justice' (2017: 337). Here I am uneasy, since 'gendered lenses' are always available, and I might be wearing them! They may be distorting my own vision, romanticising and (continuing the ocular metaphor) rendering picturesque and tranquil the huge struggle still required to achieve gender justice socially, ecclesially, and globally.

Whether the Christian community can ever be a chief agent for, and chief exemplification of, gender justice is beyond the remit of this book. I have tried to outline some of the theology available to forge the 'radical new Christian inclusion in the Church' (Archbishop of Canterbury 2017) that the Archbishop of Canterbury says he and the Church of England are determined to work towards, and that may already have been ushered in (or not) by the publication of a document, provisionally entitled *Living in Love and Faith*, by the time this book is published. I'm mindful of Bourdieu's contemptuous jibe at Butler's advocacy of individual resistance by 'act[s] of performative magic' and spurious 'subversive voluntarism'. Individual micropolitics are never enough. But there is disillusion, too, in both Bourdieu's and Butler's acceptance of the sheer weight and extent of patriarchy and heteronormativity stifling all voluntarist opposition to it. Cooperation between men and women in all the faiths, opposing versions of faith that separate them as fundamentally different and then exploiting the differences, is urgently needed, for justice to be obtained. Sharing power is the way to a more gender-just social order, but since men generally have more of it than women, conflict is inevitable.

Each of us inherits the exaggerated social practice of sexual difference, so our lives will already have been shaped by it. To some extent, at least, we will have internalised, naturalised, and operationalised it. From each unique starting point we may be attempting our own living out of gender justice within all the groups to which we belong. I have tried to show in this book that the male–female, heterosexual–homosexual, and masculine–feminine binaries tend to be harmful, and often result in violence. I have also offered an alternative view, a more plausible theological anthropology, which incorporates sex and gender difference, and that we exist within and along a continuum. This alternative account of ourselves, made, sustained, and redeemed by a loving God, requires no major theological innovation whatsoever, since it rests on doctrinal assumptions basic to Christian self-understanding. Indeed the masculine–feminine binary hardly needs representation in the human continuum since it is a shadow of the male–female binary and perpetuates it. The biggest step the churches could take towards gender justice is to allow their theological thinking to be determined by the doctrinal prompts I have suggested in this work. They are not mine at all, of course. They belong to the heritage of all Christians already. I have merely reread and reconsidered them. I have tried to show how the human continuum contributes to peace in all three areas of gender specified earlier – in the relations between women and men, in our symbolic systems of thought, and in our own gender identities.

It has been suggested to me in conversation that the theological method that I like to use, and have used in this and the previous two chapters, is open to at least two difficulties. The first difficulty is that I find in Christian doctrines only what I want to find, so that the handling of, say, the image of God, the doctrine of the Trinity, or of God as Love, or the meaning of gender-justice, and so on, has already been decided on other grounds. Doctrines serve to provide a warrant for beliefs that have already been adopted and borrowed from the surrounding intellectual and cultural context. Second, why labour with revisionary accounts of doctrines at all when the Jesus of the Gospels is better able to demonstrate the inclusion of marginalised groups of people than doctrines ever can, however skilfully they are presented or recast?

In reply to the first difficulty I plead humility, at least in my aims. I don't claim to have a right interpretation of any doctrine. I offer only arguments open to criticism and scrutiny from within the circle of faith as well as beyond it. I hope to demonstrate plausibility, no more, by the arguments that are offered. I own my indebtedness to my cultural context. I am puzzled about how it could be otherwise. When the context cries out with the anguish of marginalised people, that same anguish becomes the stimulus for reading the tradition differently, more hopefully and inclusively. I emphasise doctrines not simply because they belong to the church's faith, but because they give the ultimate grounds for moral communication and practice and render unnecessary and secondary liberal attempts to baptise or incorporate secular understandings of gender and its violence.

Second, why not base a non-violent, inclusive hermeneutic on Jesus, rather than on doctrine, especially since within the church and widely outside of it, there is much sympathy for Jesus and little sympathy for the church's doctrine? Put that way, the objection is unanswerable. Robin Gill has done something similar in another contribution to this series. In *Health Care and Christian Ethics* he found the virtues of humility, compassion, care, and faith in his analysis of the Gospels and the healing stories they contain, and these became principles that, he convincingly urged, had 'a distinctive and important contribution to make to health care ethics today even within the public forum of a Western, pluralistic society' (Gill 2006: 93). Could I not have found 'Kingdom values' in the Gospels, and based my arguments on these?

I have discussed the remarkable relationship of Jesus to and among women elsewhere (Thatcher 2016: 115–36). It is not Jesus, but cruel readings of biblical texts, and Christian doctrines warped by patriarchal assumptions, that cause gender trouble (and much other trouble as well). The doctrines of the church enable the church to live out its faith and present it as an attractive option for every generation of potential believers to embrace. What happens when doctrines and the practice that flows from them become a hindrance to belief? This is when the reshaping or revisioning of them becomes appropriate, and I have attempted such a process in Part III. Just how doctrine is to be revised and reshaped is of course another story.

There is one remaining task to be accomplished. We have found violence in all three areas of gender. In the final chapter I will attempt to contribute to a hermeneutic – an elementary method of interpretation of the Bible and tradition – that can never condone discrimination or oppression (aim 4).

CHAPTER 10

# *The Continuum and Sacred Texts*

## A Hermeneutic of Analogy

The links between beliefs and violence at the conceptual and structural levels of religious systems became clearer to me during the writing of this book. They so disturbed me that I introduced an additional aim, 'to contribute to a hermeneutic – an elementary method of interpretation of the Bible and tradition – that can never condone discrimination or oppression'. This chapter is my attempt to address this last aim. When I wrote my book, *The Savage Text*, about the misuse of the Bible and the responsibility of its readers for untold religiously inspired violence against all kinds of 'others', I had not fully appreciated the depths of the roots of violence located deep in religious systems of thought. In the last few years I also began to read some of the remarkable work of Muslim women scholars, and their battles with harsh, standard, androcentric interpretations of the Qur'an, with inevitable negative consequences for women. As we shall see, they too battle with the male–female binary in original ways. Their work confirms much of what I want to say about the *peaceful* reading of sacred texts.

The title of this section, 'a hermeneutic of analogy', and the shape of the chapter, borrow a phrase used in a discussion between three feminist theologians – one a Jew, one a Muslim, one a Christian – regarding three patriarchal texts about marriage, one from the Hebrew Bible, one from the Qur'an, and one from the New Testament. The theologians asked 'what happens when *women* read such texts as scripture' (Chaudry, Muers, and Rashkover 2009: 191, authors' emphasis)? Ayesha Chaudry speaks for them all when she asks,

> What if these texts do, in fact, say what their literal reading suggests, and do not offer us positive ways of reading them? Is the problem with the reasoner or with the text itself? What makes us question our own reasoning with regard to the text? Why do we find ourselves so beholden to these texts that

we are willing to engage in all sorts of hermeneutical acrobatics in order to tweak out liberatory understandings of these texts that sometimes appear dishonest, *even to ourselves*? What does it mean to ask these questions and do these questions only make us unfaithful? Or is it possible that they are a manifestation of our faith – a faith in God that incites us to ask these questions of ourselves and of God, and still manage to believe, despite these texts? (2009: 202–3, authors' emphasis)

The contributors were impressed with 'the commonality of issues presented for women scholars of the sacred texts', yet equally aware of the need for different, tradition-based solutions (Chaudry, Muers, and Rashkover 2009: 208). Ongoing conversation, they say, about reading Scriptures and resolving the problems found there, 'functions through a hermeneutic of analogy'. I am struck by the very 'commonality' of problems within the three traditions regarding the apparent scriptural authorisation of gender violence.

## Convergent Problems

Reading Asma Barlas's *'Believing Women' in Islam: Unreading Patriarchal Interpretations of the Qur'an* (Barlas 2002) convinced me, and some of my medical students (pursuing comparative cultural studies in a tiny corner of the small Medical Humanities curriculum), that the sacred text influencing the lives of many of their future patients need not be read as a patriarchal book that oppresses women. We have already noted Barlas's contention that the Qur'an does not define women and men in terms of binary oppositions. That was one of the reasons why I invited her to contribute an essay to the *Oxford Handbook of Theology, Sexuality and Gender*. In this essay she explains that God is 'incomparable' (Barlas 2015: 432: see Barlas 2002: 15), and must therefore be beyond 'masculinizations' (Barlas 2015: 433) either of language or of image. '[M]asculinizations of God never shade into representations of God as father since the Qur'an strictly forbids Muslims to call God that, in both a literal and a metaphorical sense' (Barlas 2015: 433). The Qur'an provides 'categorical rejections of the patriarchal imaginary of God-the-Father', which 'make[s] it impossible to ascribe readings of Islam as a patriarchy to its idea of the divine' (Barlas 2015: 434).

Barlas finds a 'coherence between divine ontology and discourse; that is between who (we believe) God *is* and what (we believe) God *says*' (Barlas 2015: 434, author's emphasis). The Qur'an, then, must be read by Muslims now, in accordance with the character of the God who gave the

Qur'an long ago. Divine ontology also lies at the root of sexual difference, or rather at the lack of it. 'The most significant Qur'anic teaching which demonstrates that sexual equality in Islam is ontological is that God created women and men from a single self' (Barlas 2015: 437).

> Reverence
> Your [Creator], Who created you
> From a single *Nafs*
> Created, of like nature,
> (its) *zawaj* [mate] and from them twain
> Scattered (like seeds)
> Countless men and women;
> (Q.4.1, in Barlas 2015: 437)

The derivation of men and women from a single self or person allows her to speak of 'the ontological identity of men and women' (2015: 437; and see Barlas 2002: 133), thereby ruling out all later justifications of moral superiority of men over women. The association of sex with sin, and sin with women's bodies, is repudiated. Alternative interpretations of notorious patriarchal verses are available. So the word *harth* in the saying 'Your women are a *harth* for you (to cultivate) so go to your *harth* as ye will' (Q.2.222–3), does *not* mean 'property' or 'land' (Barlas 2015: 442) but is a metaphor for something else. The polygyny allowed in the Qur'an 'is not meant to accommodate men's sexual needs or their desire to produce male heirs; it is simply a way to secure the interests of female orphans' (2015: 443). The wearing of the veil was once appropriate advice, for it 'set[s] apart free women from slaves' (2015: 444). That men 'are a degree [*darajah*]' above women (Q.2.228) may refer only to the 'advantage' a husband has in 'being able to *rescind* a divorce he has pronounced' (2015: 445, author's emphasis). The so-called 'beating verse' is open to a different and non-violent interpretation:

> And, as for those women whose [*nushuz*] you have reason to fear, admonish them [first]; then leave them alone in bed: then [*idribuhunne*] them; and if thereupon they pay you heed, do not seek to harm them. (Q.4.34) (in Barlas 2015: 446)

Despite the 'entire ontology of abuse' built on *idribuhunne* ('beat'), it has several other non-violent meanings, such as '"ignore", "leave/go/travel", "set an example", "take away"' (2015: 446), while *nushuz* (which Barlas translates as 'marital discord') is also used of men.

Barlas advocates what she calls 'an "open" hermeneutic' when reading the Qur'an. The Qur'an itself confirms that it may be read in different ways, and that not all interpretations are equally good. 'Rather, it is for Muslims to pick the best, a concept whose meaning is open to continual redefinition, making an interpretive closure of the Qur'an hermeneutically impossible and ethically indefensible' (Barlas 2015: 447). Echoing 'theological' or 'canonical' attempts to read the Christian Scriptures when considered as a whole, or through a theological lens, Barlas has tried throughout her academic career 'not only to challenge patriarchal readings of the Qur'an but also to propose a method for interpreting it that can lead to better ones. For instance, I read the Qur'an by the Qur'an, which is an old method in Islamic theology' (2015: 448). Yes, there are strong patriarchal elements within the Qur'an, but that is because 'men *were* the locus of power and authority in the seventh-century tribal Arab patriarchy to which the Qur'an first spoke' (2015: 447, author's emphasis). 'Tying the meanings of the Qur'an irrevocably to the imaginations of Muslims who lived a millennium ago not only forecloses its own liberatory promise but also ignores basic hermeneutic principles' (2015: 447).

The commonality between the problems on her agenda and the problems discussed in this book is striking. She locates sexual difference in her doctrine of God, and so approaches it at the appropriate ontological level. Since God is incomparable and beyond distinctions of sex, the idea of God cannot be used to endorse male superiority. She rejects the male–female binary. She speaks of the ontological *identity* between women and men, of their ontological *equality*, of their *similarity*. She does not deny sexual difference, but does not allow it to become the basis of an ideology. '[D]ifferences in the Qur'an are not meant to establish hierarchies based in race, sex, nationality, or class ... Such differences... are immaterial from God's perspective in which the only "distinguishing value" is that of *taqwá* and, for believers, God's perspective is the only real perspective.'

Jerusha Lamptey, a feminist Muslim theologian, explains. Barlas, she says, introduces 'two distinct genres of difference' (Lamptey 2014: 139). There is lateral difference, which 'distinguishes groups without attaching an evaluative measure to that distinction' (2014: 140), and hierarchical difference. Lateral difference belongs to groups of people with particular characteristics. It is 'divinely intended', and it 'never serves as the basis of evaluation' (2014: 140). Hierarchical difference, however, judges people by ranking them in some way. But only God is able to judge people. Thus, 'the sole function of [hierarchical] difference in the Qur'an is to differentiate between belief and unbelief' (Barlas 2002: 146). Sex and gender differences are lateral, and therefore cannot be ranked. The Qur'anic derivation of women and men from a single *nafs* matches my treatment of the Hebrew Bible statement that God created the human (*ha'adam*) in God's own image (Gen. 1.27). While *ha'adam* is a collective noun in Hebrew, and *nafs* is a plural feminine noun in Arabic (Barlas 2015: 437), both accounts of the creation of humanity assume God creates the human as a singularity prior to sexual difference.

Barlas's way of dealing with human difference confirms my earlier treatment of Balthasar, Barth, and the complementarians of Catholic and Protestant thought. They too elide lateral and hierarchical difference but without deploying those terms. The importance of this distinction has been taken up in Lamptey's *Muslima* 'theology of religious pluralism' (*Muslima* means 'a female Muslim'; Lamptey 2014: 7). One of the 'foundational insights' of Muslima theology is the distinction between lateral and hierarchical difference, borrowed from Barlas and others. But these distinct genres of difference, deriving from discussions about gender, are significant enough to be applied to the relation between Islam and the non-Islamic religions of the world, that is, to *religious* difference. While her theology of religious pluralism is beyond the scope of this book, I mention it in passing for two reasons. The two types of difference are being used in highly creative ways, replacing opposition and absolutism between the world faiths with a lateral commonality, together with hierarchical inter-sections between the religions that are not absolute or closed, but dynamic, multiple, partial, and ongoing (2014: 171). Another binary (that between Islam and 'other religions') is removed and replaced by the recognition of honest, dynamic complexity.

## Commonalities and Criticisms

I greet Barlas's theology with delight, even astonishment (but have no space here to consider other comparable women interpreters of the Qur'an such as Amina Wadud, Sa'diyya Shaikh, Riffat Hassan, Kecia Ali, and a new generation of women scholars). Parallels extend also to the difficulties encountered by the scriptural passages in the Bible and in the Qur'an whose meanings are detrimental to women, causing 'hermeneutical acro-batics'. The Qur'an does not mention Eve, so does not blame her for the Fall. But Christians inherit what Phyllis Trible called 'texts of terror' (1984), which have caused much distress for women throughout the history of the Christian church. Barlas's hermeneutic may be nimble (if not acrobatic) but it is principled, and based on who God is. 'God's Self-Disclosure needs to become intrinsic to any project of Qur'anic herme-neutics' (Barlas 2002: 13). While we inherit different traditions of God's self-disclosure, we both start in the right place, with the God who is disclosed in, but not only in, the texts. The 'open hermeneutic' prevents textual arrogance, avoids claiming right answers, and seeks continuity with past traditions, even as it develops them. There are, then, many fruitful analogies between Barlas's work and the case outlined in this book, spreading beyond hermeneutics to the theological reading of Scriptures and the starting point of inquiry in God's own self-revelation, and what follows from it. There are analogies too between the operations of androcentrism in both faiths and the methodologies required to resist them.

Nonetheless, Barlas's work (put together with the work of other women interpreters) has been criticised on several counts by other women scholars, and the analogies I am drawing *will extend to the criticisms of her work as well.* In *Feminist Edges of the Qur'an*, Aysha Hidayatullah argues that Barlas and other 'feminist' (her word) interpreters are not radical enough. They have 'generally ignored theoretical issues around gender essentialisms, binaries, and social construction' (Hidayatullah 2014: 129). They 'do not deconstruct ... the kinds of masculinity and femininity (and their relational formation) that persistently inform the verses of the Qur'an they are responding to; rather, they take them for granted' (2014: 129). They do not interrogate 'the commensurability of concepts of equality in the contemporary context with conceptions of male-female relations in a text revealed in the seventh century' (2014: 131). In other words, they impose 'contemporary conceptions of equality on a sacred text revealed in a premodern society where such a notion was hardly a concern to anyone in the way it is today' (2014: 131). Key concepts become essences, fixed and everlasting (like the Vatican understanding of male and female).

The new feminist *tafsir* (Qur'anic exegesis) is said to be unable to entertain the possibility that the Qur'an itself may be responsible for its misreading and for the misogyny it undoubtedly generates. For Barlas, the Qur'an is the divine Word of God, 'God's Speech'. While it cannot err, interpreters certainly can, and retrieving its meaning is beset by many problems – historical, philological, traditional, and cultural, and so on. The women exegetes are said to make a distinction that 'asserts that some parts of the Qur'an are for all times and places (universal), and others are specific to the time of Prophet Muhammad (particular)' (Lamptey 2017: 31). But perhaps this startlingly new but stubbornly traditional feminist *tafsir* is unable 'to account for the existence of certain Qur'anic statements that appear to be neglectful or harmful to women despite the application of the historical contextualization, intratextual, and tawhidic paradigm approaches' (Hidayatullah 2014: 132) (*tawhid* means God's unity, indivisibility, and incomparability). Kecia Ali argues, against Barlas, that passages in the Qur'an 'undeniably "presuppose male agency and female passivity with regard to the initiation of sex"' (in Hidayatullah 2014: 134), and that the *harth* verse 'objectifies women in the most literal sense', confirming that 'the presumption of male control over women is entrenched within these verses to such an extent that the recognition of the patriarchal historical context of revelation does not alleviate the impact of the text's content' (2014: 134). Barlas's translation (and others) of *daraba* (in the beating verse) does not address the propriety of physical chastisement within marriage *at all*. Wadud and Hidayatullah agree: 'in the case of *daraba*, the text of the Qur'an itself proves problematic for feminist exegesis, since no alternative translation or interpretive device can alleviate the possibility of it being read abusively' (2014: 137–8).

Hidayatullah *wants* 'feminist *tafsir*' to be effective, and offers her 'critical reassessment' of it in her attempt to reduce its vulnerabilities and to make it harder for patriarchal authorities to reject. And there is a lot more reassessing to be done. She is willing to conclude that 'our critics' continued abrasiveness' (Hidayatullah 2014: 150) towards them may not be due to their inherent sexism but to mistakes in feminist *tafsir* itself. High on the list of mistakes is that 'in placing feminist demands on the Qur'an, we have projected a historically specific (and at the same time theoretically unclear) sense of "gender justice" onto the text without fully considering how our demands might, in fact, be anachronistic and incommensurate with Qur'anic statements' (2014: 150). The whole strategy of interpretation overlooks and 'obfuscates the inclinations of the Qur'an that may be irreparably nonegalitarian from our contemporary perspective' (2014: 151). While the Qur'an 'makes numerous pronouncements that are indeed compatible with our contemporary understandings of sexual mutuality, reciprocity, kindness, female inclusion, and reverence for women, the Qur'an also endorses notions of male domination that ultimately make parts of the text incommensurate with our contemporary understandings of sexual equality and justice' (2014: 152).

In support of her critical reassessment she finds both mutuality and hierarchy in sexual relations in the Qur'an and observes that while feminist *tafsir* struggles to resolve the tension between them, the tension in the Qur'an itself is unproblematic. It is simply there, unresolved, like the unresolved problem, analysed several times in this book, of women and men being simultaneously different yet equal. 'Different' turns out to be 'inferior' and 'equal' turns out to be 'equal in some respects'. While the Qur'an 'demonstrates remarkable restraint in assigning specific social roles and characteristics to men and women', it 'does, in fact, assign some gender roles in certain circumstances' (Hidayatullah 2014: 155). While the possibility of men having up to four wives is restricted, in the case of polygyny, together with men's permitted sexual access to female slaves, no qualification removes the immoral character of the permission given:

> No matter how many historical and conditional limitations may be attached to the allowances for male sexual access to women in the interpretation of these verses to mitigate their scope and impact, there is no getting around the fact that these allowances exist in some form (no matter how limited) that is stubbornly asymmetrical in comparison to the treatment of women's sexual allowances. (2014: 163)

With regard to a hermeneutic, Hidayatullah places herself on 'the feminist edges of the Qur'an' (the title of her book). '[W]e ought not to continue to appeal to and thus reinforce the authority of a text that cannot definitively support our demands for feminist justice and the authority of an exegetical tradition that is perhaps constitutionally averse to them' (Hidayatullah 2014: 193). She and her colleagues must 'sustain some hope that God's justice upholds the equality of men and women and that the text is divine' (2014: 194). She is prepared to ask, 'What does it mean that we seek a standard of justice that is "beyond" the Qur'anic text? What does it mean to stop handing ultimate authority to the text in this particular way?' However, contemplating these questions enables her 'to look into the abyss of uncertainty and see it as a place of life and not only death' (2014: 194), 'as a mercy in the face of the daunting finality of certainty and the permanence of its limits' (2014: 195). A place of hope and new beginnings, it may enable the pursuit of gender justice in new ways.

Still pursuing a hermeneutic of analogy I will now draw attention to a last feature of Hidayatullah's critical assessment, what she calls 'the last resort of moral-ontological equality' (Hidayatullah 2014: 170). This will become a key feature within the 'divergent solutions' of the next section. We have just noted two arguments for equality. In the first, men and women are ontologically equal because they are created from the same *nafs*, 'and neither man nor woman has any essential quality of *being human* that the other does not have' (2014: 170, author's emphasis). Second, 'All people are the same in the sight of God in every way except with regard to their differing levels of *taqwa*.' Thus 'levels of *taqwa* constitute the only real difference between human beings, and that difference can be assessed by God only' (2014: 170, commenting on Barlas 2002: 146). While these arguments are said to be 'quite effective', a problem arises regarding the relation between *ontological* and *functional* equality. There are cases where women in the Qur'an are functionally unequal with men. The receipt of financial support (*qiwamah*) is one such case. Male control of women's bodies is another. This is Hidayatullah's case:

> The receipt of *qiwamah* and sexual passivity are attached exclusively to women ... When functional inequalities are assigned based on being a man or woman, they are rooted in a permanent difference of being ... If ... the Qur'an may sometimes outline functional inequalities related to being, then we must concede that ontological inequalities might also come with them. (Hidayatullah 2014: 171)

The derivation of the functional inequality of women from the basic ontological equality of women and men must bring with it, so the argument runs, the concession that there may be no ontological equality after all. 'This relationship of functional inequality to ontological inequality poses a formidable challenge to arguments for the ontological equality of men and women' (2014: 171).

These conversations are clearly vital for the status and future of women in Islam for the foreseeable future, and they are instructive also for Christians, especially feminists, who are still battling with patriarchy within their own traditions. I will now describe briefly Hidayatullah's treatment of the androcentrism of sacred texts, and then indicate a different solution open to the Christian tradition that is afflicted by similar problems.

Hidayatullah pursues 'a vision of the Qur'an as a divine text that allows us to imagine justice outside the text's limited pronouncements' (Hidayatullah 2014: 173). It is possible to uphold 'the divine guidance of the Qur'an while acknowledging the Quran's framing within the time of its revelation' (2014: 173). Not only is the Qur'an embedded in history, so also are its androcentric interpreters. But history moves on. The assumptions that textual meaning is equivalent to arriving at 'authorial intent', or that there is an objective meaning that can be discovered merely by reading, are both mistaken. Christians will know these assumptions are embedded in their own history, and are now generally abandoned, at least by theologians, even though they may be rife in theological populism. Hidayatullah writes,

> [U]nderstanding is not a passive process but rather the product of a dialogue between the text and reader, who always reads the text from within a particular history ... Thus the role of the reader (not just the author) becomes central to reading the Qur'an, and the reader can never objectively know the intent of the author/God. (2014: 183)

There are several other hermeneutical moves that are common to the strategies of Christian and Muslim reformers (and of course among feminists in all the world religions), but I want to concentrate here on learning how feminist *tafsir* handles the principal theme of this book – the removal of binaries – and the implications of what follows. Barlas insists the Qur'an 'does not define women and men in terms of binary oppositions' (Barlas 2002: 129). She finds the alternative idea of polarity' more acceptable. 'Polarity – or the interconnectedness of opposite principles – defines not only God's reality but the reality of humans as well' (2002: 103). Women and men

> do not embody mutually exclusive or opposite attributes; rather, they incorporate both masculine and feminine attributes. In a polar conception, women are not women because they manifest a lack (defined in terms of feminine traits) and men are not men because they possess what women lack (masculine traits). Rather, *each* manifests *the whole*. (2002: 103, author's emphases)

God, she says (like Nicholas of Cusa in the Christian tradition), is the 'coincidence of opposites', and among the opposites that God unites are the masculine and feminine 'principles' (2002: 101).

There are obvious similarities between the polar thinking here and the continuum in this book, not least the removal of oppositional qualities and emphasis on the holism that the polar view is thought to represent. But in the previous chapter, I argued that masculine and feminine principles were redundant. 'Masculine' and 'feminine' have culturally specific meanings, but they perpetuate the male–female binary and invite the mistaken assumption that men have a female side, and vice versa. Hidayatullah makes a similar charge against polar thinking. She proposes 'that feminist tafsir begin to treat not only gender but also sex as a fluid and historically contingent concept and sexual difference as a shifting relation of interdependence' (Hidayatullah 2014: 187). Barlas's polar thinking, she contends, still maintains 'an essentialized notion of difference between the sexes that ultimately undermines sexual equality' (2014: 187). While Hidayatullah does not use the idea of a continuum, she advocates it nonetheless in the model of sexual difference she proposes, that is, one

> based not on fixed binaries but rather on constructive, interdependent relationality ... Categories of male and female are relative and fluid; the two are interdependent because each requires the other, and neither exists within a fixed or static self. Man and woman are dependent on each other for their being: man cannot be man without woman, and woman cannot be woman without man ... Furthermore, as the relations between men and

women evolve, so do the meanings of what it means to be a woman and
a man. (2014:189)

Biological difference, she continues, 'is best treated as historically fluid,
relational, and contextual, rather than essential and stable' (2014: 191).
Dependent primarily on God, human beings become more acutely aware
of their dependence 'on their relationships to others for their being' (2014:
191). This is how self-knowledge is arrived at. 'Social relations shape how
one understands oneself; we become our "selves" through being in relation
to another' (2014: 191).

So fluid gender categories are not only admissible; they are necessary. So
are the evolving meanings of 'man' and 'woman'. I agree that 'man' and
'woman', at least without some open qualification, are no longer serviceable (at least for a Christian theology of gender). The human continuum
that embraces male and female copes better with these 'evolving meanings', and does so inclusively. While most people have no difficulty with
the classifications of 'man' and 'woman', some do, and the unexamined use
of them may, however unwittingly, replicate the binary that 'polarity' is
intended to replace. Feminist *tafsir* is concerned with gender justice.
However, the position towards which Hidayatullah is moving (very painfully, as she acknowledges) may also allow her to form a perspective on the
various issues we have examined in earlier chapters. Sexual difference
becomes one of many human differences that constitute human being. It
is lateral. Since categories of male and female are fluid, there is positive
affirmation and encouragement for intersex and trans people. Since there is
no binary, intersex people have no need to internalise it and judge
themselves to be defective in accordance with it. Since there is no binary,
trans people are free to acknowledge the unique difficulties they encounter
in relation to it. Since there is no binary, there is no 'fixed and static self',
gendered, to be preserved against the aching of gender dysphoria. Since
there is no binary, heteronormativity disappears along with it. Lesbian,
gay, and bisexual people therefore find their just place within the continuum of humanity. While Hidayatullah does not say this, it may be open to
her to develop her analysis in these additional directions.

## Divergent Solutions

I have been inspired by being able to 'eavesdrop' on a high-level discussion
between Muslim women believers, grappling with the product of centuries
of androcentrism, disagreeing openly and sometimes painfully, dedicating
their scholarship to the end of bringing about a better and more just

understanding of their faith as it describes and prescribes relations between women and men. The discussion continues, animated and unresolved (Barlas 2016). In the next section I will diverge from all of them in ways they might expect but which they cannot find acceptable, because they require belief in the Christian doctrines of incarnation and Trinity. Christians have available to them different solutions to the problems of both sexism and textual interpretation. I'm not saying they are better solutions, just different 'tradition-specific' ones.

### The Trinity and Sexual Difference

Like Barlas I concentrate on the doctrine of God as the final answer to the relegation of the status of women in relation to men (and, for me, to the relegation of sexual minorities in relation to majorities). Here, I suggest, the doctrine of the Trinity is crucial. Like her, I place God above all binaries, especially that of male and female, and agree there must be 'coherence between ontology and discourse'. Barlas makes much of her claim that 'The most significant Qur'anic teaching which demonstrates that sexual equality in Islam is ontological is that God created women and men from a single self' (Barlas 2015: 437). I locate sexual equality squarely in Godself. That is the prior reason for thinking that equality arrives with the *ha' adam* that is made in God's image. This claim is, of course, more than the claim that God is 'beyond' male or female, or neither male nor female. This still makes God an individual, albeit a divine one, unlike any other. A range of adjectives is available to express disapproval of this idea of God – 'monarchical', 'monistic', 'unitarian', and so on. I'm not using them, just saying that in Christian faith God is a unity of divine Persons; that these Persons are co-equal; that they are different from each other (each has distinct roles to play within the divine economy); and that they are simultaneously one (because they are all fully and completely God). Each is, in relation to the others, and the others contribute to the divine Personhood each has and is. Together they are a single communion of love, a love that spills over into the making, redeeming, and completing of the world, and they summon all who will listen to live a human life that is not only like the life of God but a real participation in it.

God is literally beyond binaries in that God is not two of anything. God is inseparably One in being, and separably Three in God's own triune Personhood. Hidayatullah's problem, that a binary doctrine of humanity inevitably ends up privileging men over women, cannot arise when God is understood as a Trinity and allowed to influence the theological anthropology to which it properly gives rise. The Persons are all divine, and so cannot be ranked hierarchically (despite misguided attempts to do so). Divine difference is lateral, since it operates on a single (divine) level. Any slide from ontological to functional equality can never gather momentum within Godself. What counts as equality (at least for trinitarian Christians) is located in Godself, in God's divine essence that admits difference but that cannot admit any distinctions of hierarchy whatsoever. Another advantage is that the 'interdependent relationality' that Hidayatullah argues for is built into the Christian doctrine of God already, for the divine Persons embrace each other in what Richard Rohr calls (in relation to fourth century CE accounts of the Trinity) 'a circle dance of love' (Rohr 2016: 27). Christians (like me) who argue for revisionist positions in the theology of sexuality and gender are often accused of importing 'liberal' or ill-defined notions of equality that are 'unbiblical' or a product of European Enlightenment (a damaging accusation in the postcolonial context). Hidayatullah has had to fend off similar accusations in her tradition. My reply to the Christians suspicious of gender equality is: I found my understanding of equality in the Trinity, and for a theologian there is no better or higher or more authoritative place to look.

The place of Christ in the divine economy is also crucial for understanding sexual difference. There is no need to repeat the earlier argument that Jesus Christ (and not *ha'adam*) is the full and complete image of God, and that his very being initiates a new humanity, a new creation in which sexual difference remains, but like differences of race and class, they are no longer divisive. Christians barely understand the revolutionary implications of this, even now. But the place of Christ in Christian faith also allows Christians to develop a hermeneutic that deals with the kind of problems feminist *tafsir* is grappling with, in a different way. Again the intent is not to suggest Christian solutions to Islamic problems, but to insist on solidarity with feminist *tafsir* both in the problems it encounters and in the sheer boldness of the alternative visions it enables. In the end though, our solutions will be tradition-dependent, and so different.

## The Divine Word and the 'Word of God'

For Islam the Qur'an is a divine text. It is the Word of God. It is God's own speech. Of course there are qualifications with regard to the reading of it, which will be given much, little, or no weight, depending on who the readers are. Qualifications include the limitations of language, of context, of passage through history, of outdated cultural practices, androcentric distortion, and so on. Hidayatullah asks, nervously, after feminist *tafsir*, 'In what way is the text still divine?' (Hidayatullah 2014: 194). Christians run into similar problems as well, whenever they open their Bibles. But there is a big difference. For Christians the Word of God is not a text or group of texts at all. The Word of God is Jesus Christ. Jesus didn't write anything. The arresting, mind-blowing, opening lines of the Gospel of John settle the question what the Word of God might be: it is not a text at all.

> In the beginning was the Word, and the Word was with God, and the Word was God. He was in the beginning with God. All things came into being through him, and without him not one thing came into being. What has come into being in him was life, and the life was the light of all people. (Jn 1.1–4)
> And the Word became flesh and lived among us. (Jn 1.14a)

Yes, the Word is God's self-disclosure, God's speaking to us about who and what God is, God's communicating to us how we are to understand 'God'. And that self-disclosure is Jesus Christ. Before the Word became incarnate, the Word was *already* 'the light of all people'. We can speak meaningfully of the divinity of Christ by borrowing Judith Butler's notion of gender performativity and using it in a similar manner of Jesus Christ, who performs his divinity in his humanity and his humanity in his divinity. Just as our gender is thought to be stated in constant micro-performances of who we are, so it is with Jesus, except that it is his divinity-in-humanity, rather than his gender, that he performs. His life and teaching, his ministry to the sick, his opposition to legalism, his astonishing love for people illustrated by some of his parables and supremely by his sacrificial death; these are some of the ways he performed his 'Word-ness', and showed the world that God is Love (1 Jn. 4).

The Bible, of course, cannot settle the question what the Bible is. Can the Qur'an answer the parallel question? And since none of the many biblical authors had an understanding of the Bible as a whole when they wrote, they could not have had a settled answer to the question or even understood it. The Bible doesn't *say* anything. To insist otherwise is to commit 'the personalistic fallacy' (Thatcher 2008: 141). Unlike Christ the Bible is not a person, divine or human. It cannot speak. Instead it lets itself be read. And it is often read badly. Insofar as biblical authors can help us to understand what the Bible is, none of them supports a blanket *sola scriptura* theory that assumes, like the opponents of feminist *tafsir*, that the sacred text conveniently supplies an objective meaning that can be read directly from the text. John's Gospel portrays Jesus' impatience with the assumption that Scripture is somehow an end in itself. 'You search the scriptures because you think that in them you have eternal life; and it is they that testify on my behalf' (Jn 5.39). Paul was equally frustrated with the devotion of one of the churches he founded to Scripture. Contrasting the new covenant with the former covenant between God and God's people, he calls himself and his companions 'ministers of the new covenant', which, he explains, is 'not of letter but of spirit; for the letter kills, but the Spirit gives life' (2 Cor. 3.6). We have seen his dire impatience with Christians in Galatia who insisted on the obedience of Gentile Christians to the precepts of the Hebrew Bible. Despite the universal reverence among Christians for the Ten Commandments, how many of us recall that Paul called them 'the ministry of death, chiseled in letters on stone tablets' (2 Cor. 3.7)? There could hardly be a stronger condemnation of literalism. The New Testament writers many times use allegory to support their interpretation of the Hebrew Bible; that is, they understood that it points, however obliquely, to Christ. An obvious example of allegory is the writer of the Letter to the Ephesians who suddenly announces in his discussion of the Septuagint version of Genesis 2.24 ('For this reason a man will leave his father and mother and be joined to his wife, and the two will become one flesh'), 'This is a great mystery, and I am applying it to Christ and the church' (Eph. 5.31–2). I take no issue with his interpretation of a particular verse of Scripture (Hebrew, of course, and translated into Greek), but merely note that there is nothing in the Genesis verse that suggests the Christological spin he puts upon it. Of course, there couldn't be. And even this is deliberately tentative. It remains 'a great mystery' (*sacramentum* in the later Vulgate), and the author feels he has to tell his readers how he has chosen to use it.

My point here is to explore another major difference, a *disanalogy*, between Christian and Muslim readers of Scripture. Christians do *not* give the highest authority to the Bible. We give it to Jesus Christ, and acknowledge the crucial role the Bible plays in providing the knowledge we need. Islam may have no comparable manoeuvre. We are not bound to Scripture, but to the One to whom Scripture points. We have the promise of the promptings of the Holy Spirit to guide us into all the truth (Jn. 16.13), but we haven't got there yet. We have the sources of tradition, and reason (and experience), as we often like to say. Why stop there? There is further mileage to be had in the medieval idea of God's Two Books, the Book of Scripture, and the Book of Nature. Reading 'nature' as a divinely authored 'text' allows us to rejoice, albeit cautiously, in the discoveries of science (and not least the narratives of the biological sciences as they probe the mysteries of sexual orientation, gender dysphoria, and the extraordinary sexual similarities of human beings). Whatever happened to Wisdom (Prov. 8), as God's mediation of Godself to humanity, imparting practical knowledge for living, way beyond the confines of God's covenant people? Richard Hooker, perhaps Anglicanism's foremost theologian, placed Wisdom higher than either the Book of Nature or the Book of Scripture. 'As her ways are of sundry kinds', he wrote (in *Of the Lawes of Ecclesiastical Politie*),

> so her manner of teaching is not merely one and the same. Some things she openeth by the sacred books of Scripture; some things by the glorious works of Nature; with some things she inspireth them from above by spiritual influence; in some things she leadeth and traineth them only by world experience ... [L]et all her ways be according unto their place and degree adored. (Hooker 1925[1594]: 236–7)

It appears then that the literalism that filters down to cause real violence is even less excusable among Christians than it is among Muslims, since biblical interpretation must always be carried on through a Christological framework. The divine love revealed through the cross of Christ and within the all-encompassing communion of love that is the Trinity, can never ultimately be allowed to be compromised or eclipsed by otherising anyone. Christians do not self-define as 'People of the Book' but as people of the Saviour. It would be impertinent for me to suggest that Muslim exegetes might learn from our struggles with literalism and androcentrism, yet given the universal character of both, some comparisons may be helpful. We agree that our sacred texts should be read theologically; that there must be coherence between who and what God is and what God 'says'; and that God's self-disclosure is primary, however much we differ about how that happens.

I'm unclear whether Muslims can question the divinity of the Qur'an, but if they can, they may be able to profit from Christians' wrestling with a similar problem. The Bible is still widely called the Word of God, especially by Christians who seek direct biblical authority for their beliefs. The irony is inescapable. There is no biblical authority for this belief, for the Bible 'says' the Word of God is Jesus Christ. The Bible is indispensable to us. Without it we would know next to nothing about Jesus, or about the Reign of God he proclaimed, or about the formation of the earliest churches, or about the experiences of the earliest Christians (and their deep disagreements). We thank God for the preservation of its different books and their eventual canonical form ratified in the fourth century CE. But for nearly two hundred years we have also studied the Bible critically, and of course, critical biblical scholarship is itself the fruit of the requirement of the Reformation demand that the words of Scripture be studied with renewed intensity. And Christians have responded variously to critical study. Generally lay people are still protected from its negative results. Some lose their faith when the chilly winds of higher criticism blow against it, while still others lose their faith because the contradictions and violence in the Bible, and not least the patriarchal assumptions of the text, are 'stumbling blocks' (Mk. 9.42) in the way of continuing belief. The point is that loosening the hold of belief in a divine text on its readers does not automatically lead to unbelief or infidelity to tradition (our creeds say nothing whatever about the Bible). It does not lead to a lack of gratitude or loss of reverence for it or to think we cannot be close to God or prompted by God when we read it. I do not know whether Muslims can learn from this experience.

I'm wondering whether what I have called the 'personalistic fallacy' might have a use if the divinity of the Qur'an is to be rethought? A similar idea is 'the myth of textual agency' (Martin 2006: 1). One hears and reads claims, a million times over, 'The Bible says …', 'The Bible teaches …', 'The Qur'an prohibits …', 'The Qur'an permits …', and so on. These innocent-looking locutions conceal a dubious textual practice, that of assuming a book, however holy, is not a book, but a person. The Bible says nothing. It is *readers* who say 'It says …' There are Bible teachers who teach the Bible but the Bible is not a teacher. It has no agency of itself. Augustine, for example, who believed that the main author of Scripture was the Holy Spirit, distinguished between 'literal' and 'figurative' readings. His test 'for whether a biblical text is literal or figurative is whether it accords with true doctrine or ethics' (Martin, 2006: 12). 'True' doctrine or ethics might be the demand to love our neighbours as ourselves, or that 'Allah is the compassionate, the merciful' (Q.1.1).

Hidayatullah's contention that the role of the reader is central to the reading of sacred texts will find a strong resonance among Christians. Stephen Barton once asked, 'What if the Bible is more like the text of a Shakespearean play or the score of a Beethoven symphony, where true interpretation involves *corporate performance and practical enactment,* and where the meaning of the text or score will vary to some degree from one performance to another …?' (Barton 1996: 6). The question, obviously, serves to liken readers of sacred texts to actors and musicians. They are given a priceless text, but without a competent performance it would be better not to undertake a performance at all. Interpretation of the text of each is essential. (Recent emphasis on performance in gender theory perhaps strengthens the analogy further.) The emphasis on 'corporate performance and practical enactment' is easily translatable into different contexts. It highlights that we are actively responsible together, for what we do with our sacred texts, and just like an unrehearsed orchestra or troupe of unrehearsed actors, we can reduce an inspired script to a cacophony or a travesty of itself.

## Common Themes

Throughout the book, links between beliefs and violence have been traced. I described a 'global pandemic' of violence against women in Chapter 2. Much of this is supported by beliefs about women, held by men. I have spoken of 'epistemic violence', of 'gentle violence' that is initially unnoticed, and of 'symbolic violence' (which contributed to the suicide of Lizzie Lowe). I offered a version of the Euthyphro Dilemma, in an attempt to explain how religious leaders and believers have justified crimes against humanity, believing these to be the will of God.

In my book *The Savage Text* (Thatcher 2008) I tried to face up to the conclusion that misuse of the Bible had led to untold violence in the past. I understood the debates raging then about (homo)sexuality to belong to a long line of biblical interpretative disasters that, for example, treated African peoples as tainted by the curse of Canaan, led to the torturing and murdering of heretics, demonised some women as witches, justified the ownership and trading of slaves, and so on. I asked then how Christians had found themselves able to advocate discrimination, on a global scale. The mission of the church was gravely compromised, and it remains compromised today with regard to the issues treated in previous chapters.

Listening to women Islamic scholars wrestling with gender injustice, I am struck by two related failures in our broad traditions. The first is the failure to take God seriously enough – the failure to let the performance of our faith be shaped by who and what we take God to be in God's own self-disclosure. That disclosure cannot be identical with any text. Jesus is God's Word. God is a communion of divine Persons. God is Love. Allah is the Compassionate, the Merciful. If these (and other) core convictions are to be embraced as true, then they should shape the performance of our faiths and the reading of our sacred texts. God is not confined to Scripture, nor is our understanding of God confined to Scripture. God will not be limited by Scripture. A *theological* reading of Scripture is essential. I understand feminist *tafsir* to prioritise the doctrine of God, and I have tried to do the same, but with a different understanding of God. It is by the doctrine of God that we get to the ontological similarity of human beings, stop confusing lateral and hierarchical difference, abandon forever the prejudice that women embody God's image to a lesser degree than men, come to the joyful realisation that the human race is more diverse than binary systems allow, and discover the interpretative key by which the revelatory function of our Scriptures may be unlocked.

The second failure is our lack of a hermeneutic that lets God be God. Here Christians can learn from Barlas's 'open hermeneutic' – her admission that texts are open to different, and sometimes unworthy, interpretations, together with her determination to find the 'best' interpretation available. In her case, the best interpretation is the one that best shows the mercy and compassion of Allah. Hidayatullah gropes towards a standard of justice that is 'beyond' the Qur'anic text and outside the text's limited pronouncements. Perhaps this is easier for Christians. She is prepared to look into 'the abyss of uncertainty'. These are prophetic words. There is no better place from which to practice faith. Human beings crave certainty when so much is uncertain all around them. Given the complexity of political, social, and environmental issues, the demand for simplification becomes overwhelming, while the exercise of the right of freedom of belief becomes the right to believe what we want to believe, irrespective of its truth-distorting and violence-inducing consequences. Faith *requires* uncertainty if it is to operate in a transformative way, and believing that we have arrived at positions of certainty is probably an expression of idolatry, and an identification of our minds with the mind of God. Hidayatullah bravely chooses uncertainty as a 'place of life', as 'a mercy in the face of the daunting finality of certainty and the permanence of its limits'. In this place finalities are exposed and new possibilities of faith arise.

I have sought in the book to portray an account of faith without three particular binaries. Tangled up in attempts to replace them, I repeatedly came across the power of binaries to endorse injustice and violence. I used the Euthyphro Dilemma to illustrate how religious thought is able to convince itself that God legitimises unjust actions. Perhaps all theistic religious traditions need to ask whether there are tendencies within them, and in particular in their reading of texts, which allow practices that are harsh, cruel, or unjust, on the grounds that God, through Scripture or other 'authoritative' teachings, commands them. For my own tradition, 'love is from God; everyone who loves is born of God and knows God. Whoever does not love does not know God, for God is love' (1 Jn. 4.7–8).

Divine love does not authorise injustice of any kind. The Great Commandments provide a rule beyond all rules, an obedience beyond obedience to any rule. Seeking to love our neighbours as God loves them, and to love ourselves as God loves us, is the best way I know towards a more peaceful life, a more just social order, and an honourable reading of the Scriptures God has given us.

# Bibliography

Abdelmoneim, Javid (2018). 'No More Boys and Girls: Can Our Kids Go Gender Free?' BBC2 Television. First broadcast 24 July.

Adams, Marilyn McCord (1992). 'Trinitarian Friendship: Same-Gender Models of Godly Love in Richard of St. Victor and Aelred of Rievaulx'. In Eugene F. Rogers, Jr. (ed.), *Theology and Sexuality: Classic and Contemporary Readings*. Oxford: Blackwell, 2002, 322–40.

Ainsworth, Claire (2015). 'Sex Redefined'. *Nature*, 518, 288–91.

Alcoff, Linda (2006). *Visible Identities: Race, Gender and the Self*. Oxford: Oxford University Press.

Alexander, Denis (2017). *Genes, Determinism and God*. Cambridge: Cambridge University Press.

Allberry, Sam (2015). *Is God Anti-Gay?* Epsom: The Good Book Company.

American College of Pediatricians (2017a). 'Gender Ideology Harms Children'. www.acpeds.org/the-college-speaks/position-statements/gender-ideology-harms-children. Accessed 7 November 2019.

(2017b). 'Homosexual Parenting: Is It Time for Change?' www.acpeds.org/the-college-speaks/position-statements/parenting-issues/homosexual-parenting-is-it-time-for-change. Accessed 7 November 2019.

Anderson, Pamela Sue (2012). *Re-visioning Gender in Philosophy of Religion: Reason, Love and Epistemic Locatedness*. Farnham: Ashgate.

Anderson, Siwan, and Debraj Ray (2012). 'The Age Distribution of Missing Women in India'. *Economic and Political Weekly*, 47, 1 December.

Anglican Communion (1998). Lambeth Conference 1998, Section I.10 – Human Sexuality'. www.anglicancommunion.org/resources/document-library/lambeth-conference/1998/section-i-called-to-full-humanity/section-i10-human-sexuality?author=Lambeth+Conference&year=1998. Accessed 7 November 2019.

Anglican Communion News Service (2017). 'Ordinands Boost Helps C of E Address Falling Clergy Numbers'. www.anglicannews.org/news/2017/09/ordinands-boost-helps-c-of-e-address-falling-clergy-numbers.aspx. Accessed 7 November 2019.

APA [American Psychological Association] (2006). *Report of the APA Task Force on the Sexualization of Girls*. www.apa.org/pi/women/programs/girls/report-full.pdf. Accessed 7 Nov. 2019.

Archbishop of Canterbury (2017). Statement. www.archbishopofcanterbury.org/
    speaking-and-writing/speeches/statement-archbishop-canterbury-following-
    todays-general-synod. 15 February. Accessed 7 November 2019.
Armour, Ellen T. (2010). 'Blinding Me with (Queer) Science: Religion, Sexuality,
    and (Post?) Modernity'. *International Journal for Philosophy of Religion*, 68
    (1–3), 107–19.
Balthasar, Hans Urs (1990). *Theo-Drama: Theological Dramatic Theory, Vol. II,
    The Dramatis Personae: Man in God*, tr. Graham Harrison. San Francisco:
    Ignatius Press.
    (1992). *Theo-Drama: Theological Dramatic Theory, Vol. III, The Dramatis Perso-
    nae: The Person in Christ*, tr. Graham Harrison. San Francisco: Ignatius Press.
Barker, Meg-John, and Julia Scheele (2016). *Queer: A Graphic History*. London:
    Icon Books.
Barlas, Asma (2002). *'Believing Women' in Islam: Unreading Patriarchal Interpre-
    tations of the Qur'an*. Austin: University of Texas Press.
    (2015). 'Islam'. In Adrian Thatcher (ed.), *Oxford Handbook of Theology,
    Sexuality and Gender*. Oxford: Oxford University Press, 432–49.
    (2016). 'Secular and Feminist Critiques of the Qur'an: Anti-Hermeneutics as
    Liberation?'. *Journal of Feminist Studies in Religion*, 32,2, Fall, 111–121.
Barnett, Brian S., Ariana E. Nesbit, and Renée M. Sorrentino (2018). 'The
    Transgender Bathroom Debate at the Intersection of Politics, Law, Ethics,
    and Science'. *Journal of the American Academy of Psychiatry and Law*, 46,
    232–41.
Barth, Karl (1958). *Church Dogmatics III: The Doctrine of Creation, Part 1*.
    Edinburgh: T&T Clark.
    (1961). *Church Dogmatics III: The Doctrine of Creation, Part 4*. Edinburgh:
    T&T Clark.
Barton, Stephen C. (2009). '"Male and Female He Created Them"' (Genesis
    1:27). In Stephen C. Barton and David Wilkinson (eds), *Reading Genesis
    after Darwin*. Oxford: Oxford University Press, 182–202.
    (1996). 'Is the Bible Good News for Human Sexuality? Reflections on Method
    in Biblical Interpretation?'. In Adrian Thatcher and Elizabeth Stuart (eds),
    *Christian Perspectives on Sexuality and Gender*. Grand Rapids, MI: Eerdmans,
    4–13.
Beardsley, Christina, and Michelle O'Brien (eds)(2016). *This Is My Body: Hearing
    the Theology of Transgender Christians*. London: Darton, Longman and
    Todd.
Beattie, Tina (2006). *New Catholic Feminism*. London: Routledge.
    (2010a). 'The Catholic Church's Scandal: Modern Crisis, Ancient Roots'.
    *Open Democracy* [website]. www.opendemocracy.net/tina-beattie/catholic-
    church%E2%80%99s-abuse-scandal-modern-crisis-ancient-roots. Accessed
    7 November 2019.
    (2010b). *The Tablet*, 7 August.
    (2013). *Theology After Postmodernity: Divining the Void – A Lacanian Reading of
    Thomas Aquinas*. Oxford: Oxford University Press.

Berkeley, George (1713). *Three Dialogues between Hylas and Philonous*. Project Gutenberg. www.gutenberg.org/ebooks/4724?msg. Accessed 7 November 2019.

Berra, Robert (2018). 'Men's Ministries and Patriarchy: From Sites of Perpetuation to Sites of Resistance'. In Caroline Blyth, Emily Colgan, and Katie B. Edwards (eds)(2018). *Rape Culture, Gender Violence and Religion: Christian Perspectives*. New York: Springer International, 27–51.

Berry, Jonathan (with Rob Wood) (2016). *Satisfaction Guaranteed: A Future and a Hope for Same-Sex Attracted Christians*. London: IVP.

Beste, Jennifer (2018). *College Hookup Culture and Christian Ethics: The Lives and Longings of Emerging Adults*. New York: Oxford University Press.

Bethmont, Rémy (2018). 'How Queer Can Christian Marriage Be? Eschatological Imagination and the Blessing of Same-Sex Unions in the American Episcopal Church'. In Mark D. Chapman and Dominic Janes (eds), *New Approaches in History and Theology to Same-Sex Love and Desire*. Cham, Switzerland: Palgrave Macmillan, 209–26.

Bloom, Amy (2002). *Normal: Transsexual CEOs, Cross-Dressing Cops, and Hermaphrodites with Attitude*. New York: Random House.

Blyth, Caroline, Emily Colgan, and Katie B. Edwards (eds)(2018). *Rape Culture, Gender Violence and Religion: Christian Perspectives*. New York: Springer International.

Bong, Sharon A. (2018). 'Transgender'. In Lisa Isherwood and Dirk von der Horst (eds), *Contemporary Theological Approaches to Sexuality*. London: Routledge, 40–52.

*Book of Common Prayer* (1662). http://justus.anglican.org/resources/bcp/1662/Athanasius.pdf. Accessed 7 November 2019.

Boswell, John (1995). *The Marriage of Likeness: Same-Sex Unions in Pre-Modern Europe*. London: HarperCollins.

Bourdieu, Pierre (2001). *Masculine Domination* (tr. Richard Nice). Cambridge: Polity Press; original French edition 1998.

Bracke, Sarah, and David Paternotte (eds)(2016). 'Unpacking the Sin of Gender'. *Religion and Gender*, 6.2, 143–54.

Bradley, Harriet (2007). *Gender*. Cambridge: Polity Press.

Brown, Mildred, and Chloe Ann Rounsley (1996). *True Selves: Understanding Transsexualism – For Families, Friends, Coworkers, and Helping Professionals*. San Francisco: Jossey-Bass.

Burrage, Hilary (2015). *Eradicating Female Genital Mutilation: A UK Perspective*. Aldershot: Ashgate.

Butler, Judith (1999). *Gender Trouble: 10th Anniversary Edition*. New York: Routledge.

Cahill, Lisa Sowle (1996). *Sex, Gender and Christian Ethics*. Cambridge: Cambridge University Press.

Case, Mary Anne (2016). 'The Role of the Popes in the Invention of Complementarity'. *Religion and Gender*, 6.2, 155–72.

*Catechism of the Catholic Church* (1994). London: Geoffrey Chapman.

CBE International. 'Men, Women and Biblical Equality'. www.cbeinternational
.org/sites/default/files/english_3.pdf. Accessed 7 November 2019.

CDF [Congregation for the Doctrine of the Faith] (1975). *Persona Humana*:
'Declaration on Certain Questions Concerning Sexual Ethics'. www.vatican
.va/roman_curia/congregations/cfaith/documents/rc_con_cfaith_doc_
19751229_persona-humana_en.html. Accessed 7 November 2019.

(1976). *Inter Insigniores: On the Question of Admission of Women to the Ministerial Priesthood.* www.vatican.va/roman_curia/congregations/cfaith/docu
ments/rc_con_cfaith_doc_19761015_inter-insigniores_en.html. Accessed
7 November 2019.

(1986). *Letter to the Bishops of the Catholic Church on the Pastoral Care of
Homosexual Persons.* www.vatican.va/roman_curia/congregations/cfaith/doc
uments/rc_con_cfaith_doc_19861001_homosexual-persons_en.html.
Accessed 7 November 2019.

(2003). *Considerations Regarding Proposals to Give Legal Recognition to Unions
between Homosexual Persons.* www.vatican.va/roman_curia/congregations/
cfaith/documents/rc_con_cfaith_doc_20030731_homosexual-unions_en
.html. Accessed 7 November 2019.

Chapman, Mark D. (2018). '"Homosexual Practice" and the Anglican Communion from the 1990s: A Case Study in Theology and Identity'. In Mark D.
Chapman and Dominic Janes (eds), *New Approaches in History and Theology
to Same-Sex Love and Desire*. Basingstoke: Palgrave Macmillan, 187–208.

Chaudhry, Ayesha Siddiqua, Rachel Muers, and Randi Rashkover (2009).
'Women Reading Texts on Marriage'. *Feminist Theology*, 17(2), 191–209.

Cheng, Patrick (2011). *Radical Love: An Introduction to Queer Theology*. New
York: Seabury Books.

(2015). 'Contributions from Queer Theory'. In Adrian Thatcher (ed.), *Oxford
Handbook of Theology, Sexuality and Gender*. Oxford: Oxford University
Press, 153–69.

Chesler, Phyllis (2010). 'Worldwide Trends in Honor Killings'. *Middle East
Quarterly* (Spring), 3–11. www.meforum.org/2646/worldwide-trends-in-
honor-killings. Accessed 7 November 2019.

Children's Society (2018). *The Good Childhood Report 2018, Summary.* www
.childrenssociety.org.uk/sites/default/files/the_good_childhood_summary_
2018.pdf. Accessed 7 November 2019.

Choi, Hyaeweol (2009). *Gender and Mission Encounters in Korea: New Women,
Old Ways: Seoul–California Series in Korean Studies, Volume 1*. Oakland, CA:
University of California Press.

Church of England (2012). 'Government Consultation on Same Sex Marriage':
GS Misc 1027. www.churchofengland.org/sites/default/files/2017–11/GS%
20Misc%201027%20government%20consultation%20on%20same%20sex
%20marriage.pdf. Accessed 7 November 2019.

Church Times (2015). 'Death of teenager "struggling with sexuality" prompts
soul-searching'. Jan. 9.

(2018). Letters. 29 June.

Coakley, Sarah (2013). *God, Sexuality and the Self: An Essay 'On the Trinity'.* Cambridge: Cambridge University Press.

Connell, Raewyn, and Rebecca Pearse (2015). *Gender in World Perspective.* Cambridge, UK & Malden MA: Polity Press; third edition.

Conseil Pontifical pour la Famille (2011). *Gender – La Controverse.* Paris: Téqui.

Cook, Christopher C. H. (2018). 'Science and Theology in Human Sexuality'. *Theology & Sexuality,* 24.3, (April), 1–18.

Cooper-White, Pamela (2015). 'Violence and Justice'. In Adrian Thatcher (ed.), *The Oxford Handbook of Theology, Sexuality and Gender.* Oxford: Oxford University Press, 487–504.

Cornwall, Susannah (2010). *Sexuality and Uncertainty in the Body of Christ: Intersex Conditions and Christian Theology.* London: Equinox.

   (2013). 'British Intersex Christians' Accounts of Intersex Identity, Christian Identity and Church Experience'. *Practical Theology,* 6.2, 220–36.

   (2015). 'Intersex and the Rhetorics of Disability and Disorder: Multiple and Provisional Significance in Sexed, Gender, and Disabled Bodies'. *Journal of Disability & Religion,* 19:2, 106–18.

   (2015a). 'Intersex and Transgender People'. In Adrian Thatcher (ed.), *Oxford Handbook of Theology, Sexuality and Gender.* Oxford: Oxford University Press, 657–75.

   (2015b). 'Troubling Bodies'. In Susannah Cornwall (ed.), *Intersex, Theology, and the Bible: Troubling Bodies in Church, Text, and Society.* New York: Palgrave Macmillan, 1–26.

   (2016). 'Foreword'. In Christina Beardsley and Michelle O'Brien (eds), *This Is My Body: Hearing the Theology of Transgender Christians.* London: Darton, Longman and Todd, xi–xiv.

   (2017). *Un/Familiar Theology: Reconceiving Sex, Reproduction and Generativity.* London: Bloomsbury T&T Clark.

   (2018). 'Reading the Writing in the Margins: Dysfunction, Disjunction, Disgust, and the Bodies of Others'. *Theology & Sexuality,* 24:2, 72–84.

Crammer, Corrine (2004). 'One Sex or Two? Balthasar's Theology of the Sexes'. In Edward T. Oakes and David Moss (eds), *The Cambridge Companion to Hans Urs von Balthasar.* Cambridge: Cambridge University Press, 93–112.

Crowther, Kathleen (2016). 'Sexual Difference'. In Ulinka Rublack (ed.), *The Oxford Handbook of the Protestant Reformations.* Oxford: Oxford University Press, 667–86.

Dallavalle, Nancy (2016). 'Sex and Gender and Sexuality: Competing Claims? A Catholic Response'. In James L. Heft and Una M. Cadegan (eds), *In the Logos of Love: Promise and Predicament in Catholic Intellectual Life.* Oxford: Oxford University Press.

Daniels, Martha (2010). 'Not Even on the Page: Freeing God from Heterocentrism'. *Journal of Bisexuality,* 10:1–2, 44–53.

Davison, Andrew (2016). *Amazing Love: Theology for Understanding Discipleship, Sexuality and Mission.* London: Darton, Longman and Todd.

de Glanville, Bartholomew (1495). *De Proprietatibus Rerum.*

DeFranza, Megan (2015). *Sex Difference in Christian Theology: Male, Female, and Intersex in the Image of God*. Grand Rapids, MI / Cambridge, UK: Eerdmans.

DeFranza, Megan K., Stephanie N. Arel, and Kate Stockly (2018). 'Sex on the Margins: Centering Intersex, Transgender, and Sexually Fluid Voices in Religious and Scientific Discourse'. *Theology & Sexuality*, 24:2, 65–71.

Deyoung, Kevin (2015). *What Does the Bible Really Teach about Homosexuality?* Nottingham: IVP.

Diamond, Lisa M. (2009). *Sexual Fluidity: Understanding Women's Love and Desire*. Cambridge, MA: Harvard University Press.

Diocese of Gloucester (2018). 'Liedentity'. www.gloucester.anglican.org/parish-resources/communications/liedentity/. Accessed 7 November 2019.

Dowd, Chris, and Christina Beardsley (eds) (2018). *Transfaith: A Transgender Pastoral Resource*. London: Darton, Longman and Todd.

Dreger, Alice (1998). *Hermaphrodites and the Medical Invention of Sex*. Cambridge, MA: Harvard University Press.

Dube, Musa W. (2012). 'Feminist Theologies of a World Scripture[s]'. In Mary M. Fulkerson and Sheila Briggs (eds). *The Oxford Handbook of Feminist Theology*. Oxford: Oxford University Press, 382–401.

Duncanson, Claire (2016). *Gender and Peacebuilding*. Cambridge, UK / Malden, MA: Polity Press.

Ellis-Petersen, Hannah (2018). 'Myanmar's Military Accused of Genocide in Damning UN Report'. *The Guardian*. 27 August. www.theguardian.com/world/2018/aug/27/myanmars-military-accused-of-genocide-by-damning-un-report. Accessed 7 November 2019.

Ellison, Marvin M. (1996). *Erotic Justice: A Liberating Ethic of Sexuality*. Louisville, KY: Westminster John Knox Press.

Evans, Adrienne, and Sarah Riley (2015). *Technologies of Sexiness: Sex, Identity, and Consumer Culture*. New York: Oxford University Press.

Farley, Margaret (2006). *Just Love: A Framework for Christian Sexual Ethics*. New York / London: Continuum.

Fassin, Éric (2016). 'Gender and the Problem of Universals: Catholic Mobilizations and Sexual Democracy in France'. *Religion and Gender*, 6.2, 173–86.

Fausto-Sterling, Anne (1993). 'The Five Sexes: Why Male and Female Are Not Enough'. *The Sciences*, March, 20–4.

Fawcett Society (2018). 'Majority of Young Men "More Likely to Challenge Sexual Harassment" since #Metoo'. www.fawcettsociety.org.uk/news/majority-of-young-men-more-likely-to-challenge-sexual-harassment-since-metoo. Accessed 7 November 2019.

Fee, Gordon D. (2005). *Discovering Biblical Equality: Complementarity without Hierarchy*. Leicester: Apollos; 2nd edition.

Fife, Janet, and Gilo (eds) (2019). *Letters to a Broken Church*. London: Ekklesia.

Filemoni-Tofaeono, Joan, and Lydia Johnson (2006). *Reweaving the Relational Mat: A Christian Response to Violence against Women from Oceania*. London: Equinox.

Fisher, Melissa (2017). *The Way of Hope: A Fresh Perspective on Sexual Identity, Same-Sex Marriage, and the Church*. Grand Rapids, MI: Baker Books.

Fox, Matthew (2008). *The Hidden Spirituality of Men: Ten Metaphors to Awaken the Sacred Masculine*. Novato: New World Library.

General Medical Council (2017). *The State of Medical Education and Practice in the UK*. www.gmc-uk.org/static/documents/content/SoMEP-2017-final-full.pdf. Accessed 7 November 2019.

Gibb Report (2017). *The Independent Peter Ball Review: An Abuse of Faith*. www.churchofengland.org/sites/default/files/2017–11/report-of-the-peter-ball-review-210617.pdf. Accessed 7 November 2019.

Gilchrist, Susan (2013). 'A Reassessment of the Traditional Christian Teaching on Homosexuality, Transsexuality and on Gender and Sexual Variation Using a New Neurophysiological and Psychological Approach'. www.tgdr.co.uk/documents/207P-ReassessmentPsychologyExtended.pdf. Accessed 7 November 2019.

(2016). 'Taking a Different Path'. In Christina Beardsley and Michelle O'Brien (eds), *This Is My Body: Hearing the Theology of Transgender Christians*. London: Darton, Longman and Todd, 108–18.

(2017). 'No, Pope Francis: Gender Identity Is Not a Choice'. www.tgdr.co.uk/documents/227P-No-PopeFrancis.pdf. Accessed 7 November 2019.

Gill, Robin (2006). *Health Care and Christian Ethics*. Cambridge: Cambridge University Press.

(2019). 'After the Decade of Disgrace'. *Church Times*. 16 August.

Girschik, Lori B. (2008). *Transgender Voices: Beyond Women and Men*. Hanover and London: University Press of New England.

Gonzalez, Michelle (2004). 'Hans Urs von Balthasar and Contemporary Feminist Theologies'. *Theological Studies*, 65, 566–95.

Gorringe, Timothy (1999). *Karl Barth: Against Hegemony*. Oxford: Oxford University Press.

Grenz, Stanley, J. (1990). *Sexual Ethics: An Evangelical Perspective*. Louisville, KY: Westminster John Knox Press.

(2001). *The Social God and the Relational Self: A Trinitarian Theology of the Imago Dei*. Louisville, KY: Westminster John Knox Press.

Grimes, Katie M. (2016). 'Theology of Whose Body? Sexual Complementarity, Intersex Conditions, and La Virgen de Guadalupe'. *Journal of Feminist Studies in Religion*, 32.1, 75–93.

Hagan, John L., and Jaimie Morse (2014). 'State Rape and the Crime of Genocide'. In Rosemary Gartner and Bill McCarthy (eds), *The Oxford Handbook of Gender, Sex, and Crime*. Oxford: Oxford University Press, 690–708.

Hague, William (2017a). 'It Is Time to Tackle This Intolerable Injustice'. *Church Times*, 14 July.

(2017b). 'Humanizing Hell: Our Restless Conscience and the Search for Peace'. In Claire Foster-Gilbert (ed.), *The Moral Heart of Public Service*. London: Jessica Kingsley, 24–40.

Hare, John (2007). '"Neither Male nor Female": The Case of Intersexuality'. In Duncan Dormor and Jeremy Morris (eds), *An Acceptable Sacrifice? Homosexuality and the Church*. London, SPCK, 98–111.

(2015). 'Hermaphrodites, Eunuchs, and Intersex People: The Witness of Medical Science in Bible Times and Today'. In Susannah Cornwall (ed.), *Intersex, Theology, and the Bible*. New York: Palgrave, 83–7.

Harper, Rosie, and Alan Wilson (2019). *To Heal and Not to Hurt: A Fresh Approach to Safeguarding in the Church*. London: Darton, Longman and Todd.

Hartke, Austen (2018). 'God's Unclassified World: Nonbinary Gender and the Diverse Beauty of Creation'. *Christian Century*, 135.9, April 25, 27–9.

Haslanger, Sally (2000). 'Feminism and Metaphysics: Negotiating the Natural'. In Miranda Fricker and Jennifer Hornsby (eds), *The Cambridge Companion to Feminist Philosophy*. Cambridge: Cambridge University Press, 102–26.

Hawthorne, Sîan (2011). 'Religion and Gender'. In Peter B. Clarke (ed.), *The Oxford Handbook of the Sociology of Religion*. Oxford: Oxford University Press, 134–50.

Heinämaa, Sara (2012). 'Sex, Gender, and Embodiment'. In Dan Zahavi (ed.), *The Oxford Handbook of Contemporary Phenomenology*. Oxford: Oxford University Press, 216–48.

Hemming, Laurence Paul (2006). 'Can I Really Count on You?' In Mark D. Jordan (ed.), *Authorizing Marriage: Canon, Tradition, and Critique in the Blessing of Same-Sex Unions*. Princeton: Princeton University Press, 68–80.

(2010). 'The Undoing of Sex: The Proper Enjoyment of Divine Command'. Studies in Christian Ethics, 23(1), 59–72.

Hendel, Ronald (2010). 'Introduction'. In Ronald Hendel (ed.), *Reading Genesis: Ten Methods*. Cambridge: Cambridge University Press, 1–12.

Hendel, Ronald, Chana Kronfeld, and Ilana Pardes (2010). 'Gender and Sexuality'. In Ronald Hendel (ed.), *Reading Genesis: Ten Methods*. Cambridge: Cambridge University Press, 71–91.

Henderson-Merrygold, Jo (2018). 'Queer(y)ing the Epistemic Violence of Christian Gender Discourses'. In Caroline Blyth, Emily Colgan, and Katie B. Edwards (eds), *Rape Culture, Gender Violence and Religion: Christian Perspectives*. New York: Springer International, 97–117.

Henig, Robin E. (2017). 'Rethinking Gender'. *National Geographic*. January, 48–73.

Hess, Richard S. (2005). 'Adam, Father, He: Gender Issues in Hebrew Translation'. *Bible Translator*, 56.3, 144–53.

Hidalgo, Myra L. (2007). *Sexual Abuse and the Culture of Catholicism: How Priests and Nuns Become Perpetrators*. New York: Haworth Press.

Hidayatullah, Aysha, A. (2014). *Feminist Edges of the Qur'an*. Oxford: Oxford University Press.

Hines, Melissa (2004). *Brain Gender*. Oxford: Oxford University Press.

HM [Her Majesty's] Government (2016). *Multi-agency Statutory Guidance on Female Genital Mutilation*. www.gov.uk/government/publications/

multi-agency-statutory-guidance-on-female-genital-mutilation. Accessed 7 November 2019.

HMPPS [Her Majesty's Prison and Probation Service](2019). 'The Care and Management of Individuals Who Are Transgender'. https://assets.publishing .service.gov.uk/government/uploads/system/uploads/attachment_data/file/ 825621/transgender-pf.pdf. Accessed 7 November 2019.

Hodgson, Natalie (2017). 'Gender Justice or Gendered Justice? Female Defendants in International Criminal Tribunals'. *Feminist Legal Studies*, 25.3 (November), 337–57.

Hogan, Linda (2011). 'Clerical and Religious Child Abuse: Ireland and Beyond'. *Theological Studies*, 72, 170–86.

(2015). 'Conflicts within the Roman Catholic Church'. In Adrian Thatcher (ed.), *Oxford Handbook of Theology, Sexuality and Gender*. Oxford: Oxford University Press, 323–39.

Home Office Communications Directorate (2000). *A Choice by Right: The Report of the Working Group on Forced Marriage*. Downloadable from British Association of Social Workers. www.basw.co.uk/resource/?id=509. Accessed 1 December 2018.

Hooker, Richard (1925). *Ecclesiastical Polity, Books I–IV* (ed. E. Rhys). Vol. 1. London: J. M. Dent (1907); reprinted Everyman's Library, 1925.

Horan, Daniel (2014). 'Beyond Essentialism and Complementarity: Toward a Theological Anthropology Rooted in *Haecceitas*'. *Theological Studies*, 75(1), 94–117.

House of Bishops (1991). *Issues in Human Sexuality*. London: Church House Publishing.

(2013). *Report of the House of Bishops Working Group on Human Sexuality* [*The Pilling Report*]. London: Church House Publishing.

House of Bishops Group on *Issues in Human Sexuality* (2003). *Some Issues in Human Sexuality*. London: Church House Publishing.

Hudson, Valerie et al. (2012). *Sex and World Peace*. New York: Columbia University Press.

IICSA [Independent Inquiry into Child Sexual Abuse] 2018. 'Child Sexual Abuse in the Anglican Church'. www.iicsa.org.uk/investigations/investigation-into-failings-by-the-anglican-church?tab=scope. Accessed 7 November 2019.

IKWRO (2017). 'Honour Killing Is Preventable'. July 26. http://ikwro.org.uk/ 2017/07/honour-killing-preventable/#more-2975. Accessed 7 November 2019.

International Olympic Committee (2016). 'IOC Consensus Meeting on Sex Reassignment and Hyperandrogenism'. www.olympic.org/Documents/Com missions_PDFfiles/Medical_commission/2015-11_ioc_consensus_meeting_ on_sex_reassignment_and_hyperandrogenism-en.pdf. Accessed 7 November 2019.

Irshai, Ronit (2016). 'Religion and Morality: Akedah Theology and Cumulative Revelation as Contradictory Theologies in Jewish Modern-Orthodox Feminism'. *Journal of Modern Jewish Studies*, 1–17 September.

(2018). 'Homosexuality and the "Aqedah Theology": A Comparison of Modern Orthodoxy and the Conservative Movement'. *Journal of Jewish Ethics*, 4.1, 19–46.

ISNA [Intersex Society of North America] (undated). 'How Common Is Intersex?' www.isna.org/faq/frequency. Accessed 7 November 2019.

(undated). www.isna.org/faq/what_is_intersex. Accessed 7 November 2019.

[Intersex Society of North America] (undated). 'Ovotestes'. www.isna.org/faq/conditions/ovo-testes. Accessed 7 November 2019.

ITV (2019). 'Why Are More Female Professional Footballers Openly Gay or Bisexual than Male Players?' July 7. www.itv.com/news/2019-07-07/womens-world-cup-why-are-more-female-professional-footballers-gay-or-bisexual-than-their-male-counterparts/. Accessed 7 November 2019.

Jantzen, Grace (1998). *Becoming Divine: Towards a Feminist Philosophy of Religion*. Manchester: Manchester University Press.

Jay, Alexis (2014). *Independent Inquiry into Child Sexual Exploitation in Rotherham 1997–2013* [*The Jay Report*]. www.rotherham.gov.uk/info/200109/council_news/884/independent_inquiry_into_child_sexual_exploitation_in_rotherham_1997_%E2%80%93_2013/2. Accessed 3 February 2018.

Johnson, Elizabeth (1984). 'The Incomprehensibility of God and the Image of God as Male and Female'. *Theological Studies*, 45, 441–65.

(1993). *She Who Is: The Mystery of God in Feminist Theological Discourse*. New York: Crossroad ; new edition 2002.

Jones, Bethany Alice, Jon Arcelus, Walter Pierre Bouman, and Emma Haycraft (2017). 'Sport and Transgender People: A Systematic Review of the Literature Relating to Sport Participation and Competitive Sport Policies'. *Sports Medicine*, 47, 701–16.

Julios, Christina (2015). *Forced Marriage and 'Honour' Killings in Britain*. Farnham: Ashgate.

Jung, Patricia Beattie (2017). *Sex on Earth as It Is in Heaven: A Christian Eschatology of Desire*. New York: State University of New York.

Kahl, Brigitte (2000). 'No Longer Male: Masculinity Struggles behind Galatians 3.28?' *Journal for the Study of the New Testament*, 79, 37–49.

Kassam, Zayn (2012). 'The Challenges of Globalization for Muslim Women'. In Mary McClintock Fulkerson and Sheila Briggs (eds), *The Oxford Handbook of Feminist Theology*. Oxford: Oxford University Press, 402–17.

Keenan, Marie (2012). *Child Sexual Abuse and the Catholic Church: Gender, Power and Organizational Culture*. Oxford: Oxford University Press.

Kilby, Karen (2012). *Balthasar: A (Very) Critical Introduction*. Grand Rapids, MI / Cambridge, UK.

Knust, Jennifer Wright (2011). *Unprotected Texts: The Bible's Surprising Contradictions about Sex and Desire*. New York: HarperCollins.

Kogan, T. S. (2007). 'Sex-Separation in Public Restrooms: Law, Architecture, and Gender'. *Michigan Journal of Gender and Law*, 14, 1–54.

Kraus, Helen (2011). *Gender Issues in Ancient and Reformation Translations of Genesis 1–4*. Oxford: Oxford University Press.

Lamptey, Jerusha Tanner (2014). *Never Wholly Other:* A Muslima *Theology of Religious Pluralism*. Oxford: Oxford University Press.

(2017). 'Toward a Muslima Theology: Theological, Constructive, and Comparative Possibilities'. *Journal of Feminist Studies in Religion*, 33.1, 27–44.

Laqueur, Thomas (1990). *Making Sex: Body and Gender from the Greeks to Freud*. Cambridge, MA / London: Harvard University Press.

Lingwood, Stephen (2010). 'Bi Christian Unitarian: A Theology of Transgression'. *Journal of Bisexuality*, 10:1–2, 31–43.

Loughlin, Gerard (2015). 'Gay Affections'. In Adrian Thatcher (ed.), *Oxford Handbook of Theology, Sexuality and Gender*. Oxford: Oxford University Press, 608–23.

(2018). 'Being Creature, Becoming Human: Contesting Oliver O'Donovan on Transgender, Identity and the Body'. *ABC Religion & Ethics*. www.abc.net .au/religion/being-creature-becoming-human-contesting-oliver-odonovan-on-tran/10214276. Accessed 7 November 2019.

(2018a). 'Gender Ideology: For a "Third Sex" without Reserve'. *Studies in Christian Ethics*, 31.4, 471–82. Accessed 7 November 2019.

MacCulloch, Diarmaid (2004). *Reformation: Europe's House Divided, 1490–1700*. London: Penguin Books.

Macquarrie, John (1966). *Principles of Christian Theology*. London: SCM Press.

Mannion, Gerald (2016). 'Changing the (Magisterial) Subject: Women Teaching-with-Authority – from Vatican II to Tomorrow'. *Irish Theological Quarterly*, 81.1, 3–33.

Marsden, Daphne (2018). 'The Church's Contribution to Domestic Violence: Submission, Headship and Patriarchy'. In Caroline Blyth, Emily Colgan, and Katie B. Edwards (eds), *Rape Culture, Gender Violence and Religion: Christian Perspectives*. New York: Springer International, 72–95.

Martin, Dale B. (2006). *Sex and the Single Saviour: Gender and Sexuality in Biblical Interpretation*. Louisville, KY: Westminster John Knox Press.

Matta, Christina (2005). 'Ambiguous Bodies and Deviant Sexualities: Hermaphrodites, Homosexuality, and Surgery in the United States, 1850–1904'. *Perspectives in Biology and Medicine*, 48.1, 75–82.

McDonald, Chine (2018). 'The Eye of the Beholder'. *Church Times*. 20 July.

McGowan, A. T. B. (2017). 'Human Sexuality and Christian Anthropology'. In Thomas Noble et al. (eds), *Marriage, Family and Relationships: Biblical Doctrinal and Contemporary Perspectives*. London: Apollos, 174–89.

McGrath, Alister E. (1998). *The Foundations of Dialogue in Science and Religion*. Malden, MA / Oxford: Blackwell.

McKeon, Michael (2012). 'The Seventeenth- and Eighteenth-Century Sexuality Hypothesis'. *Signs*, 37.4, 791–801.

Ministry of Defence [MOD](2018). *A Force for Inclusion: Defence Diversity and Inclusion Strategy, 2018 – 2030*. www.gov.uk/government/publications/ defence-diversity-and-inclusion-strategy-2018-to-2030-a-force-for-inclusion.

Moltmann, Jürgen (1992). *History and the Triune God*. London: SCM Press.

Monro, Surya, Daniela Crocetti, and Tray Yeadon-Lee, with Fae Garland and Mitch Travis (2017). *Intersex, Variations of Sex Characteristics, and DSD: The Need for Change*. University of Huddersfield.

Moore, Gareth, OP (2003). *A Question of Truth: Christianity and Homosexuality*. London: Continuum.

Muers, Rachel (2000). 'The Mute Cannot Keep Silent: Barth, von Balthasar, and Irigaray, on the Construction of Women's Silence'. In Susan Frank Parsons (ed.), *Challenging Women's Orthodoxies in the Context of Faith*. Aldershot and Burlington: Ashgate, 109–20.

Murray, Jacqueline (2008). 'One Flesh, Two Sexes, Three Genders?' In Lisa M. Bitel and Felice Lifshitz (eds), *Gender and Christianity in Medieval Europe*. Philadelphia: University of Pennsylvania Press, 34–51.

Narain, Vrinda (2001). *Gender and Community: Muslim Women's Rights in India*. Toronto: University of Toronto Press.

National Health Service (2015). 'Congenital Adrenal Hyperplasia (CAH). www .genomicseducation.hee.nhs.uk/resources/genetic-conditions-factsheets/item/73-congenital-adrenal-hyperplasia-21/. Accessed 7 November 2019.

(2018). 'Androgen Insensitivity Syndrome'. www.nhs.uk/conditions/androgen-insensitivity-syndrome/. Accessed 7 November 2019.

(2019). 'Delivering Same-Sex Accommodation'. September. https://improvement.nhs.uk/documents/6005/Delivering_same_sex_accommodation_sep2019.pdf. Accessed 7 November 2019.

(undated). 'Klinefelter's Syndrome'. www.nhs.uk/conditions/klinefelters-syndrome/. Accessed 7 November 2019.

(undated). 'Turner Syndrome'. www.nhs.uk/conditions/turner-syndrome/. Accessed 7 November 2019.

Nelson, James (1992). *Body Theology*. Louisville, KY: Westminster/John Knox Press.

(1992a). *The Intimate Connection: Male Sexuality, Masculine Spirituality*. London: SPCK.

Newman, David (2016). 'Desire, Intimacy and Discipleship'. In Jayne Ozanne (ed.), *Journeys in Grace and Truth: Revisiting Scripture and Sexuality*. London: ViaMedia, 56–63.

Nielsen, Cynthia, R., and Michael Barnes Norton (2015). 'Contributions from Philosophy'. In Adrian Thatcher (ed.), *Oxford Handbook of Theology, Sexuality and Gender*. Oxford: Oxford University Press, 137–52.

Nixon, David, and Susannah Cornwall (2015). 'Anglicanism in a Bottle? Theological Implications of Sexualities Education for Anglican Ordinands'. *Practical Theology*, 10:4, 383–95.

O'Brien, Michelle (2016). 'Intersex, Medicine, Diversity, Identity and Spirituality'. In Christina Beardsley and Michelle O'Brien (eds), *This Is My Body: Hearing the Theology of Transgender Christians*. London: Darton, Longman, and Todd, 45–55.

O'Donnell, John (1992). *Hans Urs von Balthasar*. London: Chapman, 1992.

O'Leary, Dale (1995). 'The Deconstruction of Women: Analysis of the Gender Perspective in Preparation for the Fourth World Conference on Women'. Georgia State University Digital Collections. http://digitalcollections.library .gsu.edu/cdm/ref/collection/boothe/id/1384. Accessed 7 November 2019.

(1997). *The Gender Agenda: Redefining Equality*. Lafayette, LA: Huntingdon House.

Oakley, Lisa, and Justin Humphreys (2019). *Escaping the Maze of Spiritual Abuse: Creating Healthy Christian Cultures*. London: SPCK.

OED [Oxford English Dictionary]. Oxford English Dictionary. www.oed.com. Accessed 7 November 2019.

Oliver, Harold H. (1978). 'Complementarity of Theology and Cosmology'. *Zygon*, 13, 19–33.

Olson, Kristina R. (2017). 'When Sex and Gender Collide'. *Scientific American*, 317.3, September, 44–9.

ONS [Office for National Statistics] (2016). *Sexual Identity, UK*. www.ons.gov .uk/peoplepopulationandcommunity/culturalidentity/sexuality/bulletins/sex ualidentityuk/2016. Accessed 7 November 2019.

(2017). *Sexual Identity, UK: 2016*. www.ons.gov.uk/peoplepopulationandcom munity/culturalidentity/sexuality/bulletins/sexualidentityuk/2016. Accessed 7 November 2019.

(2018). 'Gender Pay Gap in the UK: 2018'. www.ons.gov.uk/employmentan dlabourmarket/peopleinwork/earningsandworkinghours/bulletins/gender paygapintheuk/2018#analysis-of-the-gender-pay-gap. Accessed 7 November 2019.

Oxford Dictionaries. https://premium.oxforddictionaries.com. Accessed 7 November 2019.

Oxford Reference. www.oxfordreference.com/. Accessed 7 November 2019.

Ozanne, Jayne (ed.)(2016). *Journeys in Grace and Truth: Revisiting Scripture and Sexuality*. London: Via Media.

Pan-chiu, Lai (2002). 'Buddhist–Christian Complementarity in the Perspective of Quantum Physics'. *Buddhist–Christian Studies*, 22, 149–62.

Parliament UK (2018). www.parliament.uk/business/news/2018/december/gen der-sensitive-parliament-audit-published-today–/. Accessed 7 November 2019.

Parsons, Susan (1996). *Feminism and Christian Ethics*. Cambridge: Cambridge University Press.

Paternotte, David, Mary Anne Case, and Sarah Bracke (2016). 'The Sin of Turning Away from Reality: An Interview with Father Krzysztof Charamsa'. *Religion and Gender*, 6.2, 226–46.

Paul, Ian (2017). 'Are We Sexed in Heaven? Bodily Form, Sex Identity and the Resurrection'. In Thomas A. Noble et al., *Marriage, Family and Relationships: Biblical, Doctrinal and Contemporary Perspectives*. London: Apollos, 101–20.

Percy, Martyn (2018). 'Cricket, Elephants, Armies and other Analogies: The Church of England after IICSA'. https://modernchurch.org.uk/downloads/

send/32-articles/895-cricket-elephants-armies-other-analogies-the-church-of-england-after-iicsa. Accessed 7 November 2019.

Philosophy of Religion (n.d.). 'The Euthyphro Dilemma'. www.philosophyofreligion.info/christian-ethics/divine-command-theory/the-euthyphro-dilemma/#more-89 [no longer available].

Pontifical Council for the Family (2011). Gender, the Controversy. www.genethique.org/en/content/pontifical-council-family-gender-controversy#.WoL8oejFK70. Accessed 7 November 2019.

Pope Benedict XVI (2005). *Deus Caritas Est.* http://w2.vatican.va/content/benedict-xvi/en/encyclicals/documents/hf_ben-xvi_enc_20051225_deus-caritas-est.html. Accessed 7 November 2019.

(2008). 'Address of His Holiness Benedict XVI to the Members of the Roman Curia for the Traditional Exchange of Christmas Greetings'. https://w2.vatican.va/content/benedict-xvi/en/speeches/2008/december/documents/hf_ben-xvi_spe_20081222_curia-romana.html. Accessed 7 November 2019.

Pope Francis (2014). 'Opening Address to *Humanum* Conference'. www.catholicherald.co.uk/news/2014/11/17/full-text-pope-franciss-opening-address-to-humanum-conference/. Accessed 7 November 2019.

(2014a). 'The Role of Women in Theology'. http://en.radiovaticana.va/news/2014/12/05/pope_francis_the_role_of_women_in_theology/1113655. Accessed 7 November 2019.

(2015). 'General Audience. The Family – 10. Male and Female (I)' Online Archive. http://w2.vatican.va/content/francesco/en/audiences/2015/documents/papa-francesco_20150415_udienza-generale.html. Accessed 7 November 2019.

(2016). *Amoris Laetitia.* https://w2.vatican.va/content/francesco/en/apost_exhortations/documents/papa-francesco_esortazione-ap_20160319_amoris-laetitia.html. Accessed 7 November 2019.

Pope John Paul II (1979). 'General Audience: By the Communion of Persons Man Becomes the Image of God'. 14 November https://w2.vatican.va/content/john-paul-ii/en/audiences/1979/documents/hf_jp-ii_aud_19791114.html. Accessed 7 November 2019.

(1981). *Familiaris Consortio.* http://w2.vatican.va/content/john-paul-ii/en/apost_exhortations/documents/hf_jp-ii_exh_19811122_familiaris-consortio.html. Accessed 7 November 2019.

(1988). *Mulieris Dignitatem.* https://w2.vatican.va/content/john-paul-ii/en/apost_letters/1988/documents/hf_jp-ii_apl_19880815_mulieris-dignitatem.html. Accessed 7 November 2019.

(1995). 'Letter of His Holiness John Paul II to Mrs. Gertrude Mongella'. https://w2.vatican.va/content/john-paul-ii/en/letters/1995/documents/hf_jp-ii_let_19950526_mongella-pechino.html. Accessed 7 November 2019.

(1995a). *Letter to Women.* https://w2.vatican.va/content/john-paul-ii/en/letters/1995/documents/hf_jp-ii_let_29061995_women.html. Accessed 7 November 2019.

Porter, Fran (2015). *Women and Men after Christendom: The Dis-ordering of Gender Relationships*. Milton Keynes: Paternoster.

Porter, Jean (1999). *Natural and Divine Law: Reclaiming the Tradition for Christian Ethics*. Grand Rapids, MI / Cambridge, UK: Eerdmans.

Porter, Lawrence B. (1996). 'Gender in Theology: The Example of John Paul II's "Mulieris Dignitatem"'. *Gregorianum*, 77, 1, 97–131.

Preves, S. E. (2003). *Intersex and Identity: The Contained Self*. New Brunswick: Rutgers University Press.

Quero, Hugo Córdova, and Joseph N. Goh (2018). 'More than a Divine Ménage à Troi'. In Lisa Isherwood and Dirk von der Horst (eds), *Contemporary Theological Approaches to Sexuality*. Abingdon: Routledge, 289–312.

Raby, Elyse J. (2018). '"You Knit Me together in My Mother's Womb": A Theology of Creation and Divine Action in Light of Intersex'. *Theology & Sexuality*, 24:2, 98–109.

Rahman, Momin, and Stevi Jackson (2010). *Gender and Sexuality: Sociological Approaches*. Cambridge: Polity Press.

Rakoczy, Susan (2004). 'Religion and Violence: The Suffering of Women'. *Agenda: Empowering Women for Gender Equity*, 61, 29–35.

Rakoczy, Susan, IHM (2000). 'Mixed Messages: John Paul II's Writings on Women'. In Gerard Mannion (ed.), *The Vision of John Paul II*. Collegeville, MN, 159–83.

Ratcliff, Rebecca (2018). 'MPs Accuse Aid Groups of "Abject Failure" in Tackling Sexual Abuse'. *The Guardian*, 31 July. www.theguardian.com/global-devel opment/2018/jul/31/mps-accuse-aid-groups-of-abject-failure-in-tackling-sex ual-abuse?utm_source=esp&utm_medium=Email&utm_campaign=Morn ing+briefing&utm_term=282345&subid=13383252&CMP=ema-2793. Accessed 7 November 2019.

Ratzinger, Cardinal (1986). *Letter to the Bishops of the Catholic Church on the Pastoral Care of Homosexual Persons*. www.vatican.va/roman_curia/congrega tions/cfaith/documents/rc_con_cfaith_doc_19861001_homosexual-per sons_en.html. Accessed 7 November 2019.

Ratzinger, Joseph, and Angelo Amato (2004). *Letter to the Bishops of the Catholic Church on the Collaboration of Men and Women in the Church and in the World*. www.vatican.va/roman_curia/congregations/cfaith/documents/rc_ con_cfaith_doc_20040731_collaboration_en.html. Accessed 7 November 2019.

Ratzinger, Joseph, with Vittorio Messori (1988). *The Ratzinger Report: An Exclusive Interview on the State of the Church*. San Francisco. Ignatius Press.

Rea, Michael (2016). 'Gender as a Divine Attribute'. *Religious Studies*, 52, 97–115.

Reed, Terry (2016). 'Gender Incongruence in the Changing Social and Medical Environment'. In Christina Beardsley and Michelle O'Brien (eds), *This Is My Body: Hearing the Theology of Transgender Christians*. London: Darton, Longman and Todd, 95–100.

Reitan, Eric (2017). *The Triumph of Love: Same-Sex Marriage and the Christian Love Ethic.* Eugene, OR: Cascade Books.

Reynolds, Philip Lyndon (1988). 'Bonaventure on Gender and Godlikeness'. *Downside Review,* 106, July, 171–94.

Rhodan, Mary (2016). 'Why Do We Have Men's and Women's Bathrooms Anyway?' *Time.* May 26. https://time.com/4337761/history-sexsegregated/. Accessed 7 November 2019.

Robinson, Margaret (2015). 'Bisexual People'. In Adrian Thatcher (ed.), *Oxford Handbook of Theology, Sexuality and Gender.* Oxford: Oxford University Press, 640–56.

Rogers, Eugene F., Jr (1999). *Sexuality and the Christian Body.* Oxford: Blackwell.

Rohr, Richard (2016). *The Divine Dance.* London: SPCK.

Roughgarden, Joan (2013). *Evolution's Rainbow: Diversity, Gender, and Sexuality in Nature and People.* Oakland: University of California Press.

Rousseau, Jean-Jacques (1762 [English 1763]). *Émile, or On Education.* Trans. Barbara Foxley. www.gutenberg.org/cache/epub/5427/pg5427-images.html. Accessed 7 November 2019.

Royal College of Psychiatrists (2018). 'Statement on Homosexual Orientation'. www.rcpsych.ac.uk/college/specialinterestgroups/gaylesbian/submission tothecofe/psychiatryandlgbpeople.aspx. Accessed 7 November 2019.

Royal Commission into Institutional Responses to Child Sexual Abuse [Australia] (2017). www.childabuseroyalcommission.gov.au/. Accessed 7 November 2019.

Rubin, Gayle S. (2011). 'Thinking Sex: Notes for a Radical Theory of the Politics of Sexuality'. In Gayle Rubin (ed.), *Deviations: A Gayle Rubin Reader.* Durham, NC: Duke University Press, 137–81.

Runcorn, David (2013). 'Evangelicals, Scripture and Same Sex Relationships – An "Including Evangelical" Perspective'. In House of Bishops, Report of the House of Bishops Working Group on Human Sexuality /The Pilling Report/. London: Church House Publishing, 176–95.

Sain, Barbara K. (2009). 'Through a Different Lens: Rethinking the Role of Sexual Difference in the Theology of Hans Urs von Balthasar'. *Modern Theology* 25.1, 71–96.

Salzman, Todd A., and Michael G. Lawler (2008). *The Sexual Person: Toward a Renewed Catholic Anthropology.* Washington, DC: Georgetown University Press.

(2017). 'Amoris Laetitia and the Development of Catholic Theological Ethics: A Reflection'. In Thomas Knieps-Port le Roi (ed.), *A Point of No Return? Amoris Laetitia on Marriage, Divorce and Remarriage.* Berlin: Lit Verlag, 30–44.

Schiebinger, Londa (1989). *The Mind Has No Sex? Women in the Origins of Modern Science.* Cambridge, MA / London: Harvard University Press.

(1993). *Gender in the Making of Modern Science.* New Brunswick: Rutgers University Press.

Selby, Peter (2017). 'Hearing the Cries of the Abused'. *Church Times,* 14 July.

Sewell, W. H. (1992). 'A Theory of Structure: Duality, Agency and Transformation'. *American Journal of Sociology*, 98, 1–20.

Simin, Rahimi (2009). 'A Resolution to the "Euthyphro" Dilemma'. *Heythrop Journal*, 50.5, September, 753–66.

Sinclair, Keith (2013). 'Scripture and Same Sex Relationships'. In House of Bishops, *Report of the House of Bishops Working Group on Human Sexuality* [*The Pilling Report*]. London: Church House Publishing, 158–72.

Sloane, Andrew (2017). '"Male and Female He Created Them"? Theological Reflections on Gender, Biology and Identity'. In Thomas Noble et. al. (eds), *Marriage, Family and Relationships: Biblical Doctrinal and Contemporary Perspectives*. London: Apollos, 223–36.

Sonderegger, Katherine (2006). 'Barth and Feminism'. In John Webster (ed.), *The Cambridge Companion to Karl Barth*. Cambridge: Cambridge University Press, 258–73.

Song, Robert (2014). *Covenant and Calling: Towards a Theology of Same-Sex Relationships*. London: SCM Press.

Spivak, Gayatri Chakravorty (1988). *Can the Subaltern Speak?* Basingstoke: Macmillan, 1988.

*Stanford Encyclopaedia of Philosophy* (2015). https://plato.stanford.edu/entries/identity-personal/. Accessed 7 November 2019.

Stephenson, Lisa P. (2008). 'Directed, Ordered and Related: The Male and Female Interpersonal Relation in Karl Barth's *Church Dogmatics*'. *Scottish Journal of Theology*, 61(4), 435–49.

Storkey, Elaine (2015). *Scars across Humanity: Understanding and Overcoming Violence against Women*. London: SPCK.

Stowell, Jody (2016). 'Evangelicals, Gender and the New Jerusalem'. In Jayne Ozanne (ed.), *Journeys in Grace and Truth: Revisiting Scripture and Sexuality*. London: ViaMedia, 33–8.

Stuart, Elizabeth (1997). 'Dancing in the Spirit'. In Timothy Bradshaw (ed.), *The Way Forward? Christian Voices on Homosexuality and the Church*. London: Hodder & Stoughton, 71–87.

   (2003). *Gay and Lesbian Theologies: Repetitions with Critical Difference*. Aldershot: Ashgate.

Swancutt, Diana (2003). '"The Disease of Effemination": The Charge of Effeminacy and the Verdict of God (Romans 1:18–26)'. In Stephen D. Moore and Janice Capel Anderson (eds), *New Testament Masculinities*. Atlanta: Society of Biblical Literature, 193–234.

Taylor, Charles (2007). *A Secular Age*. Cambridge, MA: Harvard University Press, 2007.

Tentler, Leslie Woodcock (2016). 'Breaking the Silence: Sex, Gender, and the Parameters of Catholic Intellectual Life'. In James L. Heft and Una M. Cadegan (eds), *In the Logos of Love: Promise and Predicament in Catholic Intellectual Life*. Oxford: Oxford University Press, 100–23.

Thatcher, Adrian (1993). *Liberating Sex: A Christian Sexual Theology*. London: SPCK.

(1999). *Marriage after Modernity: Christian Marriage in Postmodern Times.* Sheffield: Sheffield Academic Press.

(2002). *Living Together and Christian Ethics.* Cambridge: Cambridge University Press.

(2007). *Theology and Families.* Malden, MA / Oxford: Blackwell.

(2008). *The Savage Text: The Use and Abuse of the Bible.* Chichester: Wiley-Blackwell.

(2011). *God, Sex and Gender: An Introduction.* Chichester: Wiley-Blackwell.

(2012). *Making Sense of Sex.* London: SPCK.

(2016). *Redeeming Gender.* Oxford: Oxford University Press.

(2018). 'Theological Amnesia and Same-Sex Love'. In Mark D. Chapman and Dominic Janes (eds), *New Approaches in History and Theology to Same-Sex Love and Desire.* Basingstoke: Palgrave Macmillan, 11–28.

Tonstad, Linn (2016). *God and Difference: The Trinity, Sexuality, and the Transformation of Finitude.* New York / London: Routledge.

Trible, Phyllis (1984). *Texts of Terror.* Philadelphia: Fortress Press.

Trujillo, Cardinal Alfonso López (2003). 'Preface to the Lexicon' [no longer available].

Uchem, Rose (2014). '"Becoming All Things to All Persons": Gender, Human Identity, and Language: Towards Healing and Reconciliation as Mission'. *Transformation*, 31.2, 99–115.

UNICEF (2016). *Female Genital Mutilation/Cutting: A Global Concern.* www .unicef.org/media/files/FGMC_2016_brochure_final_UNICEF_SPREAD .pdf. Accessed 7 November 2019.

United Nations Population Fund (2012). *Marrying Too Young: End Child Marriage.* New York: United Nations Population Fund. www.unfpa.org/sites/ default/files/pub-pdf/MarryingTooYoung.pdf. Accessed 7 November 2019.

UNWomen (2017). *Facts and Figures: Ending Violence against Women.* www .unwomen.org/en/what-we-do/ending-violence-against-women/facts-and-fig ures. Accessed 7 November 2019.

van Klinken, Adriaan (2013). *Transforming Masculinities in African Christianity.* Farnham: Ashgate.

Vasey, Michael (1995). *Strangers and Friends: A New Exploration of Homosexuality and the Bible.* London: Hodder and Stoughton.

Vasey-Saunders, Mark (2015). *The Scandal of Evangelicals and Homosexuality: English Evangelical Texts, 1960–2010.* Farnham: Ashgate; new edition.

Vasko, Elisabeth T. (2014). 'The Difference Gender Makes: Nuptiality, Analogy, and the Limits of Appropriating Hans Urs von Balthasar's Theology in the Context of Sexual Violence'. *Journal of Religion*, 94.4, October, 504–28.

Vigoya, Mara Viveros (2015). 'Sex/Gender'. In Lisa Disch and Mary Hawkesworth (eds), *The Oxford Handbook of Feminist Theory.* Oxford: Oxford University Press, 852–72.

Ward, Graham (1998). 'The Erotics of Redemption: After Karl Barth'. *Theology and Sexuality*, 8, 52–72.

Weaver, Darlene Fozard (2002). *Self Love and Christian Ethics*. Cambridge: Cambridge University Press.

Webster, Alison (1995). *Found Wanting: Women, Christianity and Sexuality*. London: Cassell.

Welchman, Lynn, and Sara Hossain (eds)(2005). *'Honour': Crimes, Paradigms, and Violence against Women*. London: Zed Books.

Whitehead, James D., and Evelyn Eaton Whitehead (2014). 'Transgender Lives: From Bewilderment to God's Extravagance'. *Pastoral Psychology*, 63, 171–84.

Widdows, Heather (2018). *Perfect Me: Beauty as an Ethical Ideal*. Princeton: Princeton University Press.

Wigley, Stephen (2007). *Karl Barth and Hans Urs von Balthasar: A Critical Engagement*. Edinburgh, T&T Clark.

Wilcox, W. Bradford (2004). *Soft Patriarchs, New Men: How Christianity Shapes Fathers and Husbands*. Chicago: University of Chicago Press.

Williams, Bernard (1973). *Morality: An Introduction to Ethics*. Harmondsworth: Pelican Books.

Williams, Rowan (1997). 'Knowing Myself in Christ'. In Timothy Bradshaw (ed.), *The Way Forward? Christian Voices on Homosexuality and the Church*. London: Hodder & Stoughton, 12–19.

Williams, Rowan D. (2002). 'The Body's Grace'. In Eugene F. Rogers, Jr, *Theology and Sexuality: Classic and Contemporary Readings*. Oxford: Blackwell, 309–21.

Wittgenstein, Ludwig (1953). *Philosophical Investigations*, tr. G. E. M. Anscombe. Oxford: Blackwell (repr. 1972).

Women's Aid (2018). 'How Common Is Domestic Abuse?' www.womensaid.org .uk/information-support/. Accessed June 2018 [no longer available].

Woolley, Jasmine (2016). 'The Social Construct of Gender'. In Christina Beardsley and Michelle O'Brien (eds), *This Is My Body: Hearing the Theology of Transgender Christians*. London: Darton, Longman and Todd, 45–56.

Worthley, Andrew (2017). 'A Faith Sector Equality Duty: How and Why the Church Could and Should adopt the Public Sector Equality Duty to Invigorate the Rights of Trans People'. *Modern Believing*, 58.4, 343–60.

YouGov (2015). '1 in 2 Young People Say They Are Not 100% Heterosexual'. https://yougov.co.uk/news/2015/08/16/half-young-not-heterosexual. August 16. Accessed 7 November 2019.

Zangwill, Nick (2012). 'A Way Out of the Euthyphro Dilemma'. *Religious Studies*, 48.1, March, 7–13.

# Index

For EU product safety concerns, contact us at Calle de José Abascal, 56–1°,
28003 Madrid, Spain or eugpsr@cambridge.org.